Women Alone

Women Alone

The Disaffiliation of Urban Females

Howard M. Bahr
Brigham Young University

Gerald R. Garrett
University of Massachusetts

Lexington Books
D.C. Heath and Company
Lexington, Massachusetts
Toronto

Library of Congress Cataloging in Publication Data

Bahr, Howard M.
Women alone.

Bibliography: p.
Includes index.
1. Single women–New York (City)–Case studies. 2. Social isolation–Case studies. I. Garrett, Gerald R., joint author. II. Title.
HQ800.B32 301.11'3 76-10501
ISBN 0-669-00722-6

Published simultaneously in Canada.

Printed in the United States of America.

International Standard Book Number: 0-669-00722-6

Library of Congress Catalog Card Number: 76-10501

Contents

List of Figures

List of Tables

Foreword

This book reports the results obtained in the last two years of the Columbia Bowery Project, a study of homelessness and disaffiliation we conducted in New York City from 1963 to 1970. It supplements a previously published report (Howard M. Bahr and Theodore Caplow, *Old Men Drunk and Sober,* New York University Press, 1973) that summarized the findings of the project during its first six years when the research was focused on homeless men. That earlier volume has a full account of how the research project began under the auspices of a municipal agency in response to local administrative problems and how it was continued under federal sponsorship in order to explore the wider issues that arose during the initial phase of the study. As the investigation developed, these issues compelled us to look beyond the population of homeless men on the Bowery about whom we had been initially concerned, to other populations whose experiences became relevant to the inquiry as its intellectual framework developed. In *Old Men Drunk and Sober* we compared homeless men on the Bowery with homeless men elsewhere in the city, with an institutionalized population of homeless men at Camp LaGuardia, with a population of poor but not homeless men in the Park Slope neighborhood and with a population of Park Avenue men who were neither poor nor homeless. However, the most important population for comparative purposes remained to be studied: homeless women.

Anyone who speaks in public about skid row and its peculiar culture can count on being asked during the question period, "How about skid row women?" It has not heretofore been an easy question to answer. Skid row men in the United States have been carefully and extensively studied for more than eighty years; they are very well known to sociologists. But the typical skid row population is exclusively male, except for the peripheral presence of a few landladies, prostitutes and transients. The Bowery is unusual among skid row districts in that it includes New York's only sizable facility for homeless women, but even so, they are a negligible fraction of the district's population and have little to do with its distinctive culture.

Despite a handful of useful studies—cited later in this book—homeless women have been something of a sociological mystery. A number of familiar facts suggested that they must be numerous: alcoholism is known to be widespread among women; the number of women losing spouses by separation is the same as the number of men, but women are somewhat less likely to remarry at any given age; the number of women losing spouses by death is much greater than the number of bereaved men at any given age and widows survive much longer than widowers because of the combined effects of lower age at marriage, longer life expectancy, fewer hazardous occupations, and perhaps some other factors; both employed and retired women have lower incomes on the average than men of corresponding age. These factors, taken together, seem more than sufficient to produce a sizable population of disaffiliated, if not homeless, women, but where are they to be found?

That question is answered in the following pages for a section of New York City with an abundance of statistical and narrative detail. The serious reader may find it instructive to begin his examination of the book with Appendix A on data collection, which explains how disaffiliated women were located and interviewed in three census tracts and a municipal shelter. The difficulties of making contact with reclusive and fearful women were formidable and were compounded by the protective efforts of hotel managers, doormen and social workers. These obstacles surmounted, the interview itself was a delicate situation. It demanded a full and circumstantial life history from people who were likely to be ashamed or saddened when they contemplated their past lives. The research operation described in Appendix A is a model of virtue in social research. The field staff were called on to display tact, compassion, single-mindedness, and respect for human dignity, for which, happily, their careful training had prepared them.

The results obtained from these interviews are statistically reliable and theoretically interesting. They are also unbelievably sad. Here are the lifestyles of the people for whom the metropolitan environment is least rewarding: elderly women living alone in dreary little rooms in huge shabby buildings without economic security or emotional response or personal recognition, without the gratification of familiar pleasures or the excitement of new experiences, and without the elementary protections that ought to be offered by a civilized community.

Nineteenth century students of poverty like Amos Warner in the United States and Charles Booth in England devoted considerable effort to ascertaining what proportion of the poor were responsible for their own plight and what proportion were innocent victims of circumstances. That sort of inquiry now seems hopelessly unsophisticated, since modern sociological theory accounts for nearly all individual misfortunes in terms of social process and social structure. The whole notion of blame has nearly disappeared from the scientific perspective on social problems, yet like many an ancient error, it contains some grains of truth, as the present study reminds us. The disaffiliated women (living alone, not employed, without voluntary associations) discovered by the research seemed to fall into two general categories: the great majority had been reduced to this wan lifestyle by old age, bereavement, ill health and insufficient income, but for a sizeable minority, disaffiliation culminated a long series of wrong choices and personal failures, drunkenness and desertion, shoplifting and marital violence, abused children and neglected obligations. For this group, strongly represented in the Women's Shelter sample, there is little that anybody can do in the present state of sociological knowledge that would promise more effective rehabilitation than the existing shelter program, which provides bed, board and access to television in a grudging and hostile spirit. The bleakness of the program reflects the hopelessness of the underlying social technology. Something ought to be done aabout the bleakness, for decency's sake, but the hopelessness is probably irremovable.

The prospects are much more hopeful for the larger category of disaffiliated women. They could lead happier, and more useful lives if they had higher incomes, better housing and a safer environment. Under existing demographic conditions there are bound to be more unattached women than men in the middle and older age group. Given the differences in labor force participation between men and women that prevailed in the past and the present differences as well, it is certain that unattached women will have lower average incomes and smaller savings than unattached men for the foreseeable future. Given the existing patterns of street crime and house-breaking in American metropolitan areas, it is plain that disaffiliated women are exposed to specially high risks of victimization. These disadvantages are severe, but they are at least theoretically remediable, and the information in this admirable volume will surely contribute to that goal.

Theodore Caplow

University of Virginia
May, 1976

Acknowledgments

The research reported in this volume was supported by a grant from the National Institute of Mental Health (MH 15637) and conducted through the facilities of the Bureau of Applied Social Research, Columbia University, during the years 1968-1970. Theodore Caplow was the principal investigator, and his continued guidance, example, and friendship are gratefully acknowledged. The present study represents the third stage of an eight-year program of research on transient and homeless populations in New York City supervised by Professor Caplow.

Special recognition is due certain staff members who assumed responsibility for portions of project administration, data collection, or analysis. These include: Joanne Jennings, who was field supervisor and who contacted the managers of the hotels and apartment buildings from whom we obtained names and permission to contact renters; Eugenie M.S. Hoggard, who supervised preliminary data analysis and preparation of the code book; and Marcia Garrett and Marcia J. Cebulski, who were our "interviewers of last resort," working with respondents who had refused other interviewers.

The interviewing was a particularly difficult phase of the project, and we were fortunate to have a highly motivated, very talented interviewing staff. It included Lorraine Benveniste, Mauveen S. Cogdill, Linda Joe, Laura Kemp, Annabel Kirschner, Alice Mehler, Cynthia Pyle, Judy Henderson, Frances Sharpe, and Dinah Hirschfeld Volk. In addition to her administrative responsibilities, Joanne Jennings conducted some interviews as well. At the Women's Shelter, the interviewing staff was male, and included Gerald Garrett, Howard Honigman, and John Cogdill.

Research assistants in coding and content analysis were Dorothy Frost, Barbara Kapelman, Jill Komiski, Miriam Koral, Woodrow T. Lewis, Susan Rutherford, Diana Liang Yu, Phyllis Jones, Arna Lee Reasons, and Patricia J. Styris. Valued secretarial assistance was given by Judith Kopecky, Frances S. Grossinger, Tammy Tanaka, Lee Vonne Davis, Susan Jo Mayer, Alison Olson, Janee I. Roche, and Cathy Baker. The painstaking efforts of Alison Olson and Cathy Baker during the months of typing and revision of this final report deserve special mention.

The research reported here could not have been done without the kind cooperation of Jack R. Goldberg, Commissioner, Department of Social Services, the City of New York, and Morris Chase, Director, Bureau of Shelter Services for Adults. We are also grateful for assistance from all members of the Women's Shelter staff, but especially from Vito Encantalupo and Ron Curtin, who shared with us their many insights into the lives of Shelter clients. Nor could we have succeeded without the willing cooperation of many owners and managers of hotels and apartment buildings in Manhattan. Most critical of all was the cooperation of the women themselves, and we are grateful to the 383 women who shared their experiences with us.

Portions of the manuscript were read by David Sternberg, and his helpful suggestions are acknowledged. Although field work took place in Manhattan, the analysis and write-up stages of the project were physically located at Washington State University. Computer programming assistance of Bernard Babbitt, Marlene Huntsinger, and William McMillan and the use of the facilities of the Sociological Data Processing Center are acknowledged with thanks.

Part of the research was conducted while Gerald Garrett held an NIMH grant for Social Science Research Training in the Department of Sociology at Washington State University. The final preparation of portions of this report was supported by Project 1960, Department of Rural Sociology, Agriculture Research Center, College of Agriculture, Washington State University.

Finally, the solid support of the administrative staff of the Bureau of Applied Social Research is acknowledged. We are especially grateful for the efforts of Phyllis Sheridan, Madeline Simonson, and Lily Grab, all of whom graciously bore without complaint the added inconvenience of administering a research project situated across the continent at a temporary extension of the Bureau of Applied Social Research.

Women Alone

1 The Unjoined Woman

This was the summer when for a long time she had not been a member. She belonged to no club and was a member of nothing in the world. Frankie had become an unjoined person who hung around in doorways, and she was afraid.[1]

Frankie is 12 years old. We begin with her to make the point that the human characteristic that is the object of our investigation—"unjoinedness" or disaffiliation[2]—is not limited to the elderly. The condition of disaffiliation is not uncommon among persons in transition between role-sets, as well as among those who move from a well-defined set of roles to a relatively undefined status. One may be "unjoined" at any age.

Disaffiliation as a Problem for Older Women

When disaffiliation derives from passage between roles, it tends to be temporary; this is not true of the disaffiliation stemming from the termination of roles, such as that associated with retirement or widowhood. Because role loss without replacement is more characteristic of aged persons than of adolescents or young adults, the subjects of the present study are middle-aged and elderly women who were selected in a way that ensured that fairly high proportions of them would be disaffiliated.[a] To be sure, we will find that extent of disaffiliation varies directly with age, among other things. But our major concern will not be with aging, but with disaffiliation. To twist Townsend,[3] we are not as concerned with "the family life of old people" as with the age (and other characteristics) of familyless people.

Perhaps some explanation is necessary about the choice of women as respondents. The 1964 proposal for research on the etiology of homelessness (hereafter cited as the Homelessness Project) was introduced by the statement: "In an age protected by Social Security and unemployment insurance, and organizations like Alcoholics Anonymous, it seems inconceivable that a person can still be lost." The research outlined in that proposal focused on the life histories of homeless men. In the course of that research, it became apparent that skid-row men were not the only "lost" population. In fact, because their ecological

[a]Details of sampling appear in Appendix A.

concentration heightens their visibility, skid-row men are probably not as "lost" as their female counterparts, the disaffiliated women in the metropolis.

That disaffiliation is more prevalent among women than among men is apparent from census figures. For example, in Manhattan in 1960 there were almost 100,000 more single women than single men, more than 3 times as many widows as widowers, and almost twice as many divorced women as divorced men. We would not assert that all single women, widows, or divorcees are disaffiliated. But disparity in the size of the 2 populations, coupled with the culturally prescribed greater importance of the family in the lives of women, suggests that "unjoined" women are very common in metropolitan areas. Furthermore, due to their greater longevity, the preponderance of women increases at the later ages. Thus, one reason for selecting middle-aged and elderly women as the target population for the present study was that a majority of dissaffiliates are women.

Another factor was the paucity of studies of social isolation among women. When the Homelessness Project began, there existed an extensive body of research on skid row and its denizens. There is no similar body of work about disaffiliated urban women. This is particularly true of middle-aged and elderly women, who are of greatest interest not only because their ages correspond to those of the homeless men previously studied, but also because disaffiliation at these stages of life is likely to be permanent rather than a transitional period between the parental home and marriage.

Much of what is known about disaffiliated urban women must be gleaned from research programs that had a different focus. For example, a survey of mental health in San Francisco conducted by the Langley-Porter Institute included interviews with a random sample of almost 600 San Franciscans aged 60 and over; of these, counting both "pure isolates" and a residual category that may be considered "relatively isolated," there were 76 isolated women.[4] Many insights into the behavior of isolated women may be obtained from Rosow's study of age density and local friendships among aged persons in the Cleveland metropolitan area; 918 of his 1200 respondents were women aged 62 and over, and approximately 70 percent of the total were widowed, divorced, or never married.[5] Another project that produced findings about disaffiliation among urban women is the Kansas City study of adult life, a longitudinal study of aging among a panel of middle-aged and elderly residents of that area. Reports from this study contain the initial formulation of the disengagement theory of aging.[6] One of the findings is that although the probability of solitary living increases with age for both men and women, at any given age women are much more likely than men to live alone.[7] The sample of aged isolates was fairly small–in the first wave of interviewing there were 16 women who lived alone, and in the third wave, following the addition of another group of respondents, there were 33 women living alone[8]–and isolates were more likely to withdraw from the panel than busy and involved people.[9] Nevertheless, despite the size of the sample of isolates, the study has made significant contributions to our understanding of the process of social withdrawal among aged women,[10] and its findings merit replication in a larger sample of urban isolates.

The majority of all disaffiliates are women simply because of the association between aging and disaffiliation and the preponderance of females in the aged population. However, in most areas of social inquiry, there is less social research about women than about men.[b] This is particularly true with respect to the sociology of aging, the sociology of work, and the sociology of deviance, three specialties for which the present study is particularly relevant.

Moreover, in those situations when social isolates of either sex do happen to be interviewed (they are overrepresented among respondents who refuse or are otherwise inaccessible), their characteristics tend to be obscured in analyses which treat "the aged" as a homogeneous population. Another example of researchers' neglect of the social isolate is the paucity of social research on widowhood, which has been characterized as "a neglected aspect of the family life-cycle."[11] Studies of aged divorcees or the never-married are rarer than studies of widows.

In sum, where middle-aged and elderly women have been studied at all, the samples have been small and the scope of inquiry fairly limited. A statement made fifteen years ago by Donahue and her associates remains a fairly accurate assessment:

> Unfortunately, there have as yet been no comprehensive studies of women in retirement. A number of investigators, however, have included some women in their study populations and have reported on sex differences and similarities in the meanings of work, attitudes toward retirement, and adjustment after retirement. . . .
>
> The study populations of most of these investigations have been small and non-representative.[12]

The dearth of research on disaffiliated women is particularly distressing in light of the fact that the personal consequences of disaffiliation seem to fall most heavily upon females. For one thing, they are overrepresented in the elderly population, and increasingly so at the upper ages. Consequently, they are

---

[b]One might speculate that female respondents would be ignored even more than they are if it were not for two factors in their favor. First, they are represented in that most frequently studied of all populations, the college student body (although there they tend to be treated as "college students" rather than women, and hence our knowledge of the sociology of the female is not notably enhanced), and few researchers are willing to discriminate so overtly as to exclude them. Besides, it is simpler to treat all bodies as "students" and get on with the analysis. The second "saving grace" preventing the woman from being one of the most understudied of all social categories is the fact that she is a more available respondent than her husband, who usually is away from the residence at work. Accordingly, she tends to be the typical respondent in the studies of the sociology of the family and of consumer behavior. Even then, however, she tends to be informant not because the researcher has a special interest in her as female respondent, but rather because she serves as informant for the family.

less likely than older men to have a surviving spouse to help and protect them. In addition, society seems to "expect more" from the elderly woman:

> . . . a very elderly disabled man may be culturally more acceptable than an elderly disabled woman. He is usually retired, and traditionally the domestic burden of the household does not fall on him. The elderly woman, on the other hand, . . . is expected to contribute to, or to carry on singlehandedly the maintenance of the household. There also may be less social tolerance of deviance in self and in household maintenance for women living alone than for men.[13]

There are several reasons for the lack of information about disaffiliated women. For one thing, ecological concentrations of homeless women are not perceived as threatening the social order or as neighborhood problems. There is even some question about whether they occur in residential concentrations (apart from institutions) to the extent that homeless men do. Politicians and neighborhood organizations have not been concerned with "cleaning up" areas where disaffiliated women live, and as a result, there has been little interest or financial support for the study of these women.

According to the "social visibility" hypothesis, some seriously disturbed persons escape hospitalization because they have low social visibility. Skid-row men, as individuals, fall into this category; but because their ecological concentration in skid rows causes obvious community problems, they have been studied extensively. The populations of isolated women, possibly just as poor and socially isolated as the skid-row men, have not been considered "derelicts" or perceived as social problems. As a consequence of their low visibility, they are a relatively unstudied population.

Another reason for the lack of data about female isolation is that empirical research on aging has tended to use male rather than female respondents, a situation that is self-perpetuating in the sense that researchers tend to study populations about which a fund of empirical knowledge already exists. It has been noted that women's reactions to aging are strikingly different from men's, and that their patterns of progressive disengagement differ, but these differences have not been explored in detail.

This book is based on the analysis of interviews conducted with 383 women. Most of these women were residents of three census tracts in Manhattan; 52 were clients of a shelter for homeless women. Each census tract was treated as a separate research site; thus, we have information about four distinct samples of women.

Particular census tracts were selected as research sites because there was evidence that older women living alone were more common there than in other tracts in Manhattan. We had no special interest in the tracts themselves. Each included a heterogeneous population within which the women represented by our sample are a minority. The tracts were useful as frameworks for collection of data, and, because there were clear differentials by tract in the proportion of women who might be designated as "disaffiliates," as categories for comparative analysis.

The Research Sites

Three criteria were used in identifying census tracts where a sizable proportion of disaffiliated women were likely to reside. These were a low median number of persons in occupied dwelling units, low median income of families and unrelated individuals, and high median age of females. In 1960 there were 18 census tracts in Manhattan in which the median number of persons in occupied dwelling units was less than 1.3 (tracts 21, 56, 58, 68, 74, 76, 85, 88, 92, 95, 101, 102, 103, 109, 113, 119, 127, and 197). However, most of these tracts did not satisfy the criteria of "poverty" (median incomes of families and unrelated individuals less than $4000 per year) and "age" (median age of female residents over 55). Tracts 56, 76, and 95 were the only tracts which met all three criteria.

These three potential research sites were visited by researchers who observed, interviewed neighborhood informants, and conducted a preliminary enumeration of the dwelling units in the tracts. The enumeration revealed that tracts 56 and 76 both maintained sizable populations of older women and were appropriate research sites, and data collection procedures were initiated there. However, results of the initial survey of tract 95 were less promising. The tract is a commercial district specializing in furs, flowers, and Greek restaurants, and by 1968 it contained few aged residents. Several residential buildings had been torn down since 1960, and most of the elderly people had moved away. The survey of the area uncovered a few persons living alone in lofts or other "crannies," but not enough to justify continued work in the tract. The low population of potential respondents eliminated tract 95 as a potential research site.

As the study progressed, it became clear that despite a very high sampling fraction, neither tract 56 nor tract 76 would yield a very large sample. Moreover, for comparative purposes we were interested in obtaining sizable subsamples of affiliated women and disaffiliated women at high-income levels as well as a larger sample of poor disaffiliates. Consequently, we decided to select a third research site, using a different set of criteria. These were that the tract selected have a large population, a high median age, an overrepresentation of females, and a substantial number of poor people. For a time we considered using several blocks from a tract rather than an entire tract, and so block data on average rental of dwelling units were used to indicate relative economic level of an area. In Manhattan there were six census tracts (59, 100, 104, 106, 159, and 275) in which the median age was at least 50 and the sex ratio (number of males per 100 females) 85 or less. Of these tracts, only tract 159 had a substantial number of "poverty" blocks (arbitrarily defined as having an average monthly rental per unit of $80 or less). In addition, tract 159 had the largest population of the six tracts, and we reasoned that a sizable random sample of its female residents would provide an adequate subsample of upper-income women as well as numerous isolates. Accordingly, tract 159 was selected as a third research site.

Additional details about the demographic characteristics of the three census tracts selected as research sites appear in Table 1-2.

A fourth research site was the Women's Emergency Shelter, a facility maintained by the Department of Social Services of the City of New York. No special procedures were involved in its selection. It is the only institution of its kind in the city, and was included in the present study because its clientele are feminine counterparts of the homeless men studies in a previous project.

We shall now present a very brief introduction to the three census tract research sites. Their order of discussion will be that in which field work took place: Tract 76 will be considered first, and it will be followed respectively by tract 56 and tract 159. At the time of the study, the fourth site, the Women's Shelter, consisted of a portion of the Pioneer Hotel, a large hotel in the Bowery area of Manhattan. Eligible homeless women were referred to the Shelter by the Emergency Assistance Unit, a subdivision of New York City's Department of Social Services. A detailed description of the operation of the Women's Shelter and the nature of its clients will be found in Chapter 5.

Tract 76

Tract 76 is not a neighborhood per se, but rather a business district where a comparatively small number of people live. It consists of 7 square blocks of commercial property stretching from 28th Street to 35th Street between Fifth and Sixth Avenues. There are many large office buildings in the tract, the most notable being the Empire State Building. In addition, there are several large department stores, specialty shops, and many warehouses.

The lower half of the tract borders on the flower district, and during the day the area is crowded with delivery trucks being loaded and unloaded. There are also several artist studios and nude model showrooms, some of which "welcome amateur photographers." Squeezed between the commercial buildings are 11 hotels and a few rooming houses. The total residential popualtion is about 1500. Slightly less than half of these residents are women, many of them elderly: the median age of women living in the tract is 58 years. Most of these women live alone; in 1960 the median number of residents per dwelling unit was 1.1. With one or two exceptions, the hotels in the tract are not obtrusive, and the casual visitor, distracted by the bustle of activity in the area and the movement of the masses who live elsewhere but daily come to work or shop or merely to pass through the district, can easily overlook the dwelling places in the area.

Residents of tract 76 are truly invisible people, numerically overwhelmed by the transients and commuters about them.

Most residents of tract 76 are hotel dwellers. Some understanding of their residential context may be obtained from descriptions of selected hotels. For example, there is the "Western Hotel,"[c] where plastic chairs that match the institutional green of the walls do not break the monotony of a large, stark lobby. Early in the project, one of the managers nodded toward lodgers seated in the lobby and told an interviewer: "Most of the women are on welfare; many of them are junkies or alcoholics." Later one of the residents of the hotel attempted to protect an interviewer from contact with the other residents, saying: "They are not worth anything. You wouldn't want to talk to them."

Many of the hotels were once elegant; some have elaborate external trim or other evidences of former glory. Now they tend to be delapidated and shabby, and frequently the shabbiness extends to the street and to nearby buildings. Upon leaving one of the hotels, the usual view across the street was of apparently homeless or drunken men sprawled on the sidewalk. Inside the same hotel the extent of decay varied from floor to floor. The lower floors were fairly wellkept, with large, clean, carpeted rooms. The upper floors were dirty and their rooms usually empty, and rooms that were occupied tended to have falling plaster, peeled paint, and broken furniture.

In contrast, another hotel in the tract was well kept, air-conditioned, and as full of activity as any large metropolitan hotel. It catered primarily to transients rather than permanent lodgers, but a few residents in rooms in upper floors of the hotel had been there many years and occupied all the rent-controlled rooms in the building. One of the managers indicated that he was most eager to "get these ladies out."

An interviewer's description of another hotel in tract 76 may provide further insight about the residential settings of our respondents:

The lobby of the Crystal Hotel is fairly typical of hotels that have seen better days. It is a large room, sparsely furnished and gaudily decorated. There are six huge columns painted pink which surround a plastic flower garden containing a small gold-colored elf standing on a pedestal. There are two street entrances into the lobby. One of them passes a row of phone booths (all out of order) and a small tobacco stand (now out of business). At this end of the lobby are four chairs, a desk and lamp, two large fans, a public typewriter, and a radiator (with cover) which is used for additional seating.

The main desk is near the other entrances and the two elevators. It is generally busy with residents stopping by for their mail and people signing in and out. Near the elevators are a cigarette machine and a copying machine. Also at that end of the lobby is a marble staircase leading to a dance studio on the first floor.

---

[c]Hotels, apartment buildings, and respondents have been given fictitious names throughout the book.

The residence floors are shabby but neat. All woodwork is painted light institutional green, and the floors are uncarpeted. Maids on the floors are very friendly and helpful in giving information on the comings and goings of the women. The few rooms that I saw were without baths, and the residents share facilities which are located along the corridor.

On one of my visits I met a custodian sifting sand in a cigarette receptacle on the seventh floor. He warned me to be careful when talking to the old ladies: "When you get in their room, they might die on you." He told me about an old man who had died in his room with a Do Not Disturb sign on the door. The man wasn't discovered for three or four days, and the custodian said he really smelled awful. After that, the maids were instructed to look in all the rooms at least once a day regardless of the signs on the doors.

The researcher noted that the Crystal Hotel's coffee shop, like the tobacco stand, had gone out of business. She also commented about the hotel dwellers themselves:

The income levels of residents vary. Some are receiving public assistance, some receive social security, and some, according to the management, are "loaded."... Many residents of this hotel . . , seemed severely emotionally disturbed; e.g., one woman stood in the lobby and screamed about how afraid she was that someone was after her. The manager stated that many of the isolated women in this building have severe emotional difficulties, and joked about the fact that they needed "to go to Bellevue."

Tract 56

Census tract 56 consists of 16 square blocks bounded on the north by East 28th Street, on the south by East 21st street, on the east by Lexington Avenue, and on the west by Fifth Avenue. Broadway cuts diagonally through a corner of the area from East 21st to East 23d; Park Avenue runs the length of the tract, parallel to the eastern and western boundaries; Madison Avenue runs parallel to these boundaries between 23d and 28th and Park and Lexington. A large park, Madison Square, lies between Fifth and Madison and 23d and 28th. The tract is a "transient" one in several respects. Most of its population lives in hotels where a "permanent" resident is one who stays at least 3 months. The neighborhood is also "in transition" in the sense that old buildings are being torn down and replaced by parking lots and office buildings. The tract itself is not ecologically homogeneous, but rather a collection of distinct neighborhoods or specialized areas. Some of the tract contains the midtown shopping district with large expensive stores and office buildings and no residential areas except hotels. Other portions of the tract are less imposing shopping areas. There are many factories and warehouses. Most of the permanent residential population of the tract is located in the blocks that form the eastern boundary. Nonresidential buildings in these blocks are divided between offices, small retail stores, religious and secular charities, and welfare, medical, and labor organizations. Part of the high-income area known as Gramercy Park is in the tract, and there are several luxury hotels and apartment buildings. There is also a large life insurance company complex, and during the day the area is crowded with business people.

Within the tract the atmosphere changes from midtown New York to a rundown, small business-tenement district. Much of the housing is within small, three- or four-story brownstones. One researcher noted:

> There are older men and women around the streets, and frequently the older men stopped me and wanted to strike up a conversation, asking me what I was doing, who I was, etc. The area in general appears to be a friendly one. One wonders whether or not there are as many single older women in this tract as there were in 1960 since the tract has buildings which are being demolished and is filled with hotels that are all eager to become fully transient hotels and who have pressured many of these women to move away from the area.

Informants in the tract stated that residents tended to be single people, many of them young adults. There are few families and very few children. A rental agent in the area reported that there were also many elderly people living alone, explaining:

> In any of the old buildings in this area that are rent-controlled, you can find almost all old ladies. They stay in frozen-priced buildings for years. Men tend to elevate their positions and move to better neighborhoods. A woman's income is less stable; one year up, the next year down, so they stay where the rent continues to be cheap. But for the next couple years I'm going to rent only to young people. I can rent to anybody I like.

Two male residents of the neighborhood described themselves and other single people living in the area as "powerless, exploited, and mistreated by landlords, blacks, and politicians." According to these informants, the tract contained many single men and women, most of whom were on welfare, though there was "no reason why they shouldn't be working." Apartments and hotels were described as "not fit for the roaches," and rents were said to return 300 to 400 percent profits for the landlords. There were also complaints about the danger of the streets and of Madison Square Park. One of the men stated: "I come home from work, have a cup of coffee here on the steps, and I have to be inside by 8."

The perceived lack of security in the area was also evident in a letter from a male resident who responded to our preliminary letter. He noted that he maintained his apartment as a "work spot," played no part in the social or residential life of the area, and asked that if we were still interested in interviewing him that we please telephone before coming because "I do not make it a habit to answer a doorbell in New York unless I expect someone."

A young women in the area described her neighborhood as "strange" because it was "like a truck route by day and you have to step over the winos by night." She also said that there were several older people living in her building, but that the landlord was trying to get a younger and more mobile group of residents in the building so that he could get more rent from rooms presently "frozen" under rent control for aged tenants who had lived there many years.

Some insight into the residents' perceptions of tract 56 may be gleaned from apparent fear and agitation of one apartment building resident who, after a long discussion with an interviewer, became very upset and said, "I shoudn't have said anything to you. How do I know you're not casing the place to see where people live alone so that you can burglarize them?" The managers of one of the finer hotels in the tract were reluctant to supply a list of names for the same reason. They stated that they had given out lists at other times, and that robberies often occurred in the hotel. They were not positive that their previously released lists of their residents had led to murders, burglary, or rapes, but they feared that the lists might "get into the wrong hands."

All these hotels had many permanent residents, though most were single businessmen, young secretaries, or career women. In tract 56 elderly women were clustered in only a few hotels. One of the hotels in which most of them were concentrated was clean and orderly, but certainly not elegant. The manager stressed that his establishment had a "feeling" for the elderly people and would not "turn them out" as some of the other hotels in the area had done. In addition to providing names for the sampling universe, he cited examples of severe deprivation among his clients and indicated that he wished that he could help with some of their problems. He described one guest, practically paralyzed, who wandered about the lobby and had difficulty obtaining food and other necessities. There was also a blind gentleman in the hotel who "spills food all over himself" and thus was an eyesore to the other guests. The manager claimed that:

> These older people were causing him to lose money because their appearance often was frightening or threatening to other people. He pointed out that very often they were shabbily dressed in inappropriate clothing, did not take care of their personal grooming, and had severe physical disabilities. He also mentioned that many of his guests were senile and had mental disorders. He stated that he felt that most of these people needed nursing homes or needed to be in a home of some kind, and wished that this were possible. He also stressed that in any of the other hotels in town, they "would have thrown them out long ago."

At another hotel—an elegant, well-kept place which had very few aged women in residence—the owner stated a management policy that elderly isolated women should be cleared from the neighborhood because these women were "a detriment to business" and were taking the rent-controlled rooms and not paying a fair rate for them.

Another hotel manager stated that he had less trouble with male guests than with elderly women. He emphasized that frequently women lodgers were destructive, loud, angry, upset, and in general caused a lot of trouble, including constant complaining to the management about real or imaginary problems. He said that most of the older women in the area were uncooperative, often "drunk and unruly," and probably would not be willing to talk to inteviewers.

Tract 159

Tract 159 stretches from 70th to 74th Streets between Amsterdam Avenue and the Hudson River. As in tract 56, there is considerable diversity. Hotels on 70th Street are drab and poorly kept; those on 74th Street serve a higher-class clientele and are in much better shape. Along 70th Street new construction was in process, with large new buildings under construction and brownstone houses being renovated. Overlooking the river there are luxurious apartment complexes which, according to their managers, include among their residents millionaires, movie stars, a famous athlete, and several prostitutes. One hotel "specializes" in residents who are musicians or connected with the performing arts in some way.

There are many elderly persons in the tract, and they are visible. During the day they crowd the benches in the parks and sit on the steps of their buildings. But they share the tract with a more dangerous element, and their actions are circumscribed by their fears.

The entire area, far beyond the borders of the tract itself, has a very unsavory reputation. There are many addicts and homosexuals, and muggings and robberies are commonplace. For example, the plight of the aged woman in the "high-risk" environment of a neighboring census tract was recently summarized in a national news magazine:

> On Manhattan's Upper West Side, thousands of penniless widows in dingy single-room-occupancy hotels bar their doors against the alcoholics and dope addicts with whom they share the bathroom, the padlocked refrigerator and the telephone down the hall. "Nine out of ten around here, there's something wrong with them," says a 72-year-old exhousekeeper living on welfare in a hotel on West 94th Street. "I get disgusted and just sleep every afternoon. Everybody dying around you makes you kind of nervous." Terrified of muggings and speeding cars, the disabled and disoriented do not leave their blocks for years on end, tipping anyone they can find to get groceries for them when their welfare checks arrive.[14]

Interviewers were unnerved by policemen's comments that they never entered buildings in the area alone, and consequently during the field work in the tract a male escort was provided to accompany interviewers to their evening appointments. Many of the "problems" of the neighborhood are discussed in a later section of the book. But the attitudes of many respondents toward their buildings and surroundings in tract 159 are exemplified in the statements which follow, all from the same woman:

The neighborhood is rotten. I've lived here since 1940. The worst thing is that welfare hotel, the Addison across the street. They're all on welfare. It's 100 percent Negro. You walk by and get cokes and all kinds of things thrown on you. It's only been that way for the last few months.

It's unsafe here. You can get robbed in the elevators. I used to go out at 11 or 12 at night. Now it's too dangerous. There is no one watching on the elevators at night. They switch to self-service at night. I take the express so that so many people can't get on.

There's no night clerk at night. They have three entrances open at night. They say that that's the law, that three entrances have to be open. I don't see why they can't just have one entrance open at night. Anyone can walk in now. . . . The corridors are dangerous. There are so many corridors. A woman alone doesn't know who could be standing around one of the corners. I've had to put a metal door in. I have three locks on my door. This place is rotten. It's run-down. The only way to solve the problem is to blow the building up. The manager is no good. He's only a renting agent. He'll give an apartment to the highest bidder and not care who he lets in here.

You should talk to Mr. Warble. We had an organization. He started it. We only had one or two meetings. People won't help. They all complain about the problems here—one robbery a week—but they want others to take care of the troubles. I hope you can do something about it.

West End is a completely different story. It's nice there. But around [here] . . . it's bad—bookies hang around. . . .

Many informants described how the hotels (and the neighborhood) had deteriorated during the years they had lived there. One respondent described how when new owners took over her hotel after World War II, the fine carpets and paintings were sold, the halls of the hotel became unsafe, and several "crazy" people moved in. But despite the unsavory reputation of the area, the high crime rate, the many addicts, and the flourishing male and female prostitution, many informants stressed that the "neighborhood was improving." The renovation of many of the brownstones and the recent construction of high-rise apartment buildings were cited as positive steps.

Frequently, the managers and building superintendents complained about the elderly women in their buildings. Sometimes they criticized their eccentricities as problems, but usually their main concern was that the old women were occupying rooms at ridiculously low rents because they had lived there for years, and the management defined them as a financial burden. Other complaints included the difficulties associated with getting a resident to seek either medical or psychiatric help. Some managers complained that the physical appearance of an unkempt older woman turned away potential tenants. Moreover, they said that such women "hang around" the hotel or rooming house and annoy the staff with their constant needs and complaints.

One of the hotel managers commented on the functions of the hotel for its older residents. He stated that he thought older people who lived in hotels were atypical, that they were less isolated than their counterparts living in apartments, just because of the nature of hotel life. The lobby serves as a central meeting place where they can chat with others or watch the activity, and there are maids and cleaning women available for conversation. In short, the hotels offer "a little action" for the inactive. This manager said that he thought of himself as a "father" and noted that the older residents relied on him for many kinds of help. When they are sick, he calls the doctor or their relatives. He reported that several of his guests had left the hotel to go to nursing homes and then returned because they missed the mixture of age groups that a hotel offers. He also said that the hotel was cheaper than a nursing home and that with social security and other old-age assistance supplements, one could live well in the city in a hotel.

Another hotel manager described his job as "like being mayor of a small town." He felt that the major problem of his older residents was "rooming house-itis," or lack of recreation. According to him, the women move in somewhere around age 45, while they are employed, and they plan to remain a short time but end up staying in the hotel until they die. As they get older, they tend to withdraw further into their "home," which often is merely an 8-by-10 room. Many of the elderly residents need medical and psychiatric treatment, but they refuse it. Moreover, mutual help among women tenants is rare. He contrasted this to behavior among men, who were described as more apt to help each other. Many of the women are lonely, but they have "created their own loneliness." They are "tied into their room that is home." A major reason that existing social agencies do not help these elderly people is that they do not wish to accept help, and no one presses service upon a resistant client.

In summary, most managers expressed negative feelings toward the solitary aged women who lived alone in their buildings, and wished to get rid of them. Many owners and managers stated they would prefer a "working transient" type of resident, both because such tenants pay more rent and because they do not call for as much emotional involvement on the part of the hotel staff.

Measuring Disaffiliation

In the research proposal we had designated the target populations as "disaffiliated women," and remarked their presumed possession of many of the characteristics of homelessness. Elsewhere it is suggested that the unifying element underlying the diversity of definitions of homelessness or skid-row-ness in the extensive literature on skidrow men is a "detachment from society characterized by the absence or attenuation of the affiliative bonds that link settled persons to a network of interconnected social structures" or, in a word, "disaffiliation."[15]

An operational definition of disaffiliation was needed, one that reflected "detachment from society" and "absence or attenuation of affiliative bonds." Two general approaches were considered. One was to select a single variable as the indicator of affiliation; the other was to combine several discrete characteristics into a more general index. By the first approach, those respondents who manifested a single characteristic, such as living in a hotel, living alone, being widowed, or never having been married, would be designated as disaffiliates and compared to the other respondents. The logic of this procedure would be something like this: the nature of hotel life is such that people with unstable or minimal ties to society tend to be overrepresented among hotel dwellers. Hence, by contrasting them with people who live elsewhere, we can identify those characteristics that are linked to disaffiliation. Or: widows, by definition, occupy an atypical marital stiuation, one that follows loss of the role of spouse and that is likely to be accompanied by attenuation of various other social bonds. Accordingly, a careful study of the problems and nature of the life of widows as compared to that of married persons will increase our understanding of social adaptations to loss and of the stresses associated with disaffiliation.

Among the advantages of this procedure are its simplicity and concreteness. Usually it is not difficult to identify hotel dwellers or widows; little conceptual effort is needed to understand who is being compared to whom.

The problem with the "single-indicator" approach is that it does not allow for the interchangeability of affiliative ties. Many widows may maintain strong church or occupational affiliations which continue to link them with the larger society; and hotel dwellers, the never married, or the unemployed may maintain healthy links to family members or to voluntary associations which serve to tie them to other persons and integrate them into the wider society.

The alternative "multiple-indicator" approach produces an index that is somewhat more abstract, but which takes into account in greater or lesser degree (depending on the number and nature of its components) the variety of ways one can be "bound" to other members of society. Its logic is something like this: a person can be affiliated via several types of organizations, but some tend to be more salient or binding than others. If a person is affiliated with one or more "salient" organizations, he is defined as more affiliated than one who lacks such affiliations. Moreover, if he maintains several affiliations, he may be considered more affiliated than one who maintains a single affiliation.

The "multiple-indicator" approach was adopted, but because the samples are relatively small, the typology generated by the combination of indicators was kept simple. Although in previous work we had identified seven "sectors of attachment" to society, (family, school, job, union or professional association, church and charity, recreation, and political organization), most of the analysis of life histories of homeless men had reflected three categories–family, employment, and other affiliations. The first two were recognized as generally more salient or "important" in binding one to society than the residual "other" category. The "affiliation index" for the present study was based upon these same three components, modified slightly. The category "family" was broadened to include any person living in the same household, the rationale being that the social relationships involved in living with a person are intimate and enduring enough to be considered a viable "affiliation" even if the roommate is not a relative or spouse. Also, because of problems of distinguishing the "lifetime membership" of some religious denominations with the temporary and renewable membership characteristic of others, compounded by the difficulties of separating respondents who "preferred" or identified with a particular religious body from those who maintained a formal affiliation, church attendance and membership were not included in the category of "other affiliations" but instead will be considered separately as correlates of affiliation.

In summary, the range of possible types of affiliation was divided into three categories: living with someone, being employed, and maintaining membership in voluntary associations. If it is assumed that living with someone or being employed are of equal importance, and are both more important than membership in voluntary associations in binding one to society, the following types are generated, in order of increasing degree of affiliation:

1. Lives alone, unemployed, no voluntary associations
2. Lives alone, unemployed, voluntary associations
3. Lives alone, employed, no voluntary associations; *or* lives with someone, unemployed, no voluntary associations
4. Lives alone, employed, voluntary associations; *or* lives with someone, unemployed, voluntary associations
5. Lives with someone, employed, no voluntary associations
6. Lives with someone, employed, voluntary associations

Thus, affiliation to other persons in the society was conceptualized in terms of "major" ties such as steady employment or a stable relationship with a spouse or roommate and "minor" ties which included affiliations presumably less demanding (and hence, less "binding") such as recreational organizations, political clubs, or labor unions.

Some may question the seemingly arbitrary designation of employment and sharing a household as more important than membership in voluntary associations. Granted that certain individuals may be committed to some organization or "cause" and maintain tenuous occupational ties, nevertheless for most people the occupational role tends to be the more demanding one in terms of both hours expended and the seriousness of consequences deriving from nonperformance. Similarly, while some persons may ignore their roommates or rarely speak civilly to their spouses, the pressure of another in one's household guarantees a constant, formal link, an availability of another person whose residential location defines him as bound to you.

Moreover, study of the completed interview schedules supported the perception that voluntary affiliations of all kinds tended to be less important to the women than their work and their housemates. Many of the voluntary affiliations they claimed were tenuous ties at best; frequently they asserted they were members of something but noted that they no longer took part in organizational functions.

Since most women in the United States have the option of organizing their lives about careers or husbands and families, or both, no attempt was made to distinguish between work and living with someone as important affiliations. Instead, they were weighted equally.

The various combinations of the three components of the affiliation index appear in Table 1-1 along with the number and percentage of respondents of each type. Observe the clear progression of levels of affiliation by research site, with tract 159 the most affiliated tract and the Pioneer Hotel sample the least affiliated. The proportion of disaffiliated women who maintain neither employment, household sharing, nor voluntary affiliations ranges from about one-fifth in tract 159 to two-thirds among the Shelter women. If those "partially disaffiliated" women whose only organizational tie is membership in one or more voluntary associations are included with the disaffiliates, the intersample range in proportion of disaffiliates varies from 31 percent to a high of 79 percent.

If employment and living with someone are weighted equally and more heavily than voluntary affiliations, ordinal affiliation scores or ranks may be assigned to the categories in Table 1-1. These scores, beginning with a rank of 1 for the disaffiliated category, appear in the first column of Table 1-1.

Table 1-1
Distribution of Respondents by Types of Current Affiliations Maintained, by Sample

Current Affiliations[a]	*Affiliation Rank*	*Tract 159 (N)*	*%*	*Tract 56 (N)*	*%*	*Tract 76 (N)*	*%*	*Pioneer Hote (N)*	*%*
None	1	33	18	23	28	29	45	35	67
Voluntary association(s)	2	24	13	12	15	6	9	6	12
Employed	3	26	14	8	10	18	28	7	14
Shares household	3	10	5	7	8	–	–	–	–
Employed and voluntary association(s)	4	36	20	19	23	11	17	2	4
Shares household and voluntary association(s)	4	16	9	3	4	–	–	–	–
Employed and shares household	5	21	11	1	1	–	–	2	4
Employed, shares household, and voluntary association(s)	6	19	10	9	11	–	–	–	–
Total		185	100%	82	100%	64	99%	52	101

[a]"Current" affiliations are affiliations maintained during most of the present year, even if the respond ent was no longer affiliated at the time of interview. Thus, an unemployed Shelter woman who ha been employed until a few weeks prior to the interview would be considered "employed."

The affiliation typology and ordinal ranking is a gross attempt at measurement, based as it is on respondents' reports of memberships without taking into account perceptions of the importance of an affiliation. A better index of affiliation would be weighted by a "salience" factor that took into account how important a particular affiliation was in the life-space of a respondent and how much time was devoted to it. Nevertheless, recognizing the limitations of the present measure of affiliation, we will use it in the present exploratory work. More refined studies of affiliation, which take the "importance" of a particular social bond into account, will be appropriate after the basic patterns of disaffiliation among urban women have been revealed.

Intersample Differentials in Affiliation

The four samples are clearly differentiated in terms of level of affiliation, and the disaffiliation exhibited by respondents in the Shelter sample is most severe. The Shelter women are the feminine counterparts of skid-row men, and most of them lack stable ties of any kind. The samples from the three census tracts also manifest three distinct "levels" of affiliation. In part, the differentials among the tract samples reflect differences in the population of the tracts, and in part they reflect sampling procedures which accentuated the intersample differences.

First, we will note the general differences among the tracts in extent of affiliation and in certain correlates of affiliation, as indicated in the 1960 U.S. Census reports. Certain demographic characteristics of the tracts are presented in Table 1-2. It will be observed that, taking the population of the tracts as a whole, tract 159 is a more "affiliated" tract than the other two, and in general, tract 56 manifests more affiliation than tract 76, although there are some exceptions.

For example, tract 76 is the "poorest" tract, followed by tract 56 and then tract 159 (median incomes in 1960 were \$3234, \$3611, and \$4334, respectively). Tract 76 is also the "oldest," and the other two follow in the same order as for income (median age of females was 58.4, 57.5, and 51.9, respectively). Tracts 56 and 76 both have 1.1 persons per occupied unit, a rate considerably lower than for tract 159 (1.5).

The figures in Table 1-2 also indicate that tract 76 had a slightly higher proportion of married females than did tract 56, and that a slightly lower proportion of its population consisted of unrelated individuals. But both of these samples contained substantially higher proportions of unrelated individuals than did tract 159. Thus, the population of tract 159 was clearly more affiliated than were residents of the other two tracts.

According to the census data, the population of tract 76 was not very different from that of tract 56. However, in the former, only women living alone were eligible for the sample, while in tract 56 the sampling universe consisted of all women aged 45 and over. The addition of this criterion of solitary living meant

Table 1-2
Selected Demographic Characteristics of the Manhattan Census Tracts Selected as Research Sites, 1960

Characteristics	*Tract 56*	*Tract 76*	*Tract 159*
Total Population	1169	1553	10,625
Whites	1150	1507	10,401
Blacks	4	17	97
Other races	15	29	127
Total foreign stock	610	911	6917
Median Years of School Completed, for Persons 25 and Over	12.6	12.3	12.5
Age and Sex			
Males	650	866	4860
Median age, males	55.8	57.7	50.7
Females	519	687	5765
Under 20 years	10	28	420
20-34 years	97	75	1029
35-44 years	53	74	769
45-54 years	68	104	988
55-64 years	117	190	1269
65-74 years	137	161	881
75 and over	37	55	409
Median age, females	57.5	58.4	51.9
Marital Status, Females			
Total 14 years and over	516	675	5473
Single	238	302	1597
Married	111	176	2342
Separated	16	29	132
Widowed	116	152	1189
Divorced	51	45	345
Employment Status and Occupation			
Females 14 years old and over	507	663	5473
Not in labor force	200	192	2652
Unemployed	5	28	176
Employed	302	443	2645
Professional, technical, and kindred workers	80	98	491
Managers, officials, and proprietors, including farm	3	22	289
Clerical and kindred workers	133	143	856
Sales workers	18	35	230
Craftsmen, foremen, and kindred workers	4	5	27
Operatives and kindred workers	–	25	242
Private household workers	14	13	91
Service workers, except private household	9	71	200
Laborers, except mine	–	–	7
Occupation not reported	13	31	212

Table 1-2 continued

Characteristics	*Tract 56*	*Tract 76*	*Tract 159*
Median Income			
Family and unrelated individuals	$3611	$3234	$4334
Household Relationships			
Total housing units	1049	1391	6500
Occupied housing units	1019	1311	6187
Median number of persons per occupied unit	1.1	1.1	1.5
Units occupied by renters	1005	1311	5996
Median gross rent	87	83	114
Population in households	1169	1553	10,567
Married couples	105	130	2164
Unrelated individuals	926	1149	4179

Source: U.S. Bureau of the Census, *U.S. Censuses of Population and Housing: 1960. Census Tracts.* Final Report PHC(1)-104. Part 1. Washington, D.C.: U.S. Government Printing Office, 1962, Tables P-1, P-2, P-3, H-1, and H-2.

that the tract 76 sample contained more disaffiliates than the sample of tract 56 residents, since by definition the most affiliated persons in the tract were excluded.

The extent to which the four samples represent distinct "levels" of affiliation may be seen by comparing the distribution of respondents by affiliation rank (Table 1-1). Observe that as we move from the most affiliated sample (tract 159) to the least affiliated (Women's Shelter), the proportion of respondents in the "high-affiliation" category (ranks 5 to 6) shows a consistent decline, and that in the "low" category (rank one) manifests a corresponding increase.

Throughout this book we will sometimes refer to the respondents from tract 159 as the "most affiliated" or "least disaffiliated" of the tract samples, and the respondents in the tract 76 sample as the "most disaffiliated" of the three tract populations. It should be remembered, however, that all these tracts contain much higher proportions of disaffiliates than most urban tracts. None of them should be considered a "high-affiliation" area.

Notes

1. Carson McCullers, *The Member of the Wedding,* Boston: Houghton Mifflin, 1948, p. 1.

2. For a discussion of disaffiliation as a theoretical concept, see Howard M. Bahr (ed.), *Disaffiliated Man: Essays and Bibliography on Skid Row, Vagrancy, and Outsiders,* Toronto: University of Toronto Press, 1970, pp. 39-50.

3. Peter Townsend, *The Family Life of Old People,* Glencoe, Ill.: Free Press, 1957.

4. Marjorie Fiske Lowenthal, "Social Isolation and Mental Illness in Old Age," *American Sociological Review,* 29 (February 1964): 54-70.

5. Irving Rosow, *Social Integration of the Aged,* New York: The Free Press, 1967.

6. See, for example, Elaine Cumming and William E. Henry, *Growing Old,* New York: Basic Books, 1961.

7. Ibid., pp. 42-43.

8. Ibid., p. 44.

9. Ibid., pp. 235-236.

10. See, for example, the characterization of styles of life among old people, particularly the "Living Alone and Liking It" and the "Successful Widowhood" types, in Richard H. Williams, "Styles of Life and Successful Aging" in Richard H. Williams, et al. (eds.), *Processes of Aging,* New York: Atherton Press, 1963, Vol. 1, pp. 335-371.

11. Felix M. Berardo, "Widowhood Status in the United States: Perspective on a Neglected Aspect of the Family Life Cycle," *The Family Coordinator,* 17 (July 1968): 191-203.

12. Wilma Donahue, Harold L. Orbach, and Otto Pollak, "Retirement: The Emerging Social Pattern," in Clark Tibbitts (ed.), *Handbook of Social Gerontology,* Chicago: University of Chicago Press, 1960, p. 398.

13. Marjorie Fiske Lowenthal, *Lives in Distress,* New York: Basic Books, 1964, p. 3. The reference is to mental disorders, not physical disability.

14. *Time,* August 3, 1970, p. 50.

15. See Theodore Caplow, Howard M. Bahr, and David Sternberg, "Homelessness," in David Sills (ed.), *International Encyclopedia of the Social Sciences,* New York: The Macmillan Company and The Free Press, 1968; and Howard M. Bahr (ed.), *Disaffiliated Man,* Toronto: University of Toronto Press, 1970.

2 Activities and Problems

One of the objectives of the project was to examine the social and environmental context of the women, including their homes and neighborhoods, to identify some of their major problems, and to describe their usual activities. This examination of context and activity was also to include respondents' contact with institutions such as hospitals and an assessment of the extent of their interaction with other people. In the present chapter we will consider women's descriptions of their housing, health, loneliness, major grievances about the neighborhood and their suggestions for its improvement, their personal frustrations, their income, and their usual daily activities.

Housing

The amount of available space in the home is related to the socioeconomic and affiliation levels of the neighborhood. One-fourth of the women in tract 159 had only one room, compared to half of those in tract 56 and all but two of the women interviewed in tract 76 (see Table 2-1). Availability of cooking facilities in the home paralleled the number of rooms available. Reports of dissatisfaction with housing reflected the differentials in number of rooms and presence of cooking facilities. Proportions of women who said that they were satisfied with their present housing were, respectively, 76, 65, and 43 percent. Reports of a relative decline in the quality of housing ("Would you say that your present housing is better, about the same, or worse than it was 10 years ago?") exhibited the same pattern: the percentages of women indicating "worse" were 35, 49, and 56 percent.

As might be expected, disaffiliation is inversely related to length of residence to the neighborhood. In tract 76, which had the highest proportion of disaffiliates, one of every three respondents had moved into the neighborhood within the past 2 years. In contrast, only 5 percent of the tract 56 sample and 9 percent of the tract 159 sample were that new to their neighborhood. Moreover, 70 percent of the respondents in the latter samples had lived in the same neighborhood for at least 11 years, compared to 43 percent of the tract 76 respondents.

Thus, it appears that the disaffiliated woman not only tends to lack ties to other persons or organizations in the city, but also is limited and, in comparative terms, deprived in the amount of personal space available to her. Her sense of deprivation is likely to be keen because the quality of her housing facilities has

Table 2-1
Percentage Distribution of Respondents with Respect to Selected "Problems," by Research Site

Problems	*Tract 159*	*Tract 56*	*Tract 76*	*Pioneer Hotel*
Housing				
Number of rooms				
One	25%	50%	97%	–
Two or three	49	35	3	–
Four or more	26	15	–	–
Proportion of units with cooking facilities	96	72	41	–
Quality of present housing compared to housing ten years ago				
Better	19	10	11	–
About the same	46	42	33	–
Worse	35	49	56	–
Satisfied with present housing	76	65	42	–
Health				
General Evaluation				
Excellent	26	21	17	8%
Good	48	38	38	25
Fair	16	24	31	29
Poor	10	17	14	38
Major health problem or injury within the past year	31	40	39	64
Treated in a hospital or clinic within the past year	17	30	40	67
Number of days spent home in bed because of illness within the past year				
Less than 1 week	79	71	76	59
1 to 3 weeks	16	15	15	16
4 weeks or more	5	14	8	25
Loneliness and Isolation				
Proportion of "trips"[a] on day preceding interview in which respondent was alone	81	84	83	86
Would like to know more neighbors	24	30	12	31
Have no close friends in New York City	13	22	41	59
Have no one who "understands," in whom can confide or share troubles	23	29	27	59
Lonely "often" or "sometimes"	45	50	52	54
Would like more contact with children[b]	52	54	82	84
Problems as Conversation Topics				
"Often" or "sometimes" discuss:				
Money and financial problems	48	54	41	62
Personal problems including health	53	52	44	64
Grievances about neighborhood conditions	59	44	56	53
Major Problems of the Neighborhood[c]				
No problems	10	4	6	8
Physical decay, dirty	38	51	40	13

Table 2-1 continued

Problems	*Tract 159*	*Tract 56*	*Tract 76*	*Pioneer Hotel*
Race or class of neighbors	23%	10%	24%	34%
Air pollution	4	9	4	–
Unsafe, high crime rate	45	32	24	8
Traffic, noise, commercial presence	6	17	12	–
High rents, exploitation by landlords	4	9	4	–
Best Way(s) to Improve Neighborhood[c]				
Impossible, can only destroy it or leave it	2	2	10	3
Clean it up, renovate it	22	19	24	17
More police, better laws and law enforcement	28	16	14	6
Change the government	7	11	8	–
Self-help by community residents	12	22	8	3
Evict unsavory people, carefully screen potential residents	1	–	10	11
Make jobs, education more available	–	–	–	11
Attitudes toward Neighborhood Organization				
Would join a neighborhood organization to improve conditions	58	71	43	68
Would favor such an organization whether or not she joined personally	91	94	90	90
Frustrations				
Disappointed in the way life turned out	40	57	48	–
Would have preferred a different occupation	41	46	44	60
Views self as a failure	7	12	19	50
Mentioned death in connection with plans for the coming year	5	9	13	18
Income				
Current income under $200 per month	11	21	34	94
Presently receives welfare or old age assistance	5	12	32	4
(*N*)[d]	(185)	(82)	(64)	(52)

[a]Each "trip" counted as a separate unit; thus respondents who left their homes several times are over-represented, and those who did not leave at all are not included.

[b]Mothers with living children.

[c]Proportions do not total 100 percent because respondents were allowed more than one response; also, only most frequent responses are included in the table.

[d]Number of respondents varies slightly from item to item due to missing data.

declined appreciably in recent years. Not only is she worse off than her more affiliated counterparts in the present, but also with respect to the quality of housing experienced in her own past.

Health

Table 2-1 also contains information about the health of respondents in the four samples. Note that the proportions of respondents reporting "excellent" health (percentages are 26, 21, 17, and 8) are congruent with the "levels of affiliation" of the samples.

One of the most striking things about the health statistics is the degree to which Shelter women are sick. They are more than twice as likely as respondents in any of the census tracts to claim "poor" health, and almost two-thirds of them have had a "major" health problem or injury within the past year. One of every four Shelter women had spent at least one of the previous 12 months in bed.

The intersample differences between the proportion of women reporting a major health problem or injury and the proportion treated in a hospital or clinic may prompt some interesting speculation. Although 31 percent of the tract 159 respondents reported a major health problem, only 17 percent had been treated in a hospital or clinic. The difference was not so striking in tract 56, but there too more women reported major injuries or problems than received treatment. However, in the low-affiliation, low-income tracts, the proportions of respondents reporting major injuries and hospital or clinic treatment within the year are nearly the same. On the face of it, these figures suggest that the disaffiliates may be receiving better health care than the higher-income, more affiliated women in tracts 159 and 56. It may be that the ready access to free medical treatment that accompanies residence in the Women's Shelter facilitates the treatment of the women's medical problems, and that persons on welfare, knowing that their clinic and hospital bills will not have to be paid by themselves, are more apt to seek hospital or clinic aid than women supporting themselves who may not wish to risk the possibility of costly medical bills. The cliche′ about good health care being available to the poor and the well-to-do but not the middle class may have some empirical support in these findings.

Loneliness and Isolation

The samples did not differ in the proportion of women whose activities outside their apartments were in the company of friends or acquaintances. Approximately four of every five "trips" out of the apartment were solitary excursions. These "trips" included walks, going to work, going shopping, visits to parks, seeing friends, and so on. The variety of activities carried out by the women are described in detail later, in the section on "Daily Activities."

Responses to the question "Would you like to know more people in this neighborhood?" did not reveal consistent variations by affiliation level of tract. Between one-fourth and one-third of the women in three of the samples answered postively. The exception was tract 76, where only one out of 8 indicated a desire to know more of her neighbors. The spontaneous comments elicited by the question revealed among tract 76 women an alienation from neighbors and neighborhood at least as intense as among the skid-row women. Comments such as the following were common:

I know enough. I have enough to do without new people.

I don't care for New York people.

Not in this neighborhood.

This is not a residential area . . . people are not stable enough.

Good Lord, no, this is a real nuthouse.

I'd like to know less. Each person I meet is another problem.

I don't mix in much and am afraid of New Yorkers.

About one-fifth of the tract 76 respondents made similar negative comments, and approximately the same proportion of Shelter women had similar unkind words for their neighbors. For comparison, here are a few of their comments:

They take their bitterness out on the person next to them.

It's not good to get involved with too many people, because they can't really be trusted.

Not the people I see. Winos.

I don't feel at ease in this neighborhood.

I am nervous, and want to stay away from people.

Although there were no consistent intersample differentials in the extent to which the women had companions in their activities outside their households, or in their "valence" for new acquaintances in their neighborhood, the answers to a question about close friends in the city revealed the now-familiar progression parelleling each tract's level of affiliation. The question was: "About how many close friends do you have here in the city? I mean, people who know you well, who you see often, and who you can rely on." As the figures in Table 2-1 reveal, all but 13 percent of the tract 159 women had at least one close friend. At the other extreme, 59 percent of the Shelter women had no close friends in the city.

Another question having to do with close interpersonal relationships was: "Do you have someone you can confide in and tell your troubles to, someone who understands you?" Again, the results illustrate the extreme isolation of the Shelter women, but the differentials among the census tracts are not as striking as in the case of "close friends." Percentages of respondents having no confidant were, respectively, 23, 29, 27, and 59. The main reason for the difference between these proportions and those for the "close friend" question is that relatives could be counted as understanding confidants, but were not considered "friends." In the census tract samples, between 34 and 38 percent of those women who said they had a confidant identified a relative as the confidant. The detachment of Shelter women from their families is highlighted by the fact that of the 20 women who claimed a confidant, only 3 named a relative.

Another indication of the isolation from family that characterizes both the Shelter women and the tract 76 sample is the fact that over 80 percent of the mothers with living children stated that they desired more contact with their children. In the samples containing higher proportions of affiliated respondents, only about half of the mothers indicated that they felt their contact with their children was too infrequent.

Finally, there was the direct question: "Some of the people we talk to speak of being lonely. Would you say you are lonely often, sometimes, or never?" The relative frequencies of "often" or "sometimes" responses again parallel the affiliation levels of the samples, although the differences are not great. Percentages of respondents admitting loneliness at least sometimes were 45, 50, 52, and 54. One of every four Shelter women said that she was often lonely; in the other tracts this proportion was much lower, ranging from 7 percent in tract 56 to 14 percent in tract 76.

The Neighborhood

In a sequence of items about conditions in the neighborhood, the women were questioned about major problems, possible ways to improve conditions, and whether they would join or support a neighborhood organization if one were formed. The level of verbal support for an organization designed to improve the neighborhood was extremely high in all the samples, with at least 90 percent of the respondents stating they would support such an organization. However, there were sizable differences among the samples in the percentages of respondents who said they would join the organization, ranging from a low of 43 percent in tract 76 to a high of 71 percent in tract 56. In all samples except tract 76, over half of the respondents said they would join a neighborhood organization made up of people like themselves. These findings may be seen as indicating that a solid base of attitudinal support for such organizations exists, but it would be a mistake to use them to estimate the potential membership of a neighborhood organization. It is one thing to say that one would join an imaginary organization, and quite another to actually affiliate with a group. The contrast between the high level of verbal support for the hypothetical organization and the present low level of involvement in existing organizations in at least two of the samples serves as a basis for considerable skepticism about the extent of congruence between the women's verbal statements and their probable affiliative behavior.[a]

---

[a]A statement by a tract 159 respondent is quite revealing in this regard. She said she would not join a neighborhood organization, but would support it. The probable extent of her support may be estimated from her comment that "Something was started here two years ago; so many people were robbed. They had a petition but I didn't sign it. I was afraid—there are so many radical groups."

Grievances about the neighborhood are a common conversation topic among the respondents. In tract 159, only politics was discussed more frequently, and in the other samples the problems of the neighborhood were also very common topics. A comparison of the proportions of women who state that they "often" or "sometimes" discussed grievances about neighborhood conditions (see Table 2-1) did not reveal substantial differences among the samples.

An analysis of the kinds of problems identified by the women as "major" showed physical decay (delapidation, unsanitary conditions, etc.) as the major problem in tracts 56 and 76, and as the second most important problem in tract 159. It is interesting to note that relatively few Shelter women (13 percent) complained about the urban blight and general untidiness of the Bowery area. Their lack of concern about this problem probably reflects differences in their expectations rather than any notable order or cleanliness in their neighborhood. In general, the Shelter women mentioned fewer neighborhood problems of any kind. In fact, they showed remarkably little concern about the neighborhood conditions.

The following comments by respondents illustrate some of the opinions about physical decay and general dirtiness of the neighborhoods studied. Each statement was made in response to the question: "What are the major problems in this neighborhood?"

Litter. My neighbor across the way—a tidy woman—airs bed clothes, dusts her window sill, and then lets the cloth go down into the street. Everyone throws things out the window; it goes into the yard between the two houses. People don't care. (tract 159)

It's unclean, it needs to be cleaned up. I don't like the drug addicts and the homosexuals and the noise. Keep the streets clean. (tract 159)

Dirty streets are the biggest problem. I don't think this is a bad neighborhood but I don't go out at night so I don't know what goes on then—but I hear about all sorts of things. (tract 159)

Decayed housing, race. The composition of the neighborhood is quite mixed and there is a great deal of hostility in relations here. (tract 159)

Dirty streets, garbage, all the dogs, . . . drunks in the alleys—the cops pass by and don't even chase them. (tract 159)

It's deplorable, discouraging. It's the filthiest place in the world. The smell is terrible, the stench. The change in the neighborhood is disheartening. It was clean once. It could be clean again. (tract 159)

The neighborhood is run-down and there are so many discontented elderly here. (tract 159)

Housing . . . old tenements with poor facilities. There has been *slight* improvement but *only* for the middle class, while the poor get *poorer* hovels. City planning goes on but people *can't* afford it. (tract 56)

The street is very dirty. They don't clean it unless the mayor is coming. And it is noisy because garbage collectors come at 4 or 5 A.M. (tract 56)

Too much noise; so many cars; they leave their motor on and go eat; dirty stink comes up to the window. They throw everything on the street. (tract 56)

Rough, bad people, drunks. It is difficult to get reasonable food, there is no place to go and rest. It is dirty, filthy, dusty all the time, and noisy. (tract 76)

Filthy living conditions, crime, and exploitation of hotel residents. People on budgets, as far as hotel owners are concerned, should die. (tract 76)

The neighborhood is all right except for the winos who are always in the park so one can't sit or walk there. (tract 76)

Everything is run-down, and needs rehabilitating. (Women's Shelter)

Another critical problem was the high crime rate and lack of personal safety in the neighborhoods. In tract 159 this was the single most important problem; 45 percent of the women interviewed mentioned it. In the other tracts it was the second most frequently mentioned problem, and among the Shelter women it ranked third. The frequency that crime was mentioned is directly related to the level of affiliation of the tract; the greater the proportion of affiliated women, the greater the concern about crime. Judging from how often fear and concern for personal safety were mentioned, the Bowery seems to be perceived as a much safer place to live than the other research sites.

Although most women in tract 159 were especially fearful, and their fears seemed well-founded, there were those who did not think the tract was particularly dangerous, and some who could identify no problems at all. In part, these intratract differences reflect the diversity in the tract. It includes several neighborhoods, and some are much safer than others. Some women noted that things had been worse in the past, but that since certain buildings had been torn down and new, fairly expensive housing built, their neighborhood was much improved. A very high proportion of tract 159 respondents were fearful, but one-tenth of the women interviewed there said that their neighborhood had no problems. One lady commented: "People are afraid but that's stupid. I try not to be. It's the same all over. [This neighborhood has] no specific problem." Another asserted, "I'm not afraid to walk the streets at night. This neighborhood isn't so bad." A third woman, perhaps reflecting a very restricted sphere of social contact rather than an accurate assessment of the neighborhood, said: "There aren't actually any problems. I mind my own business."

The statements below will provide a rough idea of the kind of "safety and crime" responses given to the question about neighborhood problems.

No protection from the police. I am afraid to go home at night . . . no protection. (tract 159)

People are scared to go down at night. I was attacked once. (tract 159)

The filth and dirt, and the crime and the dope fiends and all that business. You have to be afraid to open your door and go out. (tract 159)

It isn't a nice place to live. You can't go out without being robbed. I don't delve into other people's affairs. (tract 159)

The real problem is the fear. I'm afraid to go out in the evening. I don't feel as free as I would like. (tract 159)

Dope addicts, prostitution. These people don't live in the neighborhood, they come here. (tract 159)

There are too many out-of-order people around here—queers, prostitutes, and drug addicts. (tract 159)

I am nervous on the streets at night. But that's true all over the city. (tract 56)

Breaking and entering–we have periodic spells. (tract 56)

Bums, mugging–we have lots of everthing here. Never saw anything like it. It's shocking. Everyone is scared. (tract 76)

Safety out on the streets. People can't walk alone. This hotel is held together with a rubber band, and by paying off politicians. (tract 76)

The third critical problem identified by the respondents was the nature of their neighbors. Shelter women noted the visible presence of too many drunks and homeless men as the major problem of their area. Respondents in the census tract samples objected to the addicts, thieves, alcoholics, prostitutes, and hippies that lived in or frequented their neighborhoods. Sometimes their complaints were couched in ethnic terms, especially in tracts 159 and 76. For example,

The colored people–wherever they are, there's fighting. (tract 159)

The house isn't careful enough who they rent apartments to anymore. The hippies, we even have them in this house; terrible–one colored tenant and quite a few boys. (tract 159)

They shouldn't have let the neighborhood go down so low. They [hippies] should be imprisoned. The police should have a gun and shoot them on sight. (tract 159)

Clean up the neighborhood, not have all sorts of people, and have more policemen. (tract 159)

The neighborhood's changed–different element–lots of Puerto Ricans. Like everything else, the people who don't like it move out. (tract 159)

We have people here now, hippies, they didn't have before. What do you do? (tract 159)

Encroachment of the colored on the white population. They make so much trouble if they won't rent them an apartment. (tract 159)

As far as I can say, I don't see anything wrong. People make a lot out of nothing. Just because a colored person walks down the street–you could have a white person and he could be more dangerous. (tract 159)

The hotel is becoming delapidated. Lillian Russell used to live here but now the people aren't as "old fashioned." Also, there are more blacks. (tract 76)

Bums in the park–low-class people live in this neighborhood. . . . What can you do about the chronic drunk? (tract 76)

Too much colored stuff. They throw garbage out the windows, use the windows as a bathroom. (tract 76)

People lying on the sidewalk, homeless, hungry. (Women's Shelter)

Bums on the street–layin' around drinking. They're all sick. (Women's Shelter)

Nothing too much bad. Maybe too many drunks and winos. (Women's Shelter)

Suggestions for Neighborhood Improvement

The nature of suggestions for improving the neighborhood showed considerable intersample variation. Tract 159 women had been most fearful about crime and safety in the streets, and predictably their ideas about solutions to the neighborhood problems involved better police protection before anything else. Slightly over one-fourth of them mentioned the need for more police and better law enforcement. Also frequently mentioned were the need for neighborhood clean-up or tearing down of old buildings and replacing them with better housing. One-eighth of the tract 159 women noted a need for self-help among neighborhood residents.

In tract 56 there was less concern with better police protection (16 percent of the women mentioned it, compared to 28 percent in tract 159) and more interest in local community organization and self-help. As in tract 159, about one-fifth of the women mentioned a need for neighborhood building and remodeling programs and better sanitation practices. Comments such as "They ought to stop people from throwing garbage out windows" and "Have the crazy woman at Catholic Charities told to leave. The woman hangs around the building and is an eyesore to the neighborhood" were not uncommon.

The occasional reference in the three tract samples to changing the government usually applied to city government, and had to do with replacing corrupt or do-nothing officials as well as simply replacing the party in power. Several women were quite explicit, making remarks such as "Replace Mayor Lindsay."

Respondents in tract 76 were more negative about the future of their neighborhood than women in any other sample. One of every ten of them made a statement to the effect that improving the neighborhood was impossible, and the only solutions were to leave the neighborhood or have it torn down. In the Women's Shelter the respondents talked about improving things through rehabilitation programs of various kinds, and only 3 percent of the Shelter women thought such rehabilitation impossible. In tract 76, however, the alienation or neighborhood "death wish" was very apparent. Asked about the "best way to improve conditions," the residents alienated from the neighborhood replied:

> No way. There are drunks and addicts in the park. The cops can't do anything about it.
>
> Get a match and put fire to everything.
>
> Tear down the buildings and make houses.
>
> It is impossible to improve conditions. Needs more money for better surveillance and to improve conditions, but you can't get that.

Comments about unsavory noncriminal neighbors were more common in tract 76 than in the other tracts. In fact, respondents in that sample were almost as likely to complain about the derelicts and alcoholics in their neighborhood and of the need for raising the caliber of their neighbors as were the women on skid row. One respondent had a prospective solution: "Check the people that move in. Check their backgrounds and find out how they live before taking them in."

Among the Shelter women, the need for more police officers or for self-help by neighborhood residents was rarely mentioned. Instead there were frequent suggestions that occupational, educational, and alcoholism rehabilitation programs be established, and that there be increased efforts to clean up both the physical facilities in the neighborhood and the unfortunates who live there. Note the identification with the plight of the homeless man in many of the suggestions of Shelter women:

Listen to people, help them. Do not judge them.

All I can see is medical care. Not medicine, medical care.

To be helpful to everybody regardless of race.

Rehabilitate men and women on the Bowery. Get them jobs, put them to work.

Put mental patients in the hospital.

Put the sick winos in the hospital.

Occasionally a woman verbalized the resignation reflected in the small percentage of respondents who noted a need for "self-help" programs: "There's nothing you can do. It's already set up."

Personal Frustrations

The women in the census tract samples were asked: "Has your life turned out pretty much the way you hoped it would when you were younger?" A negative response prompted a follow-up question: "How is it different?" In view of the failure manifest in residence at the Women's Shelter—it was inconceivable that a Shelter woman would have stated that she had hoped she would become a homeless woman—this question was deleted from the interview schedule used there.

Responses to the follow-up question could be either positive, neutral, or negative. For example, one respondent said, "Before I was not myself—now I am myself" (tract 76). This kind of "self-discovery" answer was considered a positive response; life turned out better than expected. There were also neutral reponses, such as "Everyone's life is pretty much a surprise to the person as it goes on" (tract 76), which suggested that the woman's life had turned out differently than she expected but did not suggest that she felt either great disappointment or elation at the end result. Finally, there were the negative responses, which indicated unfulfilled aspirations and disappointment. The widow who sadly said, "I thought I would get old with my husband" (tract 76) exemplifies the "disappointed" category.

Approximately two-thirds of the women in the three tract samples said that their lives had *not* turned out as they expected. But when the ways in which the present status differed from the expectation were examined, it was found that the women in the high-affiliation tract were least disappointed in life. Proportions of respondents assessed as expressing disappointment were, respectively, 40, 57, and 48 percent.

Between 41 and 46 percent of the women in the tract samples answered yes to the question: "Looking back, is there another type of job you would rather have had?" The Shelter women manifested more occupational dissatisfaction; 60 percent of them would rather have had a different kind of occupational history (see Table 2-1). These findings will be considered in greater detail later in the chapter on careers and mobility patterns. Here it is sufficient to note that when controls are added for occupational status, these proportions of "dissatisfied" people probably are not unusual. Havemann and West reported that among professionals, dissatisfaction with the academic field in which they had majored varied from 9 to 33 percent, with 30 percent of the professionals who had majored in social sciences or business administration wishing they had taken a different program, and 33 percent of the pharmacists and history or language majors regretting their choice of a professional field.[1] Since the majority of our respondents were not professionals, a somewhat higher percentage of dissatisfied workers was expected, and the 41-to-44 percent range for the tract samples does not seem at all out of line.

The instrument also contained several attitude scales. In one of these scales appeared the item, "All in all, I am inclined to feel that I am a failure." It is of interest that although a substantial proportion of the women in the tract samples were disappointed with the outcome of their lives, and a similar proportion expressed regret over the nature of their occupational careers, there were relatively few who considered themselves to be failures. Moreover, the intertract differentials in the percentage of women who stated that they *did* view themselves as failures showed a consistent positive relationship with the affiliation levels of the samples (proportions of "failures" were 7, 12, 19 and 50 percent).

These proportions may take on greater meaning when viewed in a comparative perspective. During the research conducted as part of the Homelessness Project, the same question was put to two groups of skid-row men, and 50 percent of the Camp LaGuardia residents (the group most comparable to Shelter women) agreed that they defined themselves as failures. In a lower-income sample, the proportion was 12 percent. Thus, the range of self-defined failures (7 to 19 percent) in the relatively low-income census tracts studied in the present research is comparable to that found among non-skid-row men, and it appears that perceptions of failure are about as frequent among homeless women as homeless men.

Another question included both in the interview schedules used in the study of homeless men and in those of the current project was: "Where do you think you will be a year from now?" If a nongeographic answer were given, the interviewer probed: "Do you think you'll be living here in this area, or somewhere else?" In interviewing male samples it had been discovered that initial responses to the question often were very revealing. Sometimes they had to do with hopes for the future, and often contained references to the possibility of reaffiliation or even of death. More than 25 percent of the Bowery men and 19 percent of the Camp LaGuardia residents had mentioned the possibility of their deaths within the coming year. One-sixth of the lower-income males and 6 percent of the upper-middle-class males interviewed as part of the control samples likewise had mentioned death.

As is apparent in Table 2-1 the proportion of women mentioning death in connection with their plans for the coming year showed a smaller range than in the samples of males interviewed during the Homelessness Project. Anticipation of death was most frequent among the Shelter women, where 18 percent of the respondents mentioned death in some way. Note how closely this agrees with the results for Camp LaGuardia men (19 percent), and that it is somewhat lower than the figure for Bowery men as a whole (25 percent). The most striking thing about the findings with respect to the mentioning of death is that once again, the perfect consistency with affiliation level appears; the higher the affiliation level of the tract, the lower the percentage of respondents whose answers indicated anticipation of death within the coming year. The findings among the male samples studied previously had revealed the same trend.

Income

The figures in Table 2-1 on current income and welfare assistance provide striking evidence of the relationship between affiliation and income. Once again the consistent trend appears: one-ninth of the tract 159 women, one-fifth of the tract 56 respondents, and one-third of those in the tract 76 sample receive less than $200 per month, and almost everyone in the Women's Shelter is below that income level.

Similarly, the proportion receiving welfare assistance of some kind increases with the impoverishment of the neighborhood. The apparent inconsistency in the trend with respect to Shelter women should be explained. The type of aid they receive technically is neither welfare nor old age assistance, but it does derive from the Department of Social Services, and might properly be considered welfare assistance. All of them by virtue of their residence in the Shelter receive such aid.

Daily Activities

Each of the respondents was asked to describe activities on the day preceding the interview, beginning with the time she awoke in the morning and ending at bedtime. There were specific probes about how the morning was spent, activities of the early and late afternoon, dinner, and the evening. The summaries of women's days derived from these questions were coded with reference to the number and kind of specific activities reported.

The coding of the daily activities was not limited in advance to a standardized set of activities. Instead, each distinct type of activity mentioned generated an additional coding category. Apart from activities which were classified as general self-maintenance, such as eating meals, washing one's hair, showering, and bathing, all distinct kinds of activity were indicated separately in the preliminary coding. A total of 54 kinds of activity were identified.

Some further evidence about the relationship between affiliation rank and diversity of life experience may be obtained by contrasting the various subsamples in terms of the number of different activities mentioned. The distribution of mean number of activities, by affiliation rank and sample, appears in Table 2-2. The figures there show that the number of activities mentioned by respondents varies directly with the affiliation "level" of the tract. Women in tract 159 reported an average of 4.09 daily activities, compared to 3.92, 3.55, and 2.46, respectively, in the other samples. Moreover, in three of the samples, the disaffiliates (affiliation rank 1) reported fewer activities than the more affiliated women. The only exception to this finding is tract 159, where respondents in all three subsamples reported approximately the same number of different activities.

Those activities mentioned most frequently are listed in Table 2-3, and the proportion of respondents at selected affiliation ranks who reported each activity is given.

Several important findings are contained in Table 2-3. The first is that among all subsamples, watching television is a most important pastime. The proportion of women who watched television the preceding day ranged from about one-third among the more affiliated Shelter women to a high of 64 percent

Table 2-2
Mean Number of Distinct Activities Mentioned in Recounting the Experiences of the Previous Day, by Affiliation Rank, Four Samples

Sample	*Affiliation Rank*	*Mean Number of Activities*
Tract 159	1–6 (total sample)	4.09
Tract 159	5–6	4.08
Tract 159	2–4	4.06
Tract 159	1	4.15
Tract 56	1–6 (total sample)	3.96
Tract 56	2–6	4.19
Tract 56	1	3.30
Tract 76	1–6 (total sample)	3.55
Tract 76	2–6	3.97
Tract 76	1	3.03
Women's Shelter	1–6 (total sample)	2.46
Women's Shelter	2–6	2.76
Women's Shelter	1	2.31

Table 2-3
Percent of Respondents Engaging in Selected Activities on the Day Preceding the Interview, by Affiliation Rank

Sample	*Tract 159*			*Tract 56*		*Tract 76*		*Women's Shelter*	
Affiliation Rank	*1*	*2-4*	*5-6*	*1*	*2-6*	*1*	*2-6*	*1*	*2-6*
Watching television	64	57	45	39	47	37	40	51	35
Listening to radio	30	14	13	9	15	34	31	–	–
Going to movies	12	9	3	4	7	–	–	3	6
Going to theater	–	–	10	–	3	3	2	–	–
Reading	61	55	60	61	54	55	74	14	24
Writing	27	12	15	22	17	10	8	9	–
Conversation	42	40	43	43	32	27	28	23	24
Walking	18	9	8	17	8	31	17	46	47
Visiting the park	9	10	–	17	8	17	25	34	29
Cleaning	55	48	48	22	39	31	34	14	29
Shopping	48	45	40	26	37	24	31	3	–
Working	3	40	68	9	39	–	54	–	24
Sewing	6	10	13	13	10	13	8	6	–
Attending church	3	2	–	13	5	10	17	–	–
(*N*)	(33)	(112)	(40)	(23)	(59)	(29)	(35)	(35)	(17)

among the least affiliated residents of tract 159. The striking thing, however, is the fact that in every subsample watching television was one of the three activities recorded most frequently.

A second somewhat unexpected finding is the apparent importance of reading in the women's lives. In all three tract samples, between half and three-fourths of the women reported reading as one of the activities of the previous day. In fact, in tract 56 and tract 76 reading was mentioned more frequently than watching television.

A third point is that the likelihood that "cleaning" and "shopping" will be mentioned increases with the affiliation level of the sample. For example, in all three subsamples of tract 159, cleaning and shopping were mentioned by 40 percent or more of the respondents. In none of the other samples were they mentioned that frequently, and when they are mentioned, they tend to be mentioned by the more affiliated women in the tracts.

Also receiving support from Table 2-3 is the finding mentioned above: the higher the affiliation level of the tract, the greater variety in activities mentioned. Thus, 40 percent or more of the women in tract 159 reported at least five of the activities listed, but only two or three of the activities were participated in that frequently by respondents in the other tract samples. Perhaps this finding can be illustrated best by referring to the specific activities, and designating as an "important" activity any activity participated in by one-third or more of the women in any of the samples. Accordingly, it can be seen that the activities which dominated the life of the Shelter women were watching television, walking, and visiting the park. The major differences between the totally disaffiliated and somewhat affiliated Shelter respondents was that the latter were less likely to watch television, more likely to read, to work, and to spend some time cleaning their rooms. The dominant activities of the tract 76 respondents were watching television, listening to the radio, reading, cleaning, and working. As with the Shelter women, the more affiliated respondents were more likely to read, and, of course, to work. The activity patterns in tract 56 parallel those for tract 76, with the exception that conversation and shopping were mentioned more frequently in the tract 56 sample. Finally, the most important activities of tract 159 respondents were watching television, reading, conversation, cleaning, shopping, and working.

Listening to the radio was important in all tract samples but was not mentioned by the Shelter women; apparently the latter are below the threshold of economic power necessary to buy or maintain a radio. Also, walking is much more important an activity for the disaffiliated than the other women. In all the tract samples the disaffiliates are twice as likely to report walking as an activity of the previous day than are the more affiliated women. Among the Shelter women, walking was far more frequent than in the other samples; in fact, it was the activity most frequently mentioned by the "more affiliated" subsample of Shelter women. Also the Shelter sample was the only one in which visiting the park was one of the three most "important" activities.

One way to judge a woman's satisfaction with her activity level was the direct question, which appeared near the end of the inteview schedule: "For yourself, do you think you should be more or less active than you are now?" The proportions of women who stated that they thought they should be more active were, respectively, 43, 58, 59, and 66 percent. Thus, there seemed to be an inverse relationship between the mean number of daily activities that characterized members of a sample and the probabilities that they would indicate that they were less active than they should be. Among Shelter women, who averaged only 2.5 activities per day, two-thirds of the respondents said they thought they should be more active.

In their summaries of the previous day's activities, there was no direct stimulus for an evaluation of the extent of their involvement, but there were occasional responses to the probe questions, especially the last one ("Was yesterday an unusual day, or was it about typical?"), which indicated the respondent's feelings about her degree of social involvement. For example, note the following comments from tract 159 respondents:

[After morning grocery shopping] I go back to bed just to waste time because there is nothing else to do. . . . I go to bed early because I can't read or watch TV and get bored. (Age 69, affiliation rank 1)

No social life . . . can't go out unless you have a car. Very dull. (Age 71, affiliation rank 1)

Up half the night, played solitaire . . . that's my hobby in my old age. . . . Same old thing every day–solitaire and TV, things are so bad around here, I'm afraid to go out. (Age 73, affiliation rank 1)

Sat out after dinner. I am afraid to come back after 8:30–everybody is frightened to death to come up the elevators. (Age 70, affiliation rank 1)

Up at 5:00 or 5:30. I make coffee, drink it, smoke eight cigarettes and stare at the wall. [After working all day] Sometimes watch TV, sit alone, or get up and prowl in the night. (Age 65, affiliation rank 3)

Talking on the telephone is my only amusement. (Age 66, affiliation rank 1)

The comments by women obviously unsatisfied focused on the obstacles to their increased involvement, and a major obstacle was their fear for personal safety. An obvious solution to a good deal of the involuntary disaffiliation would be to create a setting in which women would take advantage of the city's cultural and social opportunities without having to risk their lives in the process. Other women living in the same neighborhood do get out and participate in organized recreational and cultural activities. To some extent, the ability to get around the neighborhood and the city safely may be purchased. Women who can afford to use cabs and to live in apartments with high security can go out alone and return and not ever be without a "guardian" cabdriver or doorman. To some extent, perceptions of security derive from the presence of a companion, usually a spouse, relative, or close friend. The impoverished woman who lives alone lacks the first of these sources of security, and is less likely to find the second readily available.

That some elderly women who live alone are able to manage fairly extensive involvement is apparent from the following statements by women in tract 159:

Went to a matinee with a relative; met another friend for dinner . . . went to another friend's home and played cards for the evening. (Age 68, affiliation rank 1)

Got dressed, got on bus, went to Museum of Modern Art; sat in the garden, then went to a film. Then came home and went across the street and got a book from the library. (Age 69, affiliation rank 2)

I had dinner at home, and spent the evening talking and playing bridge. Went to bed at 11:30. It was an unusual day; usually I do more exciting things in the evening. (Age 62, affiliation rank 2)

So some women, despite age and disaffiliation from formal associations, do manage to find activities exciting to them. Others maintain their formal affiliations into their eighties. But the general picture which emerges among those women who live alone is a decline in involvement, accompanied by a sense of futility and personal insecurity.

In concluding this discussion of daily activities, we will present several examples of women's summaries of their day, drawing upon respondents in samples other than tract 159.

I get up sometime between 8 and 9 A.M., get dressed, and go out for breakfast somewhere close. Then I spend an hour to an hour-and-a-half in the bath because it helps my leg [Fourteen months before the interview she had broken her leg in six places]. I take a nap, and read sometimes. For lunch I go to the automat or somewhere close. I usually eat around 2. Then I go out and walk up to the corner and take another bath. In the late afternoon I sometimes read or just lie and rest. I have dinner in the automat, and after dinner I sit in the automat and look at people. I don't know anyone. In the evening I may take another bath, for one to one-and-a-half hours. I sit in the lobby for a few minutes, go out to get the newspaper and practice walking, putting more weight on my leg. I go to bed at around 11 P.M.; sometimes I just lie there and never go to sleep. This is all I ever do here. (tract 76, age 45, affiliation rank 1) [Six months after the interview this respondent was found dead in her hotel room.]

This morning the respondent got up at 6 A.M., cleaned her room, and went to a nearby restaurant for breakfast. She goes to mass every morning. This particular morning she lit a candle for her next door neighbor, who had been raped earlier in the week. The morning was spent reading, knitting, and crocheting. She eats lunch in a nearby cafe, "I eat when I get hungry." Then she took a long walk in Central Park. The late afternoon she described as "same as morning—knitting, crocheting, reading, walks." Following supper she reads, may visit her friends next door, and retires by 10 P.M. (tract 76, age 64, affiliation rank 1)

I got up at 11 A.M. and had breakfast in the lobby. During the morning I stayed in my room, sitting in the chair. I had lunch in the room; took something up for lunch from the lobby. After lunch I looked at the walls. Had dinner in the lobby. After dinner came back to the room and listened to the radio. Went to bed at 10 P.M. (tract 76, age 84, affiliation rank 1)

Got up at 8 o'clock and ate breakfast downstairs in the lobby. Then made my bed, cleaned the room, listened to the radio, and read. Had lunch in the room, and spent the afternoon the same as the morning—stayed in the room, read, took a nap. I had dinner in my room. After dinner I talked to a friend who dropped in. In the evening I cold-creamed my face and listened to the radio. Just call me the loafer. I worked for 50 years and now I can do as I please. I'd rather work but that's the way it is. Went to bed between 1 and 2 A.M. (tract 76, age 70, affiliation rank 1)

I slept in the 7th Avenue subway, and got up at noon. Had coffee and a donut in the subway station for lunch. I walked around, sat on steps in the forties [streets], then went to Union Square. I talked with people, bought a loaf of bread at 14th Street. I ate half of it and gave the rest to a dog. I spent the evening walking around between 14th Street and 47th, talking to people. Finally slept in the subway at 3:30 A.M. In a way, yes, it was typical; but not like most of my life. (Women's Shelter, age 69, affiliation rank 1)

Respondent was up at 8 A.M., had breakfast. She went to the welfare center in the Bronx and was sent back to the Pioneer Hotel. She reports that she had no lunch, spent the early afternoon sitting around and slept in the late afternoon. She said she had no appetite for dinner, was too depressed. After dinnertime she sat and watched TV until 8 P.M. (Women's Shelter, age 38, affiliation rank 1)

Note

1. Ernest Havemann and Patricia Salter West, *They Went to College,* New York: Harcourt, Brace, and Company, 1952, p. 149.

3 Correlates of Affiliation

In the course of the Homelessness Project several hypotheses about the relation between aging, disaffiliation, and other aspects of the life history were tested using male subjects. One of the aims of the present project was to evaluate these hypotheses for female subjects. The specific hypotheses included the undersocialization hypothesis, the anomie hypothesis, the generational retreat hypothesis, the marginality hypothesis, the social mobility hypothesis, and the disengagement hypothesis.

Undersocialization

One of the products of the numerous studies of inebriety and homelessness among lower-class males is the "undersocialization hypothesis." According to this view, the life history of the heavy drinker tends to be "characterized by limited participation in the primary groups which are necesssary for personality formation, by minimum participation in social activities, and by inadequate opportunities for sharing experiences with others," and is "deficient in membership in those associations of sharing that are found in the family of orientation and procreation, in the peer groups that stretch from preadolescence to old age, and in community activities."[1] In other words, undersocialized persons have fewer affiliations and fewer informal ties than other people. Most tests of the undersocialization hypothesis have been limited to males. It may be assumed that women with limited participation in primary groups, minimum participation in social activities, and inadequate opportunities for sharing experiences will experience the negative consequences of these deprivations, but the extent and nature of these effects have not been demonstrated.

If "undersocialization" is conceptualized as limited participation in formal and informal ties, it is almost synonymous with the concept of disaffiliation. In fact, the only real difference is that undersocialization refers to limited social affiliations at some time prior to the point at which the respondent is characterized as disaffiliated. In other words, some support for the disaffiliation hypothesis may be claimed if it can be shown that persons deficient in affiliations during youth also manifest unusually low levels of affiliation in adult life. Usually it is understood that the undersocialization occurs during youth, although there is no impelling reason why this need be so.

Our test of the undersocialization hypothesis will be to assess whether disaffiliated women do report fewer affiliations and informal ties than other women. It is assumed that socialization occurs in the family, the school, and in voluntary organizations for young people such as extracurricular activities at school or neighborhood organizations, and a lack of involvement or low involvement in any of these will be defined as *undersocialization.* Indicators of undersocialization will be limited to extent of formal education and number of voluntary affiliations in youth. The experience of a broken home might also be considered indicative of undersocialization, but that variable is considered in detail later in the discussion of family structure.

According to the undersocialization hypothesis, affiliation and education should be positively related. Therefore, extent of educational attainment should decrease as we move "down" the continuum from higher to lower affiliation, and the expected ranking of the samples in order of decreasing educational attainment should be tract 159, tract 56, tract 76, and Women's Shelter. The data supported these expectations. The mean years of schooling for the four samples were, respectively, 13.3, 12.0, 11.7, and 10.0, and the proportion of college graduates in the samples were 22, 20, 16, and 2 percent.

The preceding sentence with its eight figures suggests that the discussion of results of analysis of data from four separate samples may pose certain problems of style. In order to avoid unnecessary confusion and repetition and at the same time to present a maximum amount of statistical evidence for the relationships being investigated, the following convention was adopted. Descriptive statistics will be presented in a series of four numbers. Each of these numbers will refer to one of the samples, and the order will be the same as in the above paragraph, that of descending affiliation rank, i.e., tract 159, tract 56, tract 76, and the Women's Shelter. Unless it is specifically noted otherwise in the text, whenever a series of four coefficients or four descriptive statistics of any kind is presented, the order will be the same. The first statistic applies to the "high-affiliation" sample (tract 159), the second to tract 56, and so on.

Some might argue that years of completed formal education is not adequate as an indicator of undersocialization because it is possible that a person with little formal education might be able to acquire in adulthood the socialization necessary to function well in society. We have no measures of the extent to which "informal" socialization in adult life occurred, but respondents did provide information about their involvement in adult education programs of any kind. The ranking of the samples on this variable is as expected, with almost two-thirds of the women residing in "more affiliated" tracts having participated in adult education, compared to half of the women in tract 76 and only one-fourth of the Shelter women (see Table 3-1).

With respect to voluntary affiliations during youth, the four samples again manifest the expected order, with the exception that among the two "more affiliated" tracts the order is reversed; i.e., a higher proportion of tract 56 women

Table 3-1
Percent of Respondents Manifesting Various "Levels" of Education and Membership in Voluntary Organizations

	Tract 159	*Tract 56*	*Tract 76*	*Women's Shelter*
Mean years of schooling	13.3	12.0	11.7	10.0
Completed college (*N*)	22% (179)	20% (82)	16% (63)	2% (50)
Participated in adult education programs (*N*)	66 (177)	64 (82)	49 (63)	24 (51)
Belonged to one or more voluntary organizations before age 20 (*N*)	56 (176)	62 (81)	52 (63)	44 (52)

reported affiliations before age 20 than did the respondents in tract 159. However, it should be noted that intersample differences in participation in youth organizations were not large. Only 18 percentage points separated the sample with the lowest participation (Women's Shelter, 44 percent) from that with the highest (tract 56, 62 percent).

Thus, there is evidence that the samples containing the highest proportion of affiliated adults also contained those persons who were most active in youth organizations and whose educational achievements were greatest, with respect to both formal schooling and participation in adult education programs.

A more definitive test of the undersocialization hypothesis was possible by examining the assocation between affiliation rank and educational attainment within each tract. In testing this hypothesis, and in subsequent tests of hypotheses involving the variable affiliation rank, we have treated affiliation rank as if it conformed to an interval scale, although in fact it is an ordinal variable. For empirical and theoretical justification for this practice, see the recent works of Labovitz.[2]

Zero-order correlations between affiliation rank and selected measures of undersocialization (years of schooling completed, years of participation in adult education programs, and number of voluntary affiliations before age 20) appear in Table 3-2. All but one of the 12 coefficients are in the anticipated direction, but most are quite low, and only five reach statistical significance. The *highest* of the 11 positive coefficients was only .44 (for years of schooling, tract 56), and a correlation coefficient of this size may be interpreted to mean that only 19 percent ($.44^2$) of the variance in affiliation rank is explainable in terms of variation in years of schooling completed. Accordingly, it is concluded that undersocialization, as indicated by educational attainment and participation in youth organizations, is only of moderate importance as a precursor of disaffiliation among urban women.

Table 3-2
Zero-Order Correlations between Affiliation Rank and Selected Measures of "Undersocialization"

	Tract 159	*Tract 56*	*Tract 76*	*Women's Shelter*
Years of schooling completed (*N*)	.18[a] (179)	.44[b] (82)	.09 (63)	.17 (50)
Years of participation in adult education programs (*N*)	.08 (185)	.28[b] (82)	-.12 (64)	.11 (52)
Number of voluntary affiliations before age 20 (*N*)	.14 (176)	.36[b] (81)	.34[b] (63)	.02 (52)

[a]Significant at the .05 level.

[b]Significant at the .01 level.

Anomie

Merton lists retreatism – the escape from the frustrations of unfulfilled aspirations by withdrawal from conventional social relationships–as a major adaptation to incongruence between cultural goals and institutionalized means for attaining them. The retreatist individual is viewed as being "asocialized," having abandoned both goals and means. Adaptive activities of psychotics, drug addicts, chronic drunkards, and vagrants are seen as examples of the retreatist pattern;[3] so, we hypothesized, are the activities of the disaffiliated urban women.

Male homelessness had been described as adaption to a situation of anomie. It could be argued that the success goals of American culture apply more to the male than to the female: men are the traditional breadwinners, and hence the strain from discrepancy between success goals and means for attaining success would be expected to affect them more than women. Nevertheless, whether in fact the strain of anomie is experienced by women and whether their adaptions to anomie parallel those of men are important research questions. For example, are women who are "unsuccessful" in achieving the approved goals for women in American society (e.g., marriage, a successful career) more likely than other women to become disaffiliates?

Our measures of the stress resulting from discrepancy between goals and means for attaining success were a number of questions which indicated the respondent's dissatisfaction with various aspects of her life. Taken together, these items might be called a "Disappointment Index." The components of the Disappointment Index were the following seven items: (1) "Are you satisfied with your present housing?" (2) "When you began working, did you intend to spend most of your working years doing what you have been doing?" (3) "Looking back, is there another type of job you would rather have had?" (4) "Some of the people we talk to speak of being lonely. Would you say you are lonely often, sometimes, or never?" (5) "Would you say that your participation in activities was more or less than that of other women your age?" (6) "For yourself, do you think you should be more or less active than you are now?" (7) "Has your life turned out pretty much the way you hoped it would when you were younger?" Three of these questions originally had three response alternatives. However, in combining the items for scale analysis, response categories were combined so that responses to all seven items were dichotomous.

Before proceeding with a discussion of the Disappointment Index, or rather, as it turned out, indices, let us review the intersample differences in responses to the items. Proportions of respondents giving the "dissatisfied" response to the seven items are presented in Table 3-3. Several consistent trends are apparent in that table. First, dissatisfaction with housing increases as we move from the higher affiliation (and economic) levels to the lower levels. Thus, over half of the tract 76 women expressed dissatisfaction with their housing, compared to one-

Table 3-3
Percent of Respondents Indicating Dissatisfaction or Disappointment with Their Present Status or Achievements

	Tract 159	*Tract 56*	*Tract 76*	*Women's Shelter*
Dissatisfied with present housing	24%	35%	57%	–[a]
Did not intend to spend working years doing what she ended up doing (*N*)	46 (167)	62 (77)	40 (60)	47 (47)
Looking back, would rather have had another type of job (*N*)	41 (172)	46 (79)	44 (61)	60 (50)
Is lonely sometimes or often (*N*)	45 (171)	50 (82)	52 (63)	54 (50)
Participates in activities less than other women her age (*N*)	32 (161)	28 (72)	45 (56)	64 (44)
Thinks that she should be more active than she now is (*N*)	43 (168)	58 (78)	59 (59)	66 (47)
Her life did not turn out as she hoped it would when she was younger (*N*)	67 (156)	70 (74)	67 (55)	–[a] –[a]

[a]Questions from which these items were derived were deemed inappropriate for women living in the Women's Shelter and were deleted from the interview schedule for that sample.

fourth of the tract 159 women. Second, the proportion of women who reported being lonely shows a small but consistent increase as the affiliation level of the sample declines. Finally, the perceptions that one participates less in "activities" than other women of the same age increase with the extent of disaffiliation which characterizes the sample as a whole. Approximately one-third of the tract 159 and tract 56 women said that they participated less than others their age, but in tract 56 the corresponding proportion was 45 percent and among Shelter women it was almost 66 percent. The same general finding appears with respect to the normative question about whether the respondent thought that she *should* be more active. Two-thirds of the Shelter women said yes, compared to slightly less than 60 percent of the tract 76 and tract 56 women and only 43 percent of the tract 159 respondents.

Just as interesting as the apparent trends are the "dissatisfaction" items which do not appear to vary by affiliation level of the sample. Shelter women were no more likely than women in the other samples to report that their work lives had been spent in activities other than they had originally intended. About 70 percent of the women in each tract sample reported that life had not turned out as they had hoped it would when they were younger. Shelter women were somewhat more apt than census tract respondents to say they would rather have had another type of job, but among the tract respondents affiliation level of the tract seemed to have no bearing on the percentage of women who indicated that they would rather have had another kind of job; slightly over 40 percent of the respondents in each tract sample said they would rather have followed a different vocation.

When responses to the seven items (five for the Shelter sample, because two of the questions were inappropriate to ask of Shelter clients) were submitted to a factor analysis,[4] six of them manifested loadings of 0.35 or better on the first unrotated factor, indicating the presence of a general "disappointment factor" of some kind. However, the analysis also revealed that there were at least three subfactors worthy of some attention, and so a varimax factor rotation was done. According to the varimax solution, the two items which loaded most heavily on factor 1 were loneliness and feelings that one participated less than other women her age. Items with high loadings on the second rotated factor were the two job-related questions. Only one item had a significant loading on the third rotated factor. For further details on the results of the factor analyses, see Table B-7 and B-8 in Appendix B. For the present, it is sufficient to say that the scores on the unrotated factor 1, which reflected inputs from all except the item about loneliness, were designated as "Disappointment Index 1," and the scores on the first two rotated factors were designated as "Disappointment Index 2" and "Disappointment Index 3," respectively. For the tract samples, the first two factors accounted for 39 percent of the total explained variance in the matrix.

In the separate analysis for the Shelter respondents, the items about fulfillment of job expectations, retrospective evaluation of the desirability of the job one had followed, and loneliness loaded on factor 1 of the principal axis (unrotated) analysis, and were designated as Disappointment Index 1. (See Tables B-9 and B-10.) However, further analysis via a varimax rotation demonstrated that each of the five component items was distinct, and hence for the Shelter sample Disappointment Index 2 reflects only the scores from responses to the retrospective evaluation of employment, and Disappointment Index 3 consists only of weighted responses to the item on whether the respondent participated in activities less than others her age. Among the Shelter respondents, the first two factors accounted for 58 percent of the explained variance.

The present test of the anomia hypothesis will use only Disappointment Index 1, which for the tract samples consists of weighted inputs from six of the seven "disappointment items," and for the Shelter sample represents three of the five possible items. The correlations between affiliation rank and Disappointment Index 1 were, respectively, -.08, -.07, .14, and -.13. None of these coefficients are statistically significant.

A related test of the anomie hypothesis may be made by viewing the intercorrelations between the anomie scale and affiliation rank. The items in the anomie scale are statements devised by Leo Srole to tap anomic attitudes,[5] and thus are distinct in content from the items used in the Disappointment Index. For details about computation of the scale scores and the specific items included in the anomia scale, see Appendix B. Mean anomie scores for the four samples were .05, .76, -47, and -.81 (with a negative score denoting high anomia). Pearsonian *r*'s for the association between affiliation rank and anomia were .26, .34, .04, and .14. The coefficients for tracts 159 and 56 are significant at the .01 level.

These findings are congruent with those of the Homelessness Project. Among the male respondents, measures of failure to achieve aspiration were not significantly correlated with disaffiliation, but there were clear intersample differences in anomia scores.[6]

In summary, measures of extent of perceived discrepancy or disappointment in achievement do not seem to be good predictors of disaffiliation. However, within the "high-affiliation" samples, a weak but significant relationship did appear between anomic attitudes and affiliation rank.

Generational Retreat

According to the "generational retreat" hypothesis, patterns of low social affiliation are transmitted from the parents to the children. George Homans has suggested that individuals whose groups have been destroyed, or who have withdrawn from their initial social groups and have not established new affiliations, will rear children of "lowered social capacity."[7] Results from the Homelessness Project provided only tentative support for the hypothesized association between the extent of one's affiliation and that of his parents. In 36 out of 41 intrasample comparisons, men with backgrounds of low parental affiliation were less affiliated than men from high-affiliation backgrounds. However, there were no intersample differences. Respondents in the control sample were just as apt to come from low-affiliation families as were the skid-row men.[8]

In the present study, the interview schedule contained two questions relevant to parental involvement with voluntary associations. One was the organization-specific query; "How often did your parents attend religious services?" The other, more general question was: "Were they active in any organizations?"

The question about attendance at religious services clearly tapped a different dimension of affiliation, and probably was subject to greater social desirability bias than the more general "organizational activity" question.

In three of the samples at least three-fourths of the respondents reported that one or both of their parents attended church regularly (almost every week). The only exception was the most affiliated sample, tract 159, where only half of the women claimed that their parents were regular church attenders. Thus, responses to the church attendance question did not provide any support for the generational retreat hypothesis.

However, the more general question did elicit trends in the expected direction. The proportions of respondents stating that their parents were active in organizations were, respectively, 52, 61, 36, and 28 percent. Except for the reversal in the two high-affiliation tracts, the intersample variations in parental involvement in associations paralleled the levels of affiliation of the respondents.

Turning to the intrasample relationships, the zero-order correlation coefficients between affiliation rank and the independent variables parental church attendance and parental activity in organizations are given in Table 3-4. The coefficients for church attendance and affiliation rank are inconsistent and reveal no particular pattern. However, all the *r*'s for parental activity and respondents' affiliation rank are positive, although only in one sample (Women's Shelter) is the relationship statistically significant.

Table 3-4
Zero-Order Correlations between Affiliation Rank and Two Measures of Parental Affiliation

	Tract 159	*Tract 56*	*Tract 76*	*Women's Shelter*
Parents' church attendance	-.11	-.33[b]	.13	.24
(*N*)	(173)	(73)	(62)	(45)
Parents' Activity in	.06	.21	.18	.31[a]
organizations (*N*)	(166)		(59)	(47)

[a]Significant at the .05 level.

[b]Significant at the .01 level.

The results parallel the findings for homeless men: there appears to be a modest positive association between the extent of parental activity in voluntary associations and the activity of their children. However, the correlation coefficients are small, usually not significant, and it must be concluded that the intergenerational transmission of propensities to disaffiliation seems relatively unimportant as a cause of disaffiliation in urban women.

Economic Marginality

Several items in the interview schedule were selected as indicators of "economic marginality." Two of these pertained to a woman's family of orientation, one to her family of procreation, and four to her own status. In the first category were the respondent's perceptions of the economic status of her parents in comparison to that of other people in her home community. The question was worded: "About how much money did your family have as compared to other families in your home community when you were growning up?" Also pertinent to the family of orientation was the father's occupational status. Each respondent was asked about the occupation of her father, and the occupation identified was assigned the appropriate index number from Duncan's Socioeconomic Index (SEI).[9] The same procedure was followed with the occupation of the respondent's husband, if she had been married.

The indicators of economic marginality which pertained to the respondent's own status were her modal lifetime SEI, her current income, her age, and a health index ranging from 1 (poor health) to 4 (excellent health). The inclusion of age and health as indicators of economic marginality was on the basis that both are indicators of the extent to which one is expected to be a productive, useful part of the economy. The sick role includes the lifting of the responsibility to be a producer, and at the same time usually relieves society of the responsibility to provide income at the level which the working person can command. Paychecks stop during prolonged or chronic illnesses unless the individual has during a productive period acquired sufficient insurance to guarantee income continuance. As for age, not only is one defined as being beyond economic usefulness at retirement age, but even before that time there may be pay cuts or an increase in "layoffs," especially for persons in low-status occupations. Moreover, the person in late middle age has a much harder time demonstrating that he is "with it," "involved," "alert," or in other ways in the mainstream of things and not marginal.

Sample means for these indicators of economic marginality, and zero-order correlation coefficients for the relationship between the various indicators and affiliation rank and economic marginality, will be considered.

There were five possible responses to the item on perceived parental economic status. There were scored from 1 to 5, with 1 representing "far less money than most people in the community" and 5 representing "far more money. . . ." Variations in sample means on this item paralleled the affiliation level of the samples, with tract 159 respondents perceiving their families most favorably with respect to the status of other families in their community, and Shelter women perceiving the status of their parents' families most unfavorably.

Within the four samples, the relationship between status of parents and affiliation rank is less clear. In two of the samples there is an inverse relationship—the higher the perceived parental status, the lower the individual's present affiliation rank—and in the other two (tract 56 and the Women's Shelter) the relationship is positive but weak. Coefficients, respectively, are -.16, .10, -.13, and .29. Only the first of these is statistically significant, and an r of that magnitude accounts for only 3 percent of the variance in affiliation rank. It is concluded that economic marginality as measured by children's perceptions of parental status in the community is a poor predictor of affiliation rank.

The apparent effects of father's occupational status parallel the findings for perceived status of parents in comparison with other families in the community. Except for an insignificant reversal between tracts 159 and 56, means for paternal status parallel the affiliation level of the samples, ranging from 56.5 for women in tract 56 to 27.8 in the Shelter sample. However, when the correlation between a woman's affiliation rank and her father's status is computed for each sample separately, a significant positive relationship appears only for tract 56 women, and the size of that relationship indicates that a knowledge of the paternal occupational status score would only explain 8 percent of the variation in scores of affiliation rank among the respondents in tract 56. Accordingly, it was concluded that father's occupational status, like perceived family status, is not particularly important as a predictor of affiliation in adult life.

The same general finding applies to husband's occupational status. In none of the samples did the husband's SEI manifest a significant correlation with affiliation rank. However, the differences in mean status of husband show sizable intersample differences—the mean SEI of husband's occupation among tract 159 women was 62.6, and the other samples, respectively, were 56.6, 47.1, and 26.9—which are consistent with the varying affiliation levels of the tracts.

With one exception, the findings for respondent's modal occupational status are congruent with those for husband's status. The intertract variations in status parallel the affiliation levels of the tracts, and only in tract 56 is there a significant correlation between affiliation rank and occupational status.

The independent variables in the last three rows of Table 3-5 are indicators of a woman's "marginality" at the time of the interview. Note that the sample means for current income and health parallel the rankings of the tracts by level of affiliation. Despite these differentials in income and health, the three tract samples appear to represent women of about the same age (means are 64, 66, and 66 years). However, the respondents at the Women's Shelter are significantly younger than women in the other samples (mean age is 47).

Table 3-5
Means for Selected Indicators of Economic Marginality, and Zero-Order Correlations between Marginality Indicators and Affiliation Rank

	Means				*Correlations with Affiliation Rank*			
Indicators of Marginality	*Tract 159*	*Tract 56*	*Tract 76*	*Women's Shelter*	*Tract 159*	*Tract 56*	*Tract 76*	*Women's Shelter*
Perceived parental economic status (*N*)	3.16 (173)	3.12 (78)	2.96 (57)	2.44 (45)	-.17[a]	.10	-.13	.29
Paternal occupational SEI (*N*)	53.4 (160)	56.5 (74)	46.4 (56)	27.8 (35)	.03	.29[a]	-.19	-.07
Husband's occupational SEI (*N*)	62.6 (135)	56.6 (50)	47.1 (39)	26.9 (36)	-.08	.14	-.14	-.10
Modal lifetime SEI (*N*)	53.4 (174)	51.4 (80)	46.2 (61)	26.6 (50)	.05	.36[b]	.00	.06
Current income (index score)[c] (*N*)	5.4	4.6	3.9	1.3	.43[b]	.58[b]	.20	.02
Age (*N*)	64.3 (185)	66.3 (82)	66.3 (64)	47.2 (52)	-.46[b]	-.62[b]	-.47[b]	-.14
Health (index score)[d] (*N*)	2.9 (185)	2.6 (82)	2.6 (64)	1.0 (52)	.26[b]	.39[b]	.29[a]	.19

[a]Significant at the .05 level.

[b]Significant at the .01 level.

[c]Categories were 1 = 0–99, 2 = 100–199, 3 = 200–299, 4 = 300–399, 5 = 400–499, 6 = 500–599, 7 = 600–999, and 8 = 1000 or more.

[d]Categories were 1 = poor health, 2 = fair, 3 = good, and 4 = excellent health.

With reference to the correlations between affiliation rank and these three independent variables, it is apparent that all these variables are very important correlates of affiliation. For the tract samples, eight of the nine coefficients are significant at the .01 level. The lack of high coefficients for the Shelter sample reflects the operation of exceptional circumstances there which minimize the apparent effects of age, health, and income. For example, the income of all the Shelter respondents is so low as to preclude any sizable association with affiliation rank, and even on the dependent variable itself there is less range of variation than in the other samples. These factors operate together to depress the magnitude of the correlation coefficient. The coefficients for the relationship between affiliation rank and both age and health are in the expected direction for Shelter women, but do not reach statistical significance. These differences between the Shelter sample and the tract samples merely reflect the obvious fact that disaffiliation among Shelter women differs in several ways from the kind of disaffiliation experienced by residents of more settled neighborhoods. The influences of age and health, in particular, operate differently for Shelter women than for women who have their own rooms or apartments in the city.

The magnitude of the correlation coefficients in the last three rows of Table 3-5 suggests that for women in the tract samples, age is a most important determinant of affiliation rank, and that current income is also a critical variable. Health also seems important, but its effects are not nearly as evident as those of the former variables. For the tract samples, the variances in affiliation rank explained by age alone were 21, 38, and 22 percent. Comparable figures for current income were 18, 34, and 4 percent. In contrast, the variance explained by the health index was never above 15 percent, and in two of the tracts was 7 or 8 percent.

The relative effects of "background" variables in contrast with "current" variables should be noted. Since the three current variables differ in content as well as recency from the background variables, no definitive statement can be made. Nevertheless, the implications of these findings are that certain aspects of a woman's current situation, such as her health and personal income, are far more important predictors of affiliation rank than the "background factors," which are beyond the control of the clinician and the therapist. This finding is particularly meaningful because "current factors" such as health and income are subject to some external control, whereas the "background" variables are beyond the reach of the therapist and clinician. In other words, it would seem that substantial increases in the affiliation of women in these samples could be achieved if their economic status were improved and if better medical care were available to them.

It should also be stressed that the present assessment of the effects of several indicators of economic marginality, like the preliminary evaluations of the operation of several other factors as antecedents or correlates of disaffiliation, has considered only the zero-order correlation coefficients. Later in this chapter the various independent variables shall be examined in multiple regression analysis, where simultaneous controls for other significant variables are part of the statistical design.

Occupational Mobility

Several studies have noted the potentially disruptive effects of vertical mobility.[10] As stated by Wilensky and Edwards, the general idea is that the mobile person "tends to lack firm ties to either the groups he has left behind or those into which he is moving."[11] In one of the papers deriving from the Homelessness Project the anticipated effects of downward mobility in the lives of skid-row men were summarized:

> One of the popular beliefs about skid-row men is that they have "skidded" or been downwardly mobile occupationally. They are visualized as men who once held normal jobs (including professional positions) but took to drink and now eke out subsistence by panhandling, dishwashing, and casual labor, or are supported by charity. . . . If downward mobility weakens or destroys the affiliative bonds that link persons to organizations in their social environment, the homelessness of skid-row men is not surprising; it is the natural consequence of their downward mobility.[12]

However, a test of the hypothesis that downward occupational mobility was directly associated with loss of affiliative ties led to the conclusion that the disaffiliation of Bowery respondents was not attributable to their downward mobility, and that whether downward mobility was accompanied by disaffiliation seemed to depend on the social context in which the mobility occurred.[13]

The effects of downward occupational mobility among women have received little attention from researchers. One of the tasks of the present study was to discover whether the alleged link between downward mobility and disaffiliation, a linkage not supported in our own previous research among homeless men, held for female respondents. A second more descriptive problem was to identify some of the correlates of occupational mobility among women. The mobility-disaffiliation hypothesis will be considered first.

The index of occupational status used was the Duncan Socioeconomic Index (SEI). The SEI status scores reflect income and education differentials in occupations as revealed in U.S. census data, weighted by the prestige rankings of occupations derived from the North-Hatt scale. There are SEI scores, ranging from 0 to 96, for each of the detailed occupational categories listed in the U.S. Census.[14]

Two measures of worklife mobility used were status loss and lifetime mobility. Status loss is the difference between one's current (or most recent) occupational status and the highest status ever attained. Lifetime mobility is the difference between a woman's initial occupational status and her current or last status. Part-time jobs while a respondent was in school were not included in the computations.

Table 3-6 presents the mean values of status loss, net lifetime mobility, and mean lifetime occupational status for the four samples. It is apparent that the three tract samples do not differ in mean status loss, but respondents in all three manifest substantially less status loss (about 6.5 SEI points) than occurs among Shelter women (12 SEI points). Similarly, Shelter women have the lowest mean net lifetime mobility scores (2.5), contrasted to mean scores ranging from 3.1 to 5.7 for the tract samples. In other words, respondents at the Women's Shelter are more likely to have experienced downward mobility, and less apt to have known improvement in status over the first full-time job, than are women in any of the tract samples. But the differentials among the latter do not correspond to their differences in level of affiliation, so little support for the downward mobility-disaffiliation hypothesis can be claimed from the intersample comparisons.

The correlation coefficients in Table 3-7 reflect the intrasample association between affiliation rank and occupational mobility. Once again, no consistent relationship appears. Only one of the eight relevant coefficients is statistically significant, and hence it is concluded that among the samples of women investigated in the present study, a history of occupational mobility in either direction does not seem related to disaffiliation.

Table 3-6
Zero-Order Correlations between Affiliation Rank and Selected Measures of Occupational Status and Mobility and Mean Values of the Occupational Variables

Correlations between Affiliation Rank and:	*Tract 159*	*Tract 56*	*Tract 76*	*Women's Shelter*
Status loss	-.09	-.20	.05	.17
Net lifetime mobility	.06	.28[a]	.19	-.13
Lifetime occupational status	.05	.36[b]	.00	.06
Mean Values				
Status loss	7.5	7.5	7.3	11.9
Net lifetime mobility	3.1	5.7	3.6	2.5
Lifetime occupational status	53	51	46	27
(*N*)	(175)	(80)	(62)	(51)

[a]Significant at the .05 level.

[b]Significant at the .01 level.

Table 3-7
Zero-Order Correlations between Status Loss and Net Lifetime Mobility and Selected Behavioral and Attitudinal Variables

	Tract 159		*Tract 56*		*Tract 76*		*Women's Shelter*	
	Status Loss	*Net Mobility*	*Status Loss*	*Net Mobility*	*Status Loss*	*Net Mobility*	*Status Loss*	*Net Mobility*
Behavioral Variables								
Education	-.11	.13	-.07	-.04	.14	-.10	.23	.05
Current income	-.09	.08	-.29[b]	.20	-.20	.18	-.01	-.04
Affiliations in youth	.13	.04	-.04	.20	.09	.04	-.02	.05
Media Use	-.11	.06	.17	-.14	.16	-.19	.20	-.02
Social Interaction Index, 1	.04	-.09	-.08	.32[b]	-.15	.15	-.17	.19
Social Interaction Index, 2	.02	.18	.09	-.01	.20	-.01	-.20	.35[a]
Attitudinal Variables								
Health	-.11	.11	-.02	-.02	.20	-.18	-.12	-.06
Anomia	-.03	.08	-.10	.09	.10	.05	.15	-.13
Misanthropy	-.09	.04	-.20	.28[a]	-.19	.23	-.16	.29
Powerlessness	-.04	-.04	.12	-.11	-.26[a]	.20	.11	.08
Self-esteem	-.09	.01	-.15	.22	-.20	.30[a]	-.12	.37[b]
Self-estrangement	-.05	.12	.09	-.01	.06	-.01	-.07	.20
(*N*)	(185)		(82)		(64)		(52)	

[a]Significant at the .05 level.

[b]Significant at the .01 level.

We will now turn to the second question, namely, What are some of the correlates of occupational mobility among women? Zero-order correlation coefficients between the two measures of occupational mobility and a series of other behavioral and attitudinal variables appear in Table 3-7.

The notable thing about the coefficients in Table 3-7 is their low value. Of the 96 coefficients, only 7 are statistically significant, and that many significant relationships out of almost 100 are to be expected by chance. In only one case is there a consistent significant relationship, i.e., a significant finding for the same two variables in more than one sample, and that is the positive relationship between self-esteem and net lifetime mobility. A consistent, parallel (but nonsignificant) relationship appears for status loss and self-esteem. Thus, there is tentative evidence that one's self-esteem is enhanced if he has experienced upward mobility, and that if he has experienced losses in status, his self-esteem has deterioated. Beyond this tentative finding, however, the matrix offers little. The general conclusion is that among the respondents in the present study, the mobility history bears little relationship to the 12 variables listed in Table 3-7.

Disengagement

The basic idea of the disengagement theory of aging is that a mutual severing of ties occurs between an aging person and others in society, and this process of disengagement leads to new levels of equilibrium between the individual and his social environment. The process is seen as self-perpetuating, and it is conceived as a normal, "healthy" stage of human life. In the formal statement of the theory, marked sex differences in the process of disengagement are delineated, and it is suggested that disengagement is more difficult for men than for women.[15]

The importance of age as a predictor of affiliation rank has already been noted in the discussion of "marginality." In the section Multivariate Analysis which follows, age emerges as the single most powerful predictor of affiliation rank. Moreover, since its predictive power is all the more impressive when it must "compete" with several other independent variables, we will not discuss it further at this point, but rather will move directly into the final portion of this chapter.

Multivariate Analysis

Up to this point we have considered each hypothesized relationship about the correlates of disaffiliation separately. With some exceptions, the results have been disappointing: Relatively little of the variance in affiliation rank has been explained by any of the independent variables. We came to essentially the same conclusion in the analysis of the antecedents of homelessness among Bowery men: No single factor explains homelessness; instead it is a consequence of the interaction of a variety of elements.

In an attempt to explain a greater proportion of the variance in affiliation rank, and at the same time to determine the relative strength of the various independent variables in accounting for the variance in affiliation rank, the data were submitted to a stepwise multiple regression analysis, which simultaneously analyzed the effects of all 17 independent variables on the dependent variable. In effect, multiple regression analysis permits the independent variables to compete with one another to determine which have the strongest relationships with the dependent variable, and it provides a cumulative measure of how much variation of the dependent variable can be explained by various combinations of independent variables.

The choice of 17 independent variables is somewhat arbitrary. The analysis of zero-order correlations identified several variables which appeared to have little explanatory power, and these were excluded from the multivariate analysis. However, six variables not discussed previously in this chapter were included as independent variables. The rationale for doing this is as follows. Having demonstrated that some of the variables identified by previous researchers as important antecedents of homelessness (e.g., undersocialization, generational retreat, occupational mobility) do not, in themselves, have much predictive power, it seemed pointless to continue to multiply text and tables in the analysis of bivariate relationships for which there was less theoretical justification than for the variables already demonstrated to be inadequate predictors of intrasample differentials in affiliation rank. Once the greater explanatory power of a stepwise multiple regression approach was recognized, the logical procedure was to include a number of variables of either demonstrated or suspected importance, and then to discard variables on the basis of their nonsignificant effects in the presence of controls for those independent variables that did manifest a significant effect.

The six independent variables not discussed previously in this chapter are two measures of affiliation during the 20-to-44 age span, two measures of current interaction, a measure of exposure to certain forms of mass media, and the respondent's estimate of her monthly expenses. The first five are summary measures, or composites of several distinct items.

The so-called "media use" scale is a summary measure which reflects the respondents' use of books and movies. The scale scores are based on the frequency of book and film use, weighted according to the loadings of those items on factor 1 of a varimax solution to the correlation matrix. For details see Appendix B, Tables B-13 and B-14.

The two measures of current interaction are derived from the varimax solution to a matrix containing the intercorrelations among these variables: number of personal letters the respondent received annually (based on the question, "How often do you receive a personal letter in the mail?"), number of persons she conversed with on the day preceding the interview, the number of persons in the neighborhood she knew by name, the number of close friends she had in New York City, and the number of times she left her room or apartment on the day before the interview. The varimax solution to the matrix showing intercorrelations among these items yielded two factors, and scores on these factors were computed for each respondent. The acquaintances, friends, and conversation items had high loadings on the first factor (Social Interaction Index, 1), and the items about personal letters and forays out of the room had higher loadings on the second (Social Interaction Index, 2). The relevant tables appear in Appendix B, Tables B-11 and B-12.

The two measures of affiliation during the 20-to-44 age span were introduced as independent variables because it was felt that the patterns of affiliation maintained during those early adult years probably had some direct consequences for the patterns of affiliation in later years, and hence the extent of affiliation at the time of interview. Church attendance histories and histories of persons lived with had been obtained from all samples. An index of church attendance over the 25-year period was obtained by computing the mean score in a four-point scale of degree of church attendance. The figures for living alone were simply the proportion of the 25-year period in which the respondent reported that she lived alone.

The bivariate correlation coefficients (Pearsonian *r*) between the 17 independent variables and affiliation rank are summarized in Table 3-8. Results of the stepwise multiple regression analysis[16] appear in Table 3-9. The number of independent variables which emerged as significant predictors of affiliation rank varied from only two among the Shelter women to eight among tract 56 respondents. In the tract samples the strongest variable was age; the amount of explained variance from this variable alone was, respectively, 22, 39, and 22 percent. Other important predictors (i.e., independent variables manifesting a significant effect in at least two of the three tract samples) were monthly expenses, monthly income, and social interaction (Index 1). The amount of intrasample variation in affiliation rank "explained" by the independent variables which entered the regression equation ranges from .30 (after correction for shrinkage)[17] in tract 159 to .59 in tract 56.

In the bivariate analysis reported in Table 3-8, six variables manifested a significant correlation with affiliation rank among tract 159 women. However, the multiple correlation analysis reveals that the influence of several of these is reduced to nonsignificance when controls for other independent variables are added. Thus, health, education, and monthly expenses—all important predictors in the bivariate analysis—drop out of the regression equation, leaving only age, income, and social interaction as significant correlates of affiliation.

For the tract 76 respondents, six independent variables had significant zero-order correlations with affiliation rank. The multiple regression analysis eliminated two of these—health and media use; age, social interaction (Index 1),

Table 3-8
Zero-Order Correlations between Affiliation Rank and 17 Independent Variables

		Sample			
Hypothesis	*Independent Variables*	*Tract 159*	*Tract 56*	*Tract 76*	*Women's Shelter*
1	Health	-.26[b]	-.38[c]	-.29[a]	-.19
2	Education	.18[a]	.44[c]	.09	.17
3	Monthly expenses	.32[c]	.48[c]	.39[b]	.17
4	Monthly income	.40[c]	.58[c]	.20	.02
5	Age	-.46[c]	-.62[c]	-.47[c]	-.14
6	Youth affiliations	.14	.35[b]	.33[b]	.02
7	Occupational status loss	-.09	-.20	.05	.17
8	Net lifetime occupational mobility	.06	.28[a]	.19	-.13
9	Modal lifetime occupational status	.05	.36[c]	.00	.06
16	Church attendance, ages 20 to 44	.06	.14	.11	-.07
17	Percent of ages 20 to 44 lived alone	-.02	-.25[a]	.12	–
18	Media use	.12	.25[a]	.36[b]	.46[c]
19	Social interaction index, 1	.28[b]	.39[c]	.39[b]	.00
20	Social interaction index, 2	-.01	.16	.24	-.16
21	Disappointment index, 1	-.08	-.07	.14	-.13
22	Disappointment index, 2	-.06	-.02	.08	-.11
23	Disappointment index, 3	.06	-.25[a]	-.00	.48[c]

[a]Significant at the .05 level.

[b]Significant at the .01 level.

[c]Significant at the .001 level.

monthly expenses, and youth affiliations remained. Of 12 independent variables in the tract 56 sample which had significant bivariate relationships to affiliation rank, four were deleted, including health, number of affiliations in youth, modal lifetime occupational status, and media use. Finally, for the tract 159 women, three of the six independent variables shown to exert significant influence in the bivariate analysis were eliminated, namely, health, education, and monthly expenses. Apparently controls for the three that remained in the equation—age, income, and social interaction (Index 1)—effectively reduced the influence of the others to nonsignificance (see Table 3-9).

Table 3-9
Stepwise Multiple Regression Analysis between Affiliation Rank and 17 Independent Variables, Four Samples

Variable	*Step*	*Partial* r	*Multiple* R	*Multiple* R^2	*Increase in* R^2	F *Ratio*	P
			Tract 76				
Age	1	–	.47	.22	–	17.5	.001
Social interaction index, 1	2	.42	.60	.36	.14	12.8	.001
Monthly expenses	3	.31	.65	.42	.06	6.4	.001
Youth affiliations	4	.24	.67	.45	.03	3.7	.01
		(C)R = .66	*(C)*R^2 = .44				
			Tract 56				
Age	1	–	.62	.39	–	50.3	.001
Monthly income	2	.45	.71	.51	.12	19.6	.001
Percent of ages 20 to 44 lived alone	3	-.28	.74	.55	.04	6.8	.001
Education	4	.25	.76	.57	.03	4.9	.01
Monthly expenses	5	.19	.77	.59	.02	2.9	.05
Disappointment index, 3	6	-.17	.78	.60	.01	2.3	.05
Net lifetime occupational mobility	7	.18	.78	.62	.01	2.5	.05
Church attendance, ages 20 to 44	8	.17	.79	.63	.01	2.3	.05
		(C)R = .77	*(C)*R^2 = .59				
			Tract 159				
Age	1	–	.46	.22	–	50.3	.001
Monthly income	2	.32	.54	.29	.08	20.1	.001
Social interaction index, 1	3	.15	.56	.31	.02	4.1	.01
		(C)R = .55	*(C)*R^2 = .30				
			Women's Shelter				
Disappointment index, 3	1	–	.48	.23	–	14.9	.001
Media use	2	.40	.59	.35	.12	9.1	.001
		(C)R = .58	*(C)*R^2 = .34				

The consistent, dominant position of age as a predictor of affiliation rank is notable; so is the consistent appearance of expenses and/or income. Two other variables identified which merit serious consideration in future studies are social interaction and disappointment or frustration with the way life turned out.

While the present findings cannot be said to provide support for the disengagement theory, the primary position of aging as the most important of the 17 independent variables certainly is consistent with the theory. However, income or expenses and extent of social interaction also exert important effects independent of the effects of aging. It is possible that both the activity theory and the disengagement theory are "right" in the sense that processes consistent with both theories may operate simultaneously, and the dominance of either process is determined, in part, by the constraints of situational variables such as the availability of financial resources.

Notes

1. David J. Pittman and C. Wayne Gordon, *Revolving Door,* Glencoe, Ill.: The Free Press, 1958, p. 10.

2. Sanford Labovitz, "The Assignment of Numbers to Rank Order Categories," *American Sociological Review,* 35 (June 1970): 515-524; "Some Observations of Measurement and Statistics," *Social Forces,* 46 (December 1967): 151-160; and "Reply to Champion and Morris," *Social Forces,* 46 (June 1968): 543-545.

3. Robert K. Merton, *Social Theory and Social Structure,* New York: The Free Press of Glencoe, 1957, p. 153.

4. For a discussion of the method used to perform the principle axis factor analysis of a correlation matrix, see S.H. Thomson, *The Factorial Analysis of Human Ability,* 4th ed., New York: Houghton Mifflin, 1950, pp. 70-74.

5. Leo Srole, "Social Integration and Certain Corollaries: An Exploratory Study," *American Sociological Review,* 21 (December 1956): 709-716.

6. Howard M. Bahr, *Homelessness and Disaffiliation,* New York: Bureau of Applied Social Research, Columbia University, 1968, pp. 281-282; Howard M. Bahr and Theodore Caplow, *Old Men Drunk and Sober,* New York: New York University Press, 1974, pp. 186-199.

7. George C. Homans, *The Human Group,* New York: Harcourt, Brace, and Co., 1950, p. 457.

8. Bahr and Caplow, *Old Men Drunk and Sober,* pp. 77-81.

9. Howard M. Bahr and Theodore Caplow, "Homelessness, Affiliation, and Occupational Mobility," *Social Forces,* 47 (September 1968): 33.

10. See, for example, Peter M. Blau, "Social Mobility and Interpersonal Relations," *American Sociological Review,* 21 (June 1956): 290; Harold L. Wilensky, "Orderly Careers and Social Participation: The Impact of Work History

on Social Integration in the Middle Mass," *American Sociological Review,* 26 (August 1961): 521-539; Harold L. Wilensky and Hugh Edwards, "The Skidder: Ideological Adjustments of Downward Mobile Workers," *American Sociological Review,* 24 (April 1959):215-231; Richard F. Curtis, "Occupational Mobility and Membership in Formal Voluntary Associations: A Note on Research," *American Sociological Review,* 24 (December 1959): 846-848.

11. Wilensky and Edwards, "The Skidder," p. 216.

12. Bahr and Caplow, "Homelessness, Affiliation, and Occupational Mobility," p. 29.

13. Ibid., p. 33.

14. Albert J. Reiss, Otis Dudley Duncan, Paul K. Hatt, and Cecil C. North, *Occupations and Social Status,* New York: The Free Press, 1961, pp. 109-138.

15. *Elaine Cumming and William E. Henry, Growing Old: The Process of Disengagement,* New York: Basic Books, Inc., 1961, pp. 210-218.

16. "This program computes a sequence of multiple linear regression equations in a stepwise manner. At each step one variable is added to (or taken from) the regression equation. The variable added is the one which makes the greatest reduction in the error sum of squares. Equivalently it is the variable which has highest partial correlation with the dependent variable partialled on the variables which have already been added and equivalently it is the variable which, if it were added, would have the highest F value. . . . Variables are automatically removed when their F values become too low." W.J. Dixon (ed.), *BMD: Biomedical Computer Programs,* Los Angeles: Health Sciences Computing Facility, Department of Medicine and Public Health, School of Medicine, University of California at Los Angeles, p. 233.

17. When multiple R is used, there is a tendency for a slightly inflated R due to the smaller number of degrees of freedom because of additional calculations. This bias toward an inflated R increases as the number of variables in the equation (n) approaches the number of cases (N). In this study, since the N's are relatively small, the bias towards an inflated R may be substantial, and a correction for shrinkage is employed. The formula is:

$$r'_{1.23\ldots n} = \sqrt{1 - (1 - r^2_{1.23\ldots n})\left(\frac{N-1}{N-n}\right)}$$

Quinn McNemar, *Psychological Statistics,* New York: John Wiley & Sons, Inc., 1962, p. 184.

4 Lifetime Patterns of Affiliation

The four major subdivisions in this chapter correspond to four types of affiliation, namely, employment, the family, voluntary associations, and the church. For each of these types of affiliation, patterns of affiliation will be discussed, and lifetime profiles will be presented for each sample.

Employment Patterns by Sample

The profiles in Figure 4-1 represent the proportion of respondents in each sample who were employed either part- or full-time between the ages of 15 and 75 (55 for Shelter women). Part-time jobs held while a woman was in school are not included. However, full-time jobs regardless of school attendance and part-time jobs after schooling terminated are represented.

In interpreting the profiles, it should be recognized that women in Manhattan and other metropolitan areas have higher than average employment rates. For example, in 1960, 46 percent of all females 14 years of age and over in Manhattan were employed, but for the remainder of the New York City SMSA the figure was only 34 percent. In our samples even the Shelter women manifested employment rates as high as the national average, and the extent of employment among women in the other samples was much higher.

When the profiles in Figure 4-1 are contrasted with the "national patterns" described in government labor force statistics, several differences other than general level of employment are apparent. The "family cycle" pattern in which labor force participation rates drop substantially between a peak around ages 18 to 24 and a second peak at ages 45 to 54 does not appear in any of the samples. In the Shelter sample, peak employment occurs at age 20 when three-fourths of the women were employed, and thereafter extent of employment declines quite sharply for about a decade, and more gradually after that. In the tract samples, peak employment occurs in middle or late middle age (ages 55, 45, and 60, respectively), but throughout the entire adult worklife, from age 25 on, the level of employment for each sample remains fairly constant. Thus, in tract 159, between ages 25 and 60 the proportion employed ranges from 65 to 73 percent; in tract 56 between ages 25 and 55 the range is 75 to 83 percent; and in tract 76 the proportion employed varies 72 to 85 percent during the 40-year period ending at age 65.

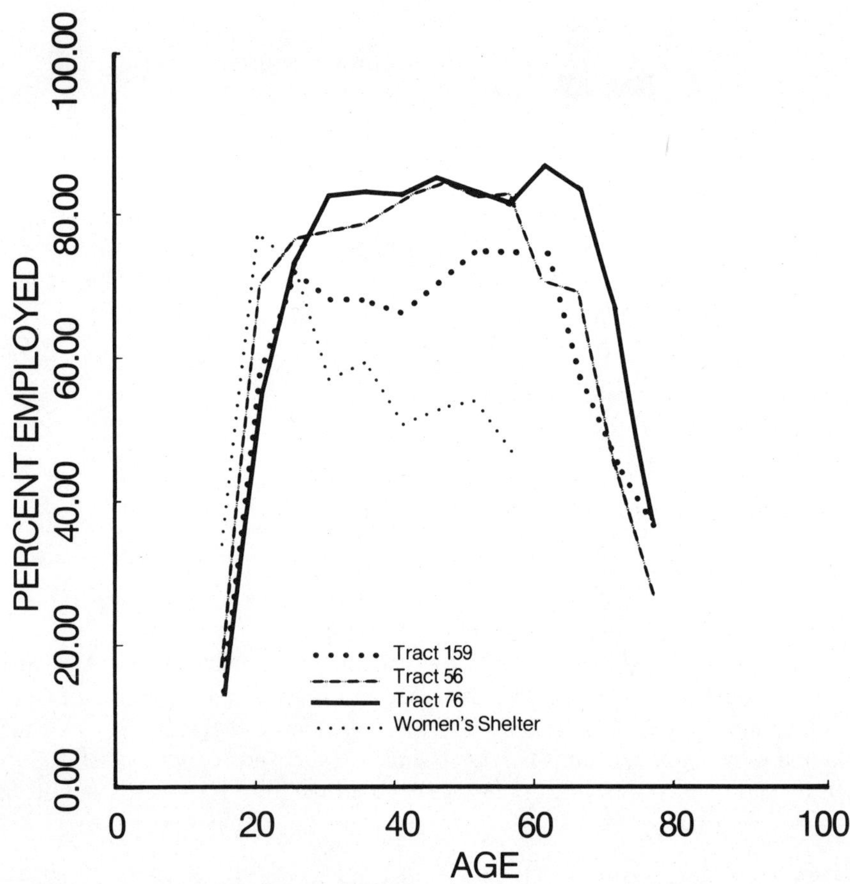

Figure 4-1. Percent of Women Employed, by Age

The decline in employment associated with aging seems to occur later in our samples than in the national samples. The national pattern[1] is as follows: (1) About 41 percent of girls of high school age work (including part-time). (2) Peak labor force participation (about 53 percent) occurs during ages 18 to 24. (3) For the next 10-year interval the proportion decreases to about 42 percent. (4) After age 35 the percentage of women working increases and reaches a second peak (52 percent) in the group aged 45 to 54. (5) After age 54 the labor force participation again declines. (6) Even after age 65 about 10 percent of women are employed.

In only one of the tract samples does a substantial decline occur as early as ages 55 to 60. In tract 56 there is a 12 percent decline between ages 55 and 60, and then no additional decline until afte age 65. Two-thirds of the tract 56 women were working right up to retirement age.

In tract 76 there is no decline until age 65; at that point 82 percent of the women were still employed. And in tract 159 there is no substantial decline until after age 60. Remarkably, in all three tract samples, between one-fourth and one-third of the women were still working at age 75.

Similar employment profiles for males were prepared as part of the Homelessness Project.[2] The profile for upper-income males manifested the same kind of stability throughout the work history as is evident in the profiles for the three tract samples, although at a higher level (above 95 percent employment). The sample of lower-income males, in contrast to the non-Shelter females in the present study, manifested a gradual decline in proportion employed from a peak of over 90 percent at age 30. In fact, from age 50 on, the lower-income males are no more likely to be employed than are women in tract 56 or tract 76. Finally, the employment profiles of Bowery men parallel those of Shelter women. At age 20, 70 percent of the Bowery men and 75 percent of the Shelter women were employed. By age 40, the proportion has dropped to about half for both samples. Between age 40 and 55 the Bowery men exhibit a continued sharp decline in employment, while among the Shelter women there is no further decline until after age 50. At age 55, the last age for which there are data on the Shelter women, their rate of employment is 39 percent, almost precisely that of the Bowery respondents.

Occupational Status Profiles

The data about employment also were coded with respect to occupational status. The measure of occupational status used, the Duncan SEI, has already been introduced in the discussion of occupational mobility in Chapter 3. The occupational status profiles in Figure 4-2 were prepared by computing means of the individual SEI scores at 5-year intervals throughout life. With the exception of the tract 76 sample, which shows increasing status until age 35 when a peak mean status of 50 is achieved, all the samples show an early achievement of a general level of status—not necessarily the *highest* point, but achievement of a status score very near the lifetime peak status—and maintenance of that level throughout most of the worklife. Thus, the tract 159 respondents attained a mean SEI of 55 at age 25, and between that time and age 70 their mean status fluctuates between scores of 50 and 56. Similarly, tract 56 women attain a mean status score of 48 at age 20, and for the next 45 years their mean scores remain within the 5-point range between 48 and 53. The Shelter women attain a much lower occupational status—at age 20 their mean score is 26—but, like the other samples, they manifest general stability in their mean status scores for the rest of the profile. The occupational status levels of all the samples, as expected, parallel their affiliation levels.

The status profiles for the male respondents interviewed in the Homelessness Project were quite different from those revealed in the present study. The

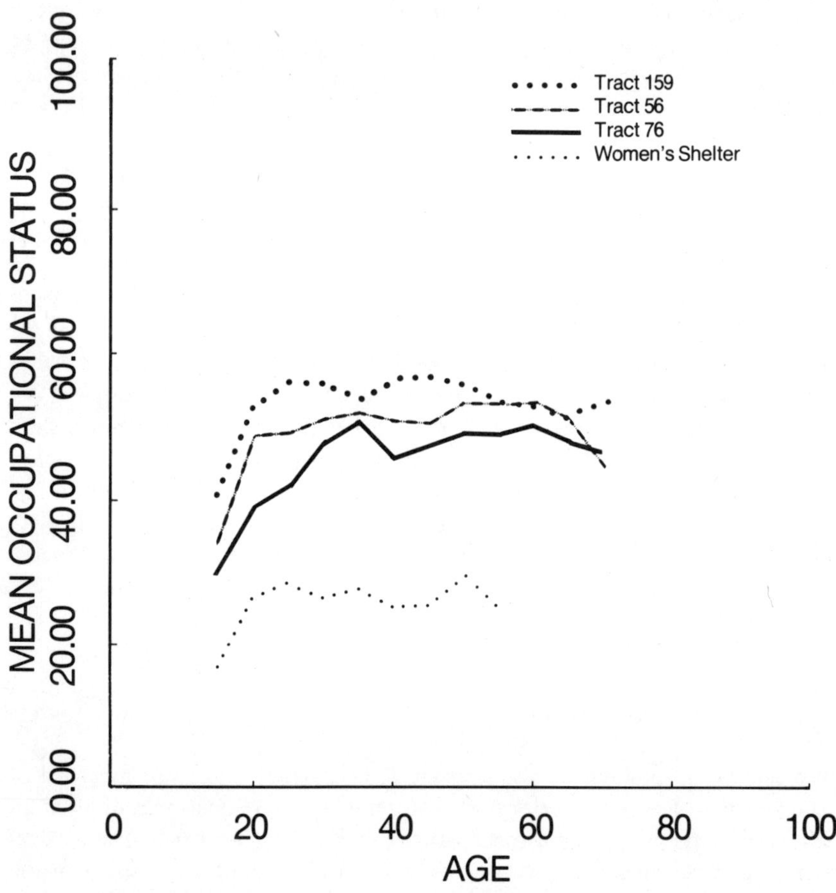

Figure 4-2. Mean Occupational Status of Employed Women, by Age

sample of upper-income males manifested increasing occupational status throughout life, with the bulk of the increase occurring by age 40, when their mean status score was 74. The lower-income males showed a continual rise in occupational status from age 15 to age 35, then a decline, and finally an increase to a peak status of 31 at age 65. The Bowery men's profile was a continuing decline with periods of stability; the highest mean occupational status ever attained was a score of 19 at age 15. By age 65 the mean score had dropped to 12.

In comparison with the women's profiles, several differences are notable. First, the women's early peak status at age 20 or 25 has no counterpart in the men's histories. Also, the general stability following attainment of the level of status characteristic of the profile as a whole is peculiar to the women's profiles and those of the Bowery men; the samples of non-skid-row males manifest substantial changes in occupational status over the life history. In addition, the occupational status of the women in the tract samples is lower than that of the upper-income men but clearly higher than that of the lower-income males. In fact, the SEI scores of the Shelter women are approximately equivalent to those of the lower-income males. Finally, none of the female samples manifested occupational status as low as that of the skid-row men.

Types of Employment

Table 4–1 presents for 10-year age intervals from 20 to 60 the percentage distribution by gross census occupational categories of employed respondents in the four samples. Substantial intersample differences are evident. In tract 159 the top three categories—professional workers; managers, officials, and proprietors; and clerical workers—are the dominant kinds of occupation with managerial and proprietory jobs much less important than professional or clerical kinds of work. The same general description fits tract 56 except for the fact that at the later ages managerial and proprietory positions increase and clerical jobs decline in importance. Also, considering the life span as a whole, professional and technical occupations are less common among tract 56 women than tract 159 women.

Tract 76 respondents were primarily clerical workers, followed by professional and technical workers, service workers, and sales workers, in that order. At ages 20 and 30 Shelter women tend to be service workers, but after age 30 they are more apt to be private household workers, operatives, or clerical workers.

The status differentials among the tracts are clearly evident in the distribution of respondents among the gross occupational categories. The proportion of women employed in the lower-status jobs increases as one moves across the table, and the proportions in the high-status categories show corresponding decreases. Among the trends apparent in two or more of the samples is a general decline with age in the proportion of respondents doing clerical work.

Family of Procreation

In all the samples, most of the women had married. The proportion ranged from 65 percent in tracts 76 and 56 to 79 percent in tract 159 and 77 percent among Shelter women. The major differences between the samples were not in the percentage of women who had married, but rather in the way marriages had terminated. In the census tract samples, between 40 and 50 percent of the marriages ended in divorce, separation, or annulment. In contrast, fully 89 percent of the Shelter women reported that their first marriage ended in divorce, separation, annulment, or desertion. The Shelter women are different in that their marriages

Table 4-1
Percentage Distribution of Respondents by Occupation and Age at 10-Year Intervals, Ages 20 to 60, Four Samples

	Tract 159					*Tract 56*					*Tract 76*					*Women's Shelter*				
	Age					*Age*					*Age*					*Age*				
Occupation	*20*	*30*	*40*	*50*	*60*	*20*	*30*	*40*	*50*	*60*	*20*	*30*	*40*	*50*	*60*	*20*	*30*	*40*	*50*	*60*
Professional, technical, and kindred workers	32%	39%	40%	31%	35%	22%	25%	28%	27%	27%	13%	17%	14%	18%	16%	8%	0%	6%	0%	0%
Managers, officials, and proprietors except farm	3	13	15	16	14	0	9	17	23	35	3	7	7	10	9	0	4	6	13	0
Clerical and kindred workers	47	30	27	35	29	55	38	33	27	14	31	48	44	44	41	11	13	6	13	25
Sales workers	7	5	6	8	11	8	7	5	6	5	16	7	7	10	22	14	0	6	0	0
Craftsmen, foremen, and kindred workers	1	3	5	2	1	0	4	4	4	6	0	2	2	3	3	0	0	0	0	0
Operatives and kindred workers	5	5	5	4	2	10	5	4	4	6	13	2	12	0	0	25	17	29	50	50
Private household workers	0	1	1	1	1	4	4	4	2	5	9	5	2	3	0	8	33	35	25	25
Service workers, except private household	4	5	3	3	5	2	7	12	8	3	16	12	12	13	9	28	33	12	0	0
Laborers, except farm and mine	0	0	0	1	2	0	0	0	0	0	0	0	0	0	0	0	0	0	0	0

frequently do not last, but they are just as likely as respondents in the other samples to have experienced marriage.

Among women who had been married, approximately one-fifth of the respondents in tracts 56 and 76 had been married more than once. In tract 159 one-fourth of the women had married two or more times, and in the Shelter sample more than one-third of the respondents had experienced a second marriage.

The Shelter sample also differed from the other samples in the incidence of consensual unions reported. In the tract samples, between 5 and 9 percent of the respondents said that at some time they had lived with a man as if they were married, but two-thirds of the Shelter women responded affirmatively to this item.

The proportion of women who had been married was about the same as for the non-skid-row males studied in the Homelessness Project (71 percent among lower-income men and 77 percent among upper-income men). However, it is plain that the respondents at the Women's Shelter are much more likely to marry than are skid-row men. Slightly less than half of the skid-row men had ever been married, compared to about three-fourths of the Shelter women. Among skid-row women, disaffiliation is more likely to occur as a consequence of a bad marriage than from no marriage at all. But among skid-row men, never marrying is a more important factor than is unsuccessful marriage.

Problems in Marriage

One portion of the interview schedule contained a series of questions about the kinds of problems that had characterized the respondent's marriage. Eight specific "things couples often have differences of opinion about" were mentioned, and for each of them the woman was asked to state whether it had been a problem in her marriage. The items included disagreements about her working, how to raise the children, differing sexual needs, drinking, either spouse being away from home too much, finances, infidelity, and in-laws. Table 4-2 shows the proportion of ever-married respondents reporting each of the problems. The figures in the table refer to first marriages only.

In the tract samples the marital problem most frequently mentioned was family finances. Even in the multiproblem marriages of the Shelter women, finances was the third most cited problem. Moreover, it is a problem mentioned by approximately one-third of the respondents regardless of the affiliation level of the tract; women in tract 159 mentioned it about as frequently as Shelter women.

The most common problems among respondents in the tract samples were mentioned by about one-third of the women. Thus, 38 percent of the tract 76 women reported disagreements on financial matters, and unfaithfulness and

Table 4-2
Percent of Ever-Married Respondents Reporting Marital Disagreements, by Type of Disagreement

Topic of Disagreement	*Tract 159*	*Tract 56*	*Tract 76*	*Women's Shelter*
Wife's working	17%	8%	5%	26%
How to raise the children[a]	20	34	19	25
Differing sexual needs	13	12	16	36
Drinking	19	22	26	36
Absences from home by either spouse	21	6	29	46
Financial matters	31	38	38	38
Unfaithfulness	31	8	32	62
In-laws	14	8	32	31
Other topics	25	24	34	38
(Lowest *N*)b	127	49	37	38

[a]Percentage of women who had had children. *N*'s, respectively, were 109, 41, 32, and 36.

[b]Number of cases varied slightly due to missing information.

in-law problems were noted by 32 percent of them. The most common problems listed by tract 56 women, financial matters and how to raise the children, were reported by 38 and 34 percent of the respondents, respectively. As for tract 159, 31 percent of the women agreed that financial matters had been problematic in their marriages, and a like proportion cited marital infidelity as a problem.

One of the striking findings apparent in Table 4-2 is the high problem content of the marriages of Shelter women. With two minor exceptions (one-third of the tract 56 women reported disagreements over child rearing, compared to one-fourth of the Shelter women, and 32 percent of the tract 76 women who had been married reported in-law problems, compared to 31 percent of the Shelter women), the Shelter women have the highest frequencies of reported marital problems for every type of problem listed. They reported marital infidelity twice as frequently as other respondents (62 percent, as compared to 32 percent in tract 76), absences of one or both spouses from home almost twice as frequently, differing sexual needs between 2 and 3 times as often, and with the exception of one of the census tract samples, the respondent's working and disagreements over in-laws at least twice as often as women in the other samples. The drinking behavior of either spouse (most frequently the husband) was listed as a marital problem in between one-fifth and one-fourth of the marriages of non-Shelter women, but it was mentioned by 36 percent of the Shelter women. However, it is noteworthy that the differentials between Shelter women and respondents in the tract samples with respect to drinking as a marital problem are not as great as for marital infidelity, differing sexual needs, absence of either spouse from home, and, with the exception of tract 76, in-law problems.

A similar series of questions had been given to the male respondents of the Homelessness Project. However, neither financial difficulties nor marital infidelity was included in the list of standard items given to all men. The number of men who mentioned these problems led to their inclusion in the present study. Among skid-row men drinking was the most frequently mentioned marital problem, followed by absence of the respondent from home; about one-third of the men mentioned absence from home as an important problem, and about half of them mentioned drinking. It is of interest that for Shelter women the order of priority is reversed, with absence from home mentioned by almost half the women and drinking by about one-third. Some of the differences may be accounted for by the fact that in questioning the skid-row men, the "absence from home" applied to his own absence, while in the present study the question was worded to include absences of either spouse. In any case, it is apparent that the marital problems identified as most common (using both the structured items and the qualitative material from the skid-row men's interviews) among skid-row men—drinking, absences from home, finances, and infidelity[3]—are also the problems most frequently identified by the Shelter women. A fifth major problem, differing sexual needs, is mentioned by the latter as frequently as drinking.

Family Affiliation throughout Life

One important section of the interview schedule was a chart on which the interviewer recorded the respondent's migration and household history (i.e., persons with whom she had lived) by year of life. For each year the interviewer entered one or more symbols (or drew a line indicating continuation of the previous year's situation) for the following categories of persons lived with: mother, father, sister, brother, child or children, extended family (all other relatives, including aunts, uncles, cousins, grandparents, etc.), husband, female friend, male friend, and alone. These data were punched on cards by year of life. By summarizing the distribution of types of persons lived with at 5-year age intervals, it was possible to prepare lifetime profiles showing the proportion of respondents living with persons in any of the original categories. In the present section, we will be concerned with lifetime patterns of living with (1) members of either the family of procreation (husband and children) or the family of orientation (parents and siblings) or (2) members of the family of procreation only.

In the Homelessness Project, similar profiles were prepared showing the percentages of respondents who lived with members of their families of orientation or procreation. The patterns discovered in that study were: (1) among skid-row men, the proportion of respondents living with family members declined consistently from age 15 until the end of the profiles at age 65; (2) among the lower-income, settled respondents in the Park Slope sample, the proportion of men living with their families declined sharply until age 25, leveled off and remained stable at about 60 percent until age 40, and then manifested another decline, ending at between 45 and 50 percent at age 65; (3) among the upper-income men in the Park Avenue sample, the proportion living with their families declined between ages 15 and 20 but after age 20 manifested a general increase throughout life, although there were some minor fluctuations, and at age 65 more than 85 percent of the Park Avenue men were living with family members.[4]

Lifetime profiles showing the percentage of respondents living with members of their families appear in Figure 4-3. Unlike the profiles for the various samples of males, all four samples of females showed the same general trend, a fairly steep decline in family affiliation throughout life. The only difference among the samples was the age at which the decline "bottomed out" and manifested either stability or a much lower rate of decrease. Among Shelter women, the period of rapid decline ends at age 40, when only one-fifth of the respondents were living with family members, and thereafter the rate of decline is much slower. The decline in living with family members among tract 76 women parallels that of the Shelter women, with the end of the "high-loss" period occurring at age 45 when 18 percent of the respondents of that age or older still lived with family members. Over the next 35 years, a slight but consistent decline in family living continues, until at age 80 only 9 percent of the respondents were living with family members. In tracts 56 and 159 the rate of decline during adult life is much slower than in the other samples, but the continuing downward trend is apparent throughout life. By age 50 the proportion of women living with family members is 39 percent for tract 56 and 58 percent for tract 159; by age 80 the corresponding proportions are 4 and 0 percent.

Figure 4-4 portrays the women's lifetime patterns of living with members of their families of procreation. The expected form of these profiles might be a sudden rise between age 15 and 25 or 30, when most women marry, and then a very gradual decline reflecting the experience of women who are widowed and divorced and do not have children who live with them after the termination of the marriage. The rate of decline in the curve should increase with age, i.e., with the increase in the probabilities of the husband dying. In addition, about 20 years after the initial upswing there should be a substantial decline, which represents the last child leaving the homes of those women already living without husbands for some reason.

The profiles for the tract 159 and tract 56 samples are roughly congruent with these expectations. In both cases a clear "family cycle" is apparent in the proportion of women living with members of their families of procreation. However, respondents in tract 76 and the Women's Shelter manifest a very different pattern. Their profiles reflect dissolution of the family of procreation fairly

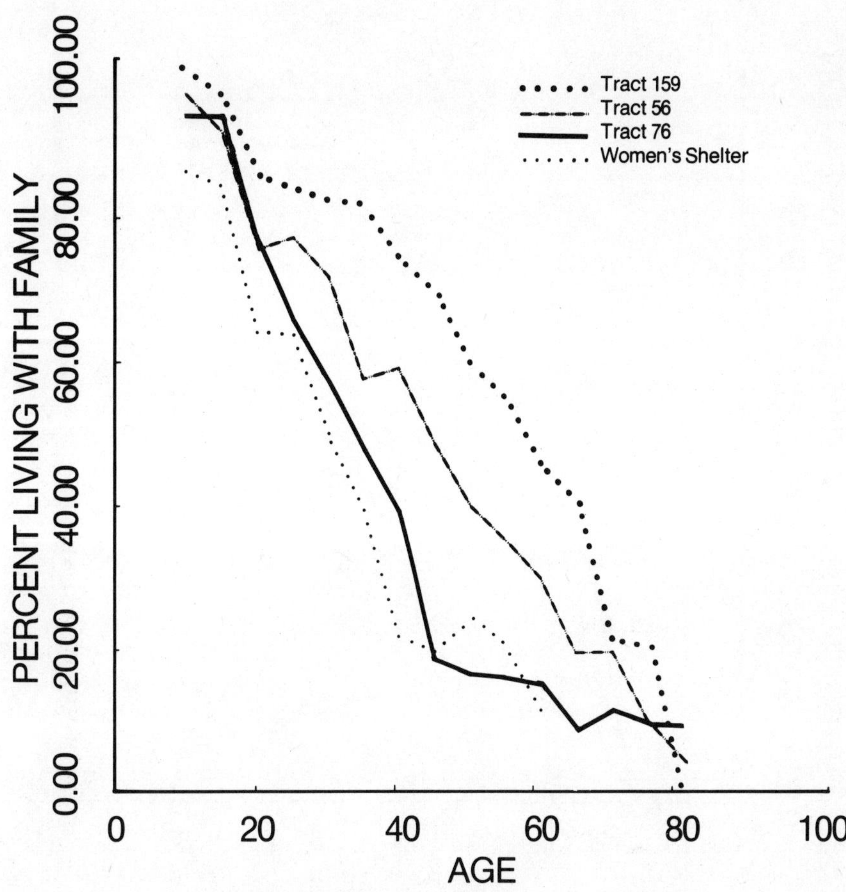

*Includes members of family of orientation and/or procreation.

Figure 4-3. Percent of Respondents Living with Members of Their Families* by Age

quickly after its formation. After a peak at age 25 or 30, the rate of decline is so rapid that by age 45 the proportion of women in these tracts living with husbands or children is comparable to that in the tract 56 and 159 samples at age 70.

The consistent decline in family affiliation throughout life may be interpreted to mean that the dissolution of ties to family of orientation among these women occurs at a more rapid rate than the formation of ties to members of families of procreation. Many of the women in all the samples married and had families, and in the tract 56 and 159 samples many women were living with family members, but the creation of marital ties or the renewal in later adult life

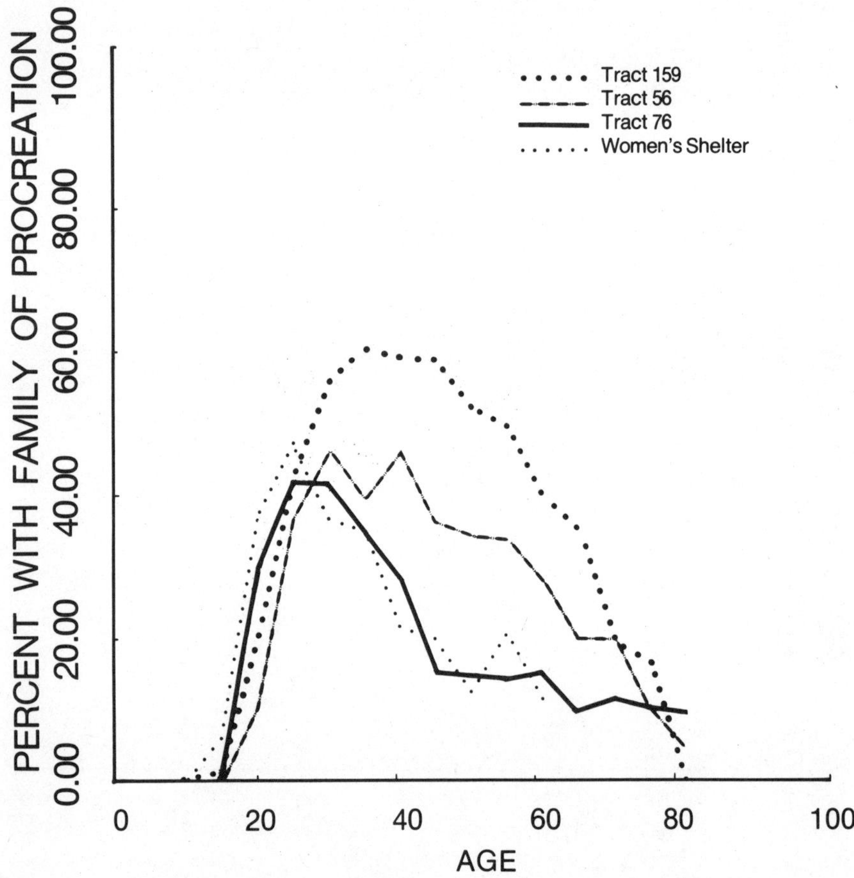

Figure 4-4. Percent of Respondents Living with Members of Their Families of Procreation, by Age

of ties to family of orientation (as in cases where sisters were living together) simply do not occur nearly as frequently as the dissolutions of ties. Thus the lifetime decline in attachment to family members, at least as measured by sharing the same household with them, characterizes all four samples. All manifest family affiliation patterns congruent with those of skid-row men, and incongruent with the profiles of either the lower-income or upper-income men studied in the Homelessness Project.

Voluntary Associations

Those memberships classed as "voluntary affiliations" included all except employment, family, and church attendance. The data came from questions in which respondents indicated whether they had ever belonged to various kinds of organizations. One series of questions applied to the woman's adult life, defined as "since you left school." Among the types of groups mentioned specifically were religious groups, fellowship organizations (Eastern Star, Rebeccas, Daughters of the American Revolution), labor unions or professional organizations, political or action organizations, recreational or social groups (athletic teams, bridge clubs, bowling leagues), music or art groups, and neighborhood organizations (PTA, Red Cross). The final question included "any other groups you haven't mentioned."

In another part of the interview schedule was a similar series of questions pertaining to the childhood and teenage years in which respondents were asked about extracurricular activities in school, organized athletic teams, YWCA, political clubs, 4-H clubs, Girl Scouts, cooking or sewing groups, charity organizations, drama groups, and church clubs. When a woman answered yes to any of the specific kinds of organization or to the residual "other clubs or groups" question, she was asked to name the organization or organizations to which she referred, the date she joined that group, the duration of her membership, and the extent of her participation in the activities of that organization.

Types of Voluntary Affiliations

The frequencies with which memberships in the various types of organizations were reported are given in Table 4-3. However, before discussing intersample variations in type of voluntary affiliation maintained, the most obvious findings in the table should be mentioned. Note that the reported youth memberships of Shelter women do not differ from those of the other respondents. The Shelter woman is just as likely as the census-tract respondent to have participated in extracurricular activities and athletic teams, and to have belonged to political groups, charity or service organizations, 4-H, WYCA, religious clubs, drama groups, or any other kind of organization. However, as an adult, her organizational participation is strikingly different from that of the other women. In every category of voluntary organization she is the least affiliated, and the differences are large. Between 23 and 41 percent of the tract respondents belong to religious groups and clubs; for Shelter women the figure is 4 percent. Between 14 and 26 percent of the other respondents belong to political or action organizations, but only 2 percent of Shelter women have such ties. Between one-fourth and one-third of the other respondents maintain memberships in community or neighborhood organizations; *no* Shelter women have memberships in organizations of this kind. Whatever else Table 4-3 may show, it is clear that with respect to voluntary organizations, the disaffiliation of Shelter women may not be attributed to their lifelong patterns of avoidance of memberships. In youth, they too were affiliated.

Table 4–3
Percent of Respondents Affiliated with Various Types of Voluntary Organizations during Youth and as Adults

Type of Organization	*Tract 159*	*Tract 56*	*Tract 76*	*Women's Shelter*
As a Young Girl or Teenager				
Clubs, sororities, or extracurricular activities	29%	29%	21%	31%
Athletic teams	14	14	10	12
YWCA	12	11	14	15
Political or action organizations	6	9	6	6
4-H club, Girl Scouts, or other outdoor or handicraft groups	12	11	11	8
Cooking or sewing clubs	3	11	13	8
Service or charity organizations	8	12	5	12
Religious groups or clubs	14	21	21	16
Drama or art groups	13	14	11	10
Other organizations	11	15	3	12
As an Adult				
Religious groups or clubs	23	41	29	4
Fellowship organizations (Eastern Star, Rebeccas, DAR, etc.)	6	10	8	4
Labor unions or professional associations	33	29	25	4
Political or action organizations	17	26	14	2
Recreation or social groups (athletic teams, card clubs, bowling leagues, etc.)	22	26	19	8
Drama or art circles, music groups, or other hobby clubs	18	25	14	0
Community or neighborhood organizations (PTA, Red Cross, etc.)	34	35	25	0
Other organizations	14	17	8	8

The affiliation patterns reported "as a young girl or teenager" are remarkably consistent from sample to sample. Most frequently reported are memberships in clubs, sororities, or extracurricular activities (21 to 31 percent of the women mentioned these), followed by affiliations in religious groups or clubs (14 to 21 percent). The least common type of affiliation was the political group; the proportion reporting such memberships was highest in tract 56 (9 percent). In the other categories of organizations mentioned, the usual proportion reporting membership was between 10 and 14 percent.

The consistency among the tract samples in types of affiliation continues into adult life. Thus, while the organizational category reported most frequently varies (in tract 159 it is community and neighborhood organizations, in tracts 56 and 76 it is religious groups and clubs) within each sample, the three categories of affiliation most frequently maintained were community and neighborhood organizations, religious groups and clubs, and labor unions or professional associations. Between one-fourth and slightly more than one-third of the respondents in the tract samples belonged to each of these types of organization.

On the basis of each woman's statement about the dates of her participation in the various kinds of organizations, lifetime profiles were prepared for each respondent showing for each year of her life the number of voluntary affiliations she maintained. Then, the individual profiles were summarized for each sample. The resulting composite profiles showed the mean number of voluntary affiliations maintained by respondents in each of the samples (Figure 4-5) and the proportion of respondents maintaining at least one voluntary affiliation (Figure 4-6).

Among the patterns of aging and participation in voluntary associations revealed by previous researchers are the "family-cycle" model, the "disengagement" model, and the "stability" or "continued engagement" model. In the family-cycle model the early adult years are characterized by low rates of membership, affiliation increases during the middle years, and then declines in the fifties and sixties.[5]

The disengagement model is derived from the disengagement theory of aging. According to this perspective, disengagement from voluntary affiliations, as well as other forms of social attachment, is a natural consequence of aging. Thus, following middle-age, affiliation in voluntary associations should show a progressive, consistent decline. Finally, there is the "stability" model, according to which participation in voluntary associations is continued throughout adult life at approximately the same level, and may even increase as changes in family responsibilities permit increased participation in organizations outside the family.[6] The continued-engagement model is congruent with the so-called "activity theory" of aging.

The profiles in Figure 4-5 reveal two distinct patterns of age-linked variation in the mean number of voluntary affiliations which characterize the four samples. In the two samples with the lowest level of current affiliations (tract 76 and

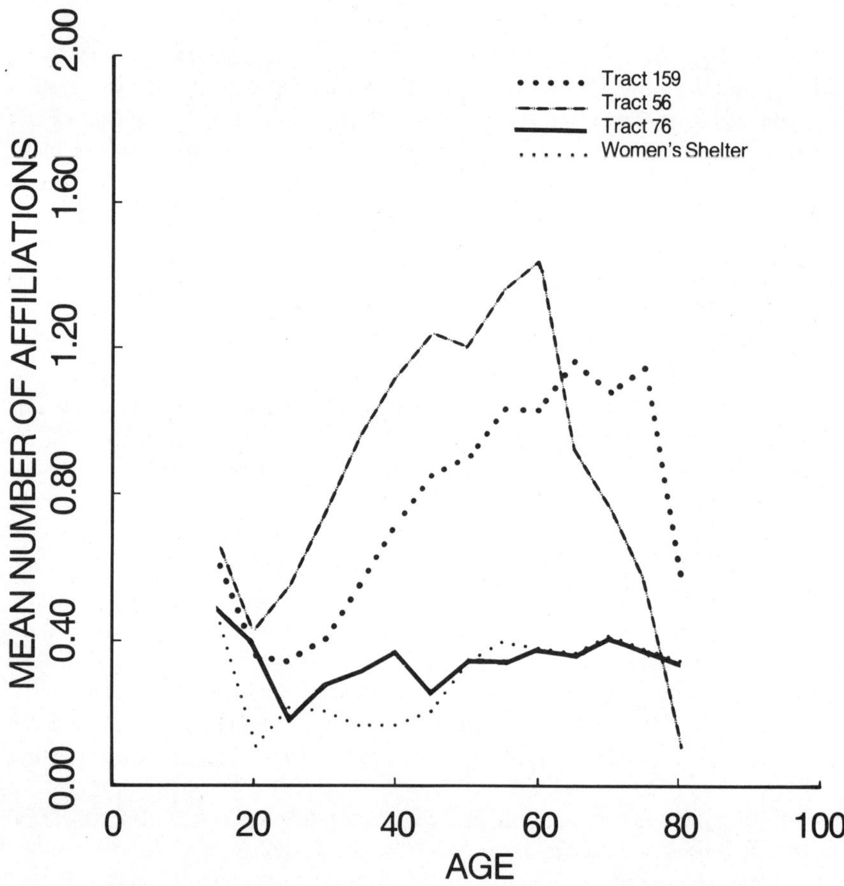

Figure 4-5. Mean Number of Voluntary Affiliations, by Age

the Women's Shelter), the most extensive involvement in voluntary associations occurs during the teenage years. Following this peak affiliation, there is a decline to a low point at age 20 or 25, and then the mean number of affiliations increases slightly. Throughout the rest of the adult life, a level of affiliation intermediate between the high point in the teen years and the low point in the following decade is maintained. Neither sample manifesting this pattern provides support for the family-cycle or disengagement models. In fact, the trend is for level of affiliation to increase slightly with advancing age. Thus, the stability or continued-engagement model is supported.

The other two samples, tract 159 and tract 56, have very different affiliation profiles. Respondents in these samples also manifest a decline in affiliation following a high point in the teenage years, but throughout the remainder of

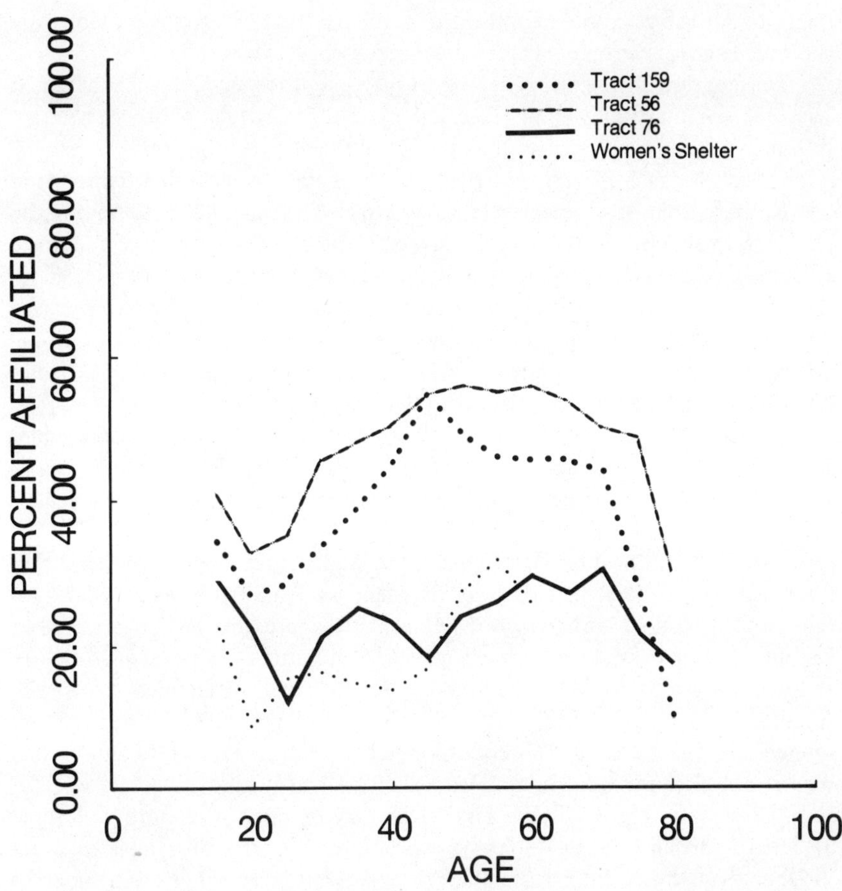

Figure 4-6. Proportion of Respondents Maintaining One or More Voluntary Affiliations, by Age

adult life they continue to add affiliations and finally reach a peak much higher than that achieved during their high school years. In tract 56 the increase in extent of affiliation continues until retirement age, and in the more affluent tract 159 it continues until age 75. Even at age 80, the mean number of affiliations maintained by women in the tract 159 sample is higher than that achieved by the tract 76 or Shelter respondents during their youth. The sharp decline in extent of affiliation after age 60 for the tract 56 women and after age 75 for the tract 159 respondents might be cited as support for the disengagement model. However, the decline among tract 159 respondents occurs later than the model would predict, and hence the support for the disengagement theory derived from the profiles in Figure 4-5 must be limited to only one of the four samples, tract 56. All things considered, the profile for the tract 159 sample supports the continued-engagement model better than the disengagement model.

Turning now to profiles reflecting proportion of respondents maintaining at least one voluntary affiliation (Figure 4-6), the congruency between the tract 159 and tract 56 samples in contrast to that of the Women's Shelter and tract 76 respondents is again apparent. In all the samples, the maximum participation in one or more voluntary associations occurs fairly late in adult life. Among the Shelter women aged 55 or more, 31 percent maintained some kind of voluntary affiliation at age 55 in comparison with 22 percent at age 15. Among tract 76 respondents the corresponding proportions are a maximum of 30 percent at age 70, compared to 28 percent at age 15. The gradual decline in extent of affiliation after age 60 might be cited as evidence for the disaffiliation model. However, the profiles are not congruent with the family-cycle model.

The "proportion affiliated" profiles for the tract 159 and tract 56 samples are very similar to those for mean number of affiliations. Thus, from a peak at age 15 there is decline to age 20, followed by an increase in the proportion of affiliated women which for tract 56 reaches a peak at age 45 and then declines, as predicted by both the disengagement and the family-cycle model. The profile for tract 159 women is somewhat less congruent with the family-cycle model because a high level of affiliation is maintained for approximately 25 years before any decline sets in, and the decline begins to occur after a peak level of affiliation at age 60, when 55 percent of the tract 159 respondents maintained at least one voluntary association. Again, it is of interest that the proportion of tract 159 respondents affiliated at age 80 corresponds to the proportion affiliated in the Women's Shelter and tract 76 samples at their peak affiliation.

In summary, the profiles in Figure 4-6 may be cited in support of all three models of participation in voluntary associations: the tract 56 sample supports the family-cycle and disaffiliation models, and through age 60 or 65 the tract 76 and 159 profiles support the continued-engagement model. In fact, since the disengagement theory assumes that the mutual withdrawal of the aging person and society occurs independently of health factors, and that the profiles do not take health into account, the substantial decline in the proportion of respondents maintaining affiliations after age 70 is, at best, only equivocal evidence for the disengagement model. The profiles for tracts 76 and 159 in Figures 4-5 and 4-6, taken together, suggest that as the woman ages, she maintains or even increases her involvement in associations outside the home until physical factors accompanying advanced age intervene and make such participation impossible. For the tract 159 women, such factors do not seem to have a substantial impact until after age 75; in tract 76 their influence is apparent somewhat earlier.

Comparisons with Samples of Males

Affiliation profiles for four samples of males, including two skid-row samples, a lower-income sample, and an upper-income sample, were prepared as part of the

Homelessness Project. The profiles for the three kinds of male respondents were quite different, with the skid-row respondents exhibiting disaffiliation throughout their lifetimes, the lower-income, "settled" sample manifesting the family-cycle pattern, and the upper-income sample exhibiting increasing participation in voluntary associations throughout adult life. Thus, in the final report of the Homelessness Project, if was noted that:

In Park Slope [the lower-income sample] the proportion of respondents who belonged to voluntary associations increased steadily from age 20 until age 40, and then declined at about the same rate until age 60, and more rapidly thereafter.

For skid-row men there is a continuous decline in participation in voluntary associations until middle age, when the decline is temporarily halted by a period of stability and even a slight increase in affiliation. Then the decline continues.[7]

The affiliation profile for the Park Avenue men [the upper-income sample] shows the expected low membership in the early adult years, but after that time the trend is toward a continuing increase in affiliation, with most of that increase coming after age 40. These respondents were most affiliated with voluntary associations at age 65, the last age appearing on the figure.[8]

Several conclusions may be derived from a comparison of the profiles for males with those for the female respondents in the present study. First, the males are more apt to belong to voluntary associations, and they belong to more of them than do the females. For example, the maximum mean number of voluntary affiliations in any of the female samples at any age was 1.4 (tract 56 respondents at age 60). In contrast, the peak for Park Avenue men was a mean 2.7 affiliations at age 65. The mean number of voluntary associations maintained throughout adult life by Bowery men was approximately 0.75; the corresponding figure for Shelter women and tract 76 respondents was only half that figure, or less. Thus, the male respondents in all socioeconomic samples seem to maintain at least twice as many voluntary affiliations as do the female respondents.

Comparisons of the percent of respondents maintaining at least one voluntary affiliation produce the same finding: until age 55 at least half of the Bowery men and much higher proportion of the other male samples have at least one voluntary affiliation, but only 20 to 23 percent of the Women's Shelter and tract 76 respondents are similarly affiliated. The differences between the upper-income males and the tract 56 and 159 respondents are not quite as dramatic; at least 80 percent of the males in the Park Avenue sample were affiliated with one or more voluntary organizations, compared to slightly over 50 percent of the tract 159 females. In summary, it appears that males are more likely than females to belong to voluntary associations, and among those maintaining voluntary affiliations, males tend to have more memberships than females.

The lack of congruence between the patterns of the lifetime affiliation among the female respondents and those of the males deserves comment. Among the samples of males, only the upper-income respondents manifested continuing increases in extent of affiliation throughout adult life. But none of the samples of females showed a consistent decline in mean number of voluntary affiliations until age 60 or after, and only the tract 56 sample showed a decline in the proportion of respondents maintaining at least one voluntary affiliation before that date. Thus, the profiles of even these samples of women designated as "most disaffiliated" manifest patterns (not levels) of participation in voluntary associations more congruent with the affiliation profiles of upper-income men than of lower-income men. This finding is particularly striking in light of the fact that none of the samples of women were upper-income samples. Although the census tract in which the upper-income males resided was selected for study primarily on the basis of its median income, a *low* median income was one of the characteristics which led to the inclusion of tract 159 (the "high-affiliation" tract) in the current study. Of course there are a number of well-to-do women in the tract 159 sample, but the sample as a whole is definitely a lower-income sample. Nevertheless, the patterns of involvement in voluntary organizations among the women in tract 159, as well as in the other female samples, parallels the experience of upper-income men more closely than that of lower-income men.

Aging and Religious Affiliation

One of the publications deriving from the Homelessness Project presented a summary of patterns of aging and church attendance from selected research studies.[9] From these studies were derived four models of the relationship between aging and church attendance. These were designated as the traditional model, the stability model, the family-cycle model, and the disengagement model. It will be recognized that three of them correspond to models already discussed in the section Voluntary Associations. The one model not introduced there, the traditional, predicts a steady increase in religious activity after age 35.

Analysis of the lifetime profiles of church attendance among the four samples of metropolitan males revealed substantial religious disaffiliation during adult life in all the samples, and demonstrated that "the model of aging and church attendance derived from the disengagement theory of aging is most congruent with the patterns of lifetime church attendance reported by the respondents."[10] The data also showed that as aging occurred, church attendance was increasingly less important as a source of voluntary affiliation among both the well-to-do men and the poor men. In other words, the fraction of total participation in organizations outside the home which was devoted to church work *declined* with age. The histories of church attendance obtained in the present study permit us to compare the findings for males with those for females.

Respondents were first asked about their religious preference. Then there was a question about when they had first attended church or synagogue, followed by a series of questions which identified periods of regular attendance. Then periods of less frequent attendance were recorded. Categories used in constructing the affiliation profiles were attendance "regularly" (almost every week), "sometimes" (more than two times a year), "infrequently" (one or two times a year), and "no attendance."

The profiles in Figure 4-7 show the proportions of respondents who reported attending church regularly at 5-year intervals over the life span. In many respects the women's lifetime attendance patterns parallel those observed among the four samples of males studied in the Homelessness Project. For example, all the profiles in Figure 4-7 reveal a high point in church attendance during the teenage years, followed by a sharp decline. In two of the samples, the most impoverished (Shelter women) and the most affluent (tract 159 respondents), the decline in regular attendance is never reversed.

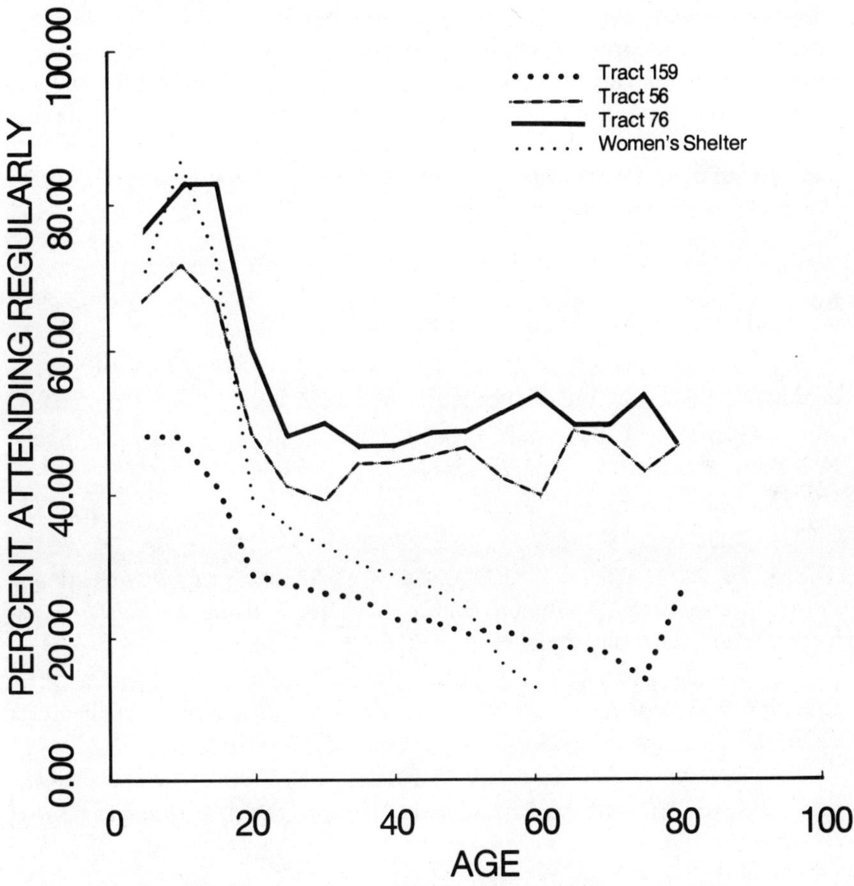

Figure 4-7. Percent of Respondents Reporting Regular Church Attendance, by Age.

Among the samples studied during the Homelessness Project, it was the upper-income respondents who showed the lowest rates of regular church attendance, and the next lowest rates characterized the Bowery men. Precisely the same pattern occurs in the present samples, where the very lowest attendance is manifested by the tract 159 respondents, and the next lowest occurs among the Shelter respondents.

For the tract 56 and tract 76 samples, the decline in regular church attendance ends at about age 25, and after that, the proportion of regular attenders remains at the same level or increases slightly throughout adult life. As late as age 80 there is no evidence of any substantial decline in attendance rates. In fact, the general trend in both these intermediate (in terms of "level" of affiliation) samples is a slight, nonsignificant increase in frequency of regular attendance as age increases. If we limit our generalizations to the adult years, two models are clearly supported by the present data. The "extreme" samples show lifetime disaffiliation, the "intermediate" samples support the stability model. In the main, the stability occurs at between 40 and 50 percent regular attendance, a level slightly above that shown by skid-row males and approximately equivalent to the manifested by the lower-income men surveyed during the Homelessness Project.

Notes

1. U.S. Department of Labor, *Manpower Report to the President,* Washington, D.C.: U.S. Government Printing Office, 1968.

2. Howard M. Bahr and Theodore Caplow, *Old Men Drunk and Sober,* New York: New York University Press, 1974, pp. 154-173.

3. Ibid., pp. 133-136.

4. Ibid., pp. 138-142.

5. Harold L. Wilensky, "Life Cycle, Work Situation, and Participation in Formal Associations," in Robert W. Kleemeier (ed.), *Aging and Leisure,* New York: Oxford University Press, 1961, p. 218.

6. Wendell Bell and M. T. Force, "Urban Neighborhood Types and Participation in Formal Associations," *American Sociological Review* 21 (February 1956): 25-34.

7. H. Bahr, *Homelessness and Disaffiliation,* New York: Columbia University, 1968, pp. 207–208; see also Bahr and Caplow, *Old Men Drunk and Sober,* pp. 219-228.

8. Bahr, *op. cit.,* pp. 285-286.

9. Howard M. Bahr, "Aging and Religious Disaffiliation," *Social Forces* 49 (September 1970): 59-71.

10. Ibid., p. 69.

5 The Women's Shelter

The remaining chapters of this report will focus on one type of disaffiliated woman, the homeless woman or Shelter resident. These women differ from the more "normal" residents of the census tracts in many ways, but perhaps the greatest difference is that they are literally homeless. The women in the tract samples all had a fixed address of their own, even if it was a very tiny hotel room; the Shelter women have no homes, but are temporarily lodged in a public facility. It seemed appropriate that a discussion of patterns of life among clients of the Women's Shelter should begin with an introduction to the Shelter itself and its relationship with certain other elements of the vast bureaucracy that is the New York City Department of Social Services.

The Emergency Assistance Unit

The Emergency Assistance Unit (EAU) in lower Manhattan operates on a 24-hour basis to provide temporary assistance for emergency cases. The EAU falls under the administrative jurisdiction of the Department of Social Services, which is the coordinating body for New York City's vast system of welfare organizations. Emergency cases handled by the EAU range from the client who requests carfare to those who are destitute and homeless. Homeless clients, provided that they meet certain eligibility requirements, are referred to the Men's or Women's Emergency Shelter, both of which are located in Manhattan's Bowery district.

No matter how critical the needs of the client, all cases must be processed in accordance with bureaucratic procedure. The flow of welfare clients proceeds as follows:

> The client reports to the intake desk which is manned with a receptionist and one or two policemen. Following a brief questioning period, the client is sent to an appropriate casework division depending upon the needs presented. If she is a homeless person, she is sent to booth one or two, where she will talk to one of two caseworkers who deal only with homeless women. Often,

---

Portions of this chapter are adapted from an earlier report by Gerald R. Garrett and Dinah H. Volk, *Homeless Women in New York City*, New York: Columbia University, Bureau of Applied Social Research, 1970. Much of the chapter was published in a slightly different form as the last portion of a chapter on "Homeless Women" in Howard M. Bahr, *Skid Row: An Introduction to Disaffiliation*, New York: Oxford University Press, 1973, and is included in the present volume by permission of Oxford University Press.

particularly during peak hours, the line at the intake desk is long and the client is usually required to wait before seeing the caseworker. Rows of chairs are provided in the center of the lobby, which is lined with casework interview booths. We observed women in the office for as long as five and six hours. The caseworker conducts an interview, fills out an intake interview form, completes an Application for Public Assistance or Request for Care, writes a Resource Summary, and has the client sign a Consent and Release Form. After each interview, the caseworker records a summary of the interview together with his comments and opinions on the History Sheet.

Despite the volume of questionnaires and interview schedules available to caseworkers in authorizing and dispensing services, EAU staff make irregular use of the official forms. In some instances, questionnaires are half completed, thereby omitting vital information about the client; in other files the standard documents are missing altogether. The extent to which EAU staff attend to official details of handling clients is reflected in comments made by caseworkers and secretarial employees:

Most of these forms are obsolete to begin with. I know the case files are disorganized. Now, this is because whether or not a worker fills out the forms is left up to him. Nobody really checks the files.

There's really no need to fiddle with most of that stuff. We don't use it anyway. Besides, the way things are around here, I, for one, don't have time to complete them anyway.

While a somewhat casual regard for processing clients in a routine way seems to promote organizational problems, the "quick pace" of operations itself, especially during the working day, makes the work situation even more difficult. These working conditions are aptly summarized in the comments of field workers:

. . . At peak periods of the day, especially during the afternoon hours, the masses of clients and workers circulating through the main intake-reception room make it almost easier for a caseworker to telephone across the hall for a file rather than make the trip in person. . . .

Today I attempted to speak with two caseworkers in their intake booths. The noise muffled most of our words. In the course of 15 minutes, the interview was interrupted eight times: five telephone calls and three interruptions by clerks.

. . . The EAU is characterized by disorganization, a lack of coordination, and a shortage of staff and facilities. This is amply illustrated by the state of the files as well as the general operational level of the agency. The outer room where clients wait is crowded so that as many as 30 must either stand or sit on the concrete floor. This is particularly so in the afternoon hours; at 9:00 in the morning when the Center opens, the line at the intake desk extends out the front door. We have observed many clients waiting for an entire morning or afternoon because there are not enough caseworkers.

The Exploratory Study

Permission to interview clients at the Women's Emergency Shelter and to examine case records at the EAU was obtained from the Commissioner of New York City's Department of Social Services. Despite this high-level approval, the idea of publicity for the Women's Shelter in particular was seen as a controversial matter by some caseworkers. On one occasion a staff member expressed the opinion that "it is not good for the women to see someone talking about them," and another worker objected to "publicizing the misery and despair of these women." Some caseworkers, however, argued that it was important that Shelter clients have exposure to publicity, visitors, and nonstaff members.

In August 1968, the exploratory investigation of the Women's Shelter and the EAU was begun. This investigation was conceived as a pilot study that would provide familiarity with the Shelter as a research setting and sensitize researchers to the problems of homeless women. Project staff were instructed to record their observations of the women at the Shelter, administrators and caseworkers, general operations at the EAU and the Shelter, and other relevant aspects of the social environment in which homeless women in New York City reside.

During the initial period of field work at the Shelter in 1968, project members reported that Shelter staff insisted each visit to the facility be authorized through the appropriate bureaucratic channels. One project worker explains the difficulty encountered in the early part of the exploratory investigation:

Yesterday I called Mrs. M, the head matron, and asked if I could visit the Shelter again. I presumed that since I had been there twice before I would not need further clearance from the Welfare Center. She informed me that I would again have to go through channels. At 3:00 I called and spoke with Mrs. M. She said that the supervisor had just left. She could not let me come over without permission from the main office. I called the supervisor in the main office. I told her I would like to go over to the Shelter in an hour and she agreed to call them. At 4:00 I went to the Shelter. The matron said Mrs. M had just left and that there was no message about me. At that moment the matron in charge for the evening came in. She said there was no message, she could not let me stay, and she was much too busy. She kept demanding, "What did Mrs. M tell you?" and saying, "During the day it's all right if someone comes in but not at 4:00 at night."

Finally, one of them found a message written on an envelope. It was from Mrs. M and it requested that I call Mr. W in the main office before staying at the Shelter. At first the matrons would not let me use their phone because they were so busy. After arguing that it would be difficult for Mr. W to speak with them if I called from an outside phone, they grudgingly agreed. The first time I called Mr. W the line was cut off. The second time we were connected, I explained the entire project to him (he has just taken over as temporary supervisor of the office and knew almost nothing about the project) and he agreed that I could stay. When I asked him to speak to the matron, she became very hostile. She asked him to explain who I was and complained angrily that she had 27 clients to take care of, that there were three matrons in the office and a patrolman and there was absolutely no room for me. I again spoke to Mr. W. He said he did not know what the matron was trying to say but that she seemed to want to cooperate. Since there were only two matrons in the office at the time, and there seemed to me to be plenty of room, I promised to give up my seat if someone came in.

While difficulties in establishing visitation privileges impeded progress of the exploratory study, a more serious problem seemed to be the reluctance of many caseworkers to express their frank and candid opinions about the welfare system. Though cooperative and helpful, many workers voiced their concern about making critical statements that might later jeopardize their professional status in the eyes of welfare administrators. As one worker put it, "Let's face it. The City Welfare setup is political."

In the summer of 1969, when the interviews were conducted with Shelter clients, field workers reported no unusual difficulties in establishing rapport with the Shelter staff. Caseworkers and matrons alike seemed particularly frank in expressing opinions about the welfare system, even those that sometimes cast the department in an unfavorable light. Reports from field workers characterized the Shelter staff in the following ways:

We have received excellent cooperation from the supervisors, caseworkers, and especially the matrons. The caseworkers and matrons have been unusually helpful in locating interviewees for us in the hotel. Yesterday the matron spent twenty minutes tracking down a woman that I had asked about earlier. The casework supervisor, who has been especially frank in divulging "inside" information about the operations of the Shelter, has given us free access to the casework files.

While the exploratory study was especially useful in highlighting potential difficulties in conducting research in the Shelter setting, more significant contributions were the insights it provided about the nature of shelter women. The importance of the shelter group as a source of data is clearly indicated in the pilot report:

. . . Observations suggest that these women represent the female counterpart to the homeless man found in the Bowery district. It seems probable that Shelter women represent a more "pure" form of female homelessness and social isolation than can be found in other districts of Manhattan. Moreover, female homelessness in this setting appears to be more visible to public observers than elsewhere in the City.

The Women's Emergency Shelter

At the time of the pilot study in 1968, the Women's Emergency Shelter[a] had just recently been placed under the jurisdiction of the EAU, and it shared the

[a]See Appendix C for a historical sketch of the Women's Shelter in New York City.

same secretarial staff, files, and facilities. Since 1968, however, a gradual shift of management to the Shelter itself has taken place; case files for almost all Shelter clients who were admitted within the past two years are kept in the Shelter's intake office.

The Neighborhood

The Women's Shelter is housed in the Pioneer Hotel, a commercial hotel establishment located in the heart of the Bowery district.[1] Nearby are the traditional institutions of skid row: bars, "flophouses," cheap restaurants, barber colleges, second-hand shops, missions, and liquor stores.

Perhaps the most distinguishing feature of the Bowery is the presence of many drunken men propped in doorways, lying in the street and on the sidewalk, and occasionally under parked automobiles. It was this feature of the Bowery, more than anything else, that seemed to irk the Shelter women (although, ironically, most of the women themselves had been intoxicated in public at one time or another). Repeatedly, comments such as the following would come out in the course of an interview.

> Bums on the street—layin' around. They're all sick—sick in the head.
>
> They're drunken bums. Always sleepin in the streets. That's the problem with the Bowery. It's no place for a lady.
>
> They're poor people, They're homeless drunks. Let's rehabilitate these God-awful winos.
>
> All you find is alcoholics down here; your derelicts. Lost men and women.

Although many women have misgivings about associating with Bowery men, only a few were afraid to roam the Bowery area. In fact, a few of the more adventuresome clients appeared to find a certain exciting quality about the neighborhood. As one woman described it, "I sit in the park sometimes, watch all the interesting people go by. And, then, there's all sorts of interesting shops—jewelry shops, the lamp store, things like that. Lot's of good bars, too [respondent laughs]."

The Bowery holds other attractions, too. Several of the Shelter women indicated that the Bowery and adjoining areas were especially good for panhandling. As one respondent explained, "You've got to know where to go, though. Myself, I make a good living down on Canal Street; sometimes on Lafayette and around Mott (Chinatown). Even better, I like the banks on Friday afternoon." Still other women commented that the Bowery was a suitable place for them because it is easy to "bum a pint off of the Bowery bums."

Facilities

The City of New York has a lease contract with the Pioneer Hotel for occupancy of most of the rooms located on the main floor. The remainder of the hotel space is handled on a commercial basis. Field workers provide a description of the layout of facilities at the Pioneer:

Men and women use the same entrance to the hotel. To the left of the lobby is a hall which leads to the hotel rooms, bathroom facilities, and offices (converted hotel rooms) for the caseworkers. On the right of the lobby, there are two sitting rooms with television sets. One of these is for the women. Most of the women remain in the television room throughout their waking hours. The matron's office adjoins the women's sitting room. There are three rooms used by the caseworkers. In addition the Shelter has eight sleeping rooms with 46 beds and several bathrooms. The remainder of the hotel is used by male guests, though the Shelter can rent these if there is not sufficient room for their population.

Since there are no dining facilities at the Pioneer Hotel, provisions for meals are handled through a local restaurant a few blocks from the Shelter. Although the restaurant operates on a commercial basis, meals for the Shelter women are obtained under a long-term contract with the city. Three meals are served; the menus are planned by a dietician in the Welfare Department. In the words of the matron:

The girls to get very good meals. For breakfast they have juice, dry cereal, a cup of milk, a scrambled egg, roll and butter and a beverage—coffee, tea, or milk. A lot of us don't get that. They get it 365 days a year. For lunch they have soup, sandwich, a cupcake and something to drink. For supper they have something like meatballs and spaghetti and bread and butter or they have baked ham sometimes and vegetables . . . dessert and coffee.

Complaints regarding the meals were not unlike those encountered in large-scale institutions. Observers reported that women typically complained that portions of the meal were too small, the meat was too fatty, tough, and occasionally unpalatable altogether.

We don't get enough fruit.
I want more salads.
Why do they burn the meat?
The coffee's worse than mudwater.

Matrons almost invariably discounted such widespread complaints in the manner of: "Well, they just have to have something to gripe about."

Although the present Shelter facilities are not elaborate, the cost of maintaining operations is reputedly high in light of the comparatively few women services. At the time of the pilot study in 1968, the daily costs were estimated at $4.50 per client.[b]

---

[b]At the time of data-gathering in 1969, an expansion of the Shelter facilities was planned. It was learned that the City was negotiating an agreement to acquire a newly renovated building located a few blocks from the present site. The new building will constitute a substantial expansion over present facilities at the Pioneer Hotel, including the addition of

Admissions and Referral to the Shelter

Women may be directed to the Shelter in a number of ways. Though the majority of cases are authorized through the central welfare office (during the day) and the EAU (after 5 P.M.), a small number of clients come to the Shelter as "self-referrals" or are referred by police officers, community charity organizations, psychiatric institutions, state or city hospitals, and particular city agencies such as the Women's House of Detention. Not all referrals, particularly those dispatched from nonwelfare organizations, are accepted as clients at the Shelter. Policy regarding accepting clients was explained by the casework supervisor:

We get lots of people, especially "after hours" who are just plain looking for a hand-out. They want something for nothing. A lot of times somebody will bring a gal here for us to take in when we can't do anything for her. I usually tell them that they should go to the Welfare center.

Even within the welfare system, the problem of inappropriate referral is evidently common:

We get four or five inappropriate referrals every two or three days, and I just won't accept them. We got rules here which we have to abide by. We got a referral from Gramercy just this morning; they should have sent her to Church Street. They should know better. So, I called up the Welfare Center and let them know about it. . . . And then, the client needed carfare to get back to her caseworker. . . . If they would just follow the rules, things would be a lot better.

Regarding the Shelter's admission procedure, a number of women with whom interviewers spoke complained that they were the victims of a disorganized and uncoordinated welfare system. One client summarized the difficulties she encountered in receiving authorization to enter the Shelter:

. . . I had lost my apartment, like I said before. I didn't have nowhere to go . . . So I went to see my caseworker at the Welfare Center on Street . . . Miss S told me to report to Pioneer Hotel on Broome at Bowery; she said I could stay there. . . . Well, I only had a quarter, and I was saving that for a coffee and donut, so I asked for carfare. Well I took the subway downtown, but you see, I didn't know exactly how to get there. . . . I got off on Houston, I think, and walked and walked and walked. You know, we'd just had that big snow the day before, and it was real hard to get around, especially with my ankle swollen like it was. I fell two or three times, I did. . . . Well, I asked an officer and he explained how I should get there. . . . By the time I arrived at the hotel it was half past noon. The caseworker made me wait for half an hour, then had the nerve to tell me I had to go to Church Street to get authorization; said my careworker, Miss S shouldn't have sent me here. . . . I walked to the Church Street Center—sat there for an hour—and then some woman told me I had to get

---

kitchen and dining accommodations. More notable, however, is the fact that recommendations for medical facilities, enlarged office space, private rooms for casework practice, psychotherapy, and individual and group counseling have received administrative approval.

authorization or something from my caseworker since I was under her care. I'm telling you the truth: I walked all the way from Church Street up to Street. When I got there, Miss S had already gone home and they said I'd have to wait until Monday to see her. I told the lady my problem and she called the office on Bowery, and he told her I had to go to Church Street . . . it was close to midnight time I got there, and then the matron says she can't take me in after 10.

In the course of reviewing files of Shelter clients at the EAU, a number of cases were uncovered in which the client had been referred from one agency to another for a variety of reasons. Perhaps the most incredible case, however, is that of Miss S, age 56, never married, who came to New York years ago from New Haven. Medical reports from New Haven (Yale Clinic for Alcoholics) and in New York indicate that she is an alcoholic of 25 years standing. Miss S's welfare history in New York dates back to 1951. From 1951 to 1955, the client's case-history log shows that she made occasional applications to the Emergency Assistance Unit for temporary relief (carfare and small amounts of public assistance), most of which she paid back in later months. Her record up until 1955, however, is not extensive, indicating that she was apparently self-supporting and in partial control of her drinking. In 1955, however, Miss S suffered some serious setbacks; her sister (her only living relative) died, and she was jilted by her boyfriend ("I loved him very much"). According to caseworker reports, her drinking increased markedly. She lost her job, encountered some serious accidents as a consequence of her heavy drinking, and was arrested at least 8 times during a period of 6 months. In January 1956, two officers brought Miss S to the EAU for help. In 1956 and 1957 the client made numerous applications for public relief, yet either her application was refused or she was referred to another agency. The following account of Miss S's tour of the welfare bureaucracy during those years is "pieced together" using a series of interdepartment memos, letters to caseworkers, and medical reports.

January 7, 1956: " . . . Please admit the above client for temporary lodging." (EAU)

January 9, 1956: "We find it impossible to work with her. She is violent, she bangs on the desk, and more recently she has been threatening the workers and other staff members. (Yesterday) . . . in one of her drunken sprees she attacked another client. Due to this type of behavior we are returning the client to your office for disposition to another agency."

October 1, 1956: (Application for assistance submitted). "Case declined. Record of abusive conduct."

November 2, 1956: (Application for assistance submitted). "Case declined. Record of abusive conduct. Referred to admitting physician, Bellevue Hospital."

November 4, 1956: (From Hospital), "Will you kindly readmit this client to the Women's Shelter?"

November 5, 1956: (Women's Shelter), "Client referred to Welfare Center." [Evening of November 5: client attempts suicide in restroom of lower Manhattan bar.]

November 6, 1956: (From EAU). "On the basis of client's irrational behavior, we ask you to readmit her (to Bellevue Hospital) at the recommendation of our Staff Physician, Dr. D, because it is necessary for her own protection that she be off the street. In previous years she has suffered many accidents while drinking, like broken arm, bruises and laceration of the scalp."

November 8, 1956: "Client released [from psychiatric ward] in care of friend."

November 9, 1956: (Client assaulted man in bar. Became violent, threw bottles through bar window. Fell on broken glass. Cut face, arms, legs badly.)

November 10, 1956: (Hospital). "We are referring the above name to your agency for public assistance."

November 11, 1956: (From Welfare Center). "The last time we sent this patient to you November 6, she was kept three days and discharged. . . . We are asking you to readmit her because of extreme behavior in the past week." [Client given carfare. Did not show up at Hospital.]

November 12 to January 1, 1957: [Client in jail. Charge not recorded.]

January 9, 1957: Client requested care (Welfare Center). "We are not referring her to the Women's Shelter due to record of abusive conduct. . . . We referred Miss S to the New York State Alcoholic Clinic in Brooklyn. Given carfare."

January 10, 1957: "Client could not make appointment due to her extreme drunkenness. . . ."

January 11, 1957: [Client attempted suicide. Details not recorded. No further entry until May 8, 1957.] [c]

While official criteria define eligibility for referral to the Shelter, it became increasingly clear throughout the study that caseworkers recognize client needs other than the objective circumstances of poverty, temporary homelessness, and so on. As one caseworker put it, "there is a 'shelter type,' I think." Comments from caseworkers and supervisors elaborate on the "informal policy" that governs referral and admission to the Shelter:

I think the Department defines the clients as you [the researcher] do. We have something known as a "shelter type." I think the Department defines them as disaffiliated, without fixed family ties and residence as opposed to people who can't manage funds. That's the way a lot of people there define it.

---

[c] At the time of data-gathering in 1969, Miss S. was an in-service client at the Women's Shelter. Her casework folder indicated that she had had almost continuous contact with the Shelter and the Welfare Department since 1957.

Most of them just aren't hospital cases. Sometimes I feel like we function like a nut hospital for those few . . . that need the security. They live alone in some furnished room sometimes. . . . Part of it is due to the fact that they're drinkers . . . it leads to emotional problems. If you're . . . how could you say it? . . . straight, . . . you could do that . . . you could live alone all right. . . . So the women are really afraid to get on public assistance.

The Shelter is designed for women who can't function in the community, who need a protective environment and supervision. Alcoholics, the mentally disturbed—these are people who can't manage their own affairs. . . . These women need the protection facilities of an institution. Left on their own they could get into trouble.

Most of the people are on the borderline between being in the community and not being in the community. Some become accustomed to shelter living. Like a club membership. It's a syndrome. Women get lonesome for companionship. They don't have to make beds,they get clean linen, there's a TV to watch, they're locked in at night, a matron turns the lights out. It's a return to a real childish state.

They are sick if they're alcoholics . . . chronically ill. They can't cope with society and they become immature. They can't seem to function on their own and they're better off in an institution with friends. . . . If they had to live in a room alone they would starve. We don't know why it is but it's a true fact. You wouldn't believe it but it's true.

You see, on public assistance they get $15 a week for a room. Where can you get a room for that? Someplace on the West Side. They're addicts, prostitutes around. The women are protected in the Shelter; they're not molested, except from the outside. Not often because the police are there. They could get mugged in an apartment. At the Shelter there's security. They have an appointment once a week with a caseworker . . . some of these women . . . if you offered them the White House they wouldn't go. They're dependent. They come to get a ticket for the Shelter where they're secure. That's a lot of them. Some just vegetate there. We don't want them to get dependent but some just sit there the whole day and don't do anything.

Welfare puts them in a room sometimes . . . it's terrible. I think it's worse than being here. They drink themselves to death then. That really happens in some cases. I remember one woman who just drank herself to death. It's worse than it is here, I think, because they're all alone.

In contradiction to what casewokers identify as "shelter types," a small proportion of women expressed hostile feelings about having shelter living thrust upon them.

What's there to like about a place like this? Nothing. The Bowery ain't no place for a lady. Them drunkards laying on the streets. Why, I'm afraid to walk down the street. And the noise with them trucks. . .

I didn't want to come here. I told my caseworker that. Soon as I get me a job, I'll be out of here. You can bet on that.

It's a place to eat and sleep. But it ain't for me. I just don't belong in a place like this.

Since the inception of the Women's Shelter, there has been an exchange of clients with Bellevue Hospital and various nursing homes in metropolitan New

York. From time to time the Shelter admits clients who are recently discharged patients from Bellevue, and Shelter clients who show signs of severe psychiatric disorders are sent to Bellevue. Commitment for psychiatric treatment, however, seems not to rest solely on medical grounds. When the Shelter psychiatrist, who spends one morning each week at the Pioneer Hotel, was asked if he often recommends hospitalization, he replied:

No. There is a reluctance . . . not that there isn't a need. Hospitals are more and more reluctant these days to admit people. . . . There's no good place to go. . . . We usually commit them only when they're a danger to themselves and others.

Daily Routine

The operations at the Shelter assume a somewhat routine nature during the regular work week. Almost without exception, a "typical" day moves accoding to the following schedule.

The client is awakened at 6 (sharp) in the morning; breakfast is at 7:30 to 8:00 in a local restaurant located two blocks from the Hotel. Meals are provided by the restaurant under a special contract with the City Welfare Department. Lunch is served at 1:00 p.m. on weekdays; twelve, on Sundays. Dinner is served at 5:30. Twice daily refreshments are served to the women by the matrons: coffee and cookies at 10 in the morning; juice and cookies in the evening.

The sleeping rooms are locked during the day; at 7:30 in the evening they are opened. Lights are put out at 10 and each woman must be in bed by then. Violation of this policy brings about cancellation of her meal and lodging privileges.

When a woman arrives at the Shelter, having first negotiated check-in procedures with the casework staff, she is required to take a bath; soap and delousing shampoo are provided. Each bath is recorded in the matron's "bath-book." Nightgowns and bathrobes are issued by the matron. A woman is never permitted to sleep in street attire; neither is she allowed to sleep nude. If an intoxicated client returns to the Shelter, her clothes are withheld until she has achieved sobriety. Sundry items and toiletries are provided by the Welfare Center; special items are obtained through a request-for-cash. The management of the Pioneer Hotel provides linens and towels as well as a housekeeper.

Aside from television, reading materials, and a few games and art supplies (which are seldom used by the women), there is little in the way of diversions to interrupt what is otherwise a monotonous routine. More than half the clients with whom interviewers spoke said they remained in the television room all day. Responses to the question "what do you do most of the day?" reflect the dismal surroundings and uninterrupted monotony:

What do I do? I sit. Period. I sit all morning before lunch; I sit all afternoon before dinner; and I sit all evening until bedtime at 10. That's all. Besides going to the cafe, 'bout the "farthest" I go is to the toilet in the other room!

What the hell *is* there to do around here? That's a better question! We don't do nothing. The same goddamn thing every day. Except, maybe the food gets worse over to the cafe each day. Why, we even get the same awful cookies every day . . . I take walks.

Well I usually sit in the dayroom, you know. I like to look out the window, out on the street. I watch them tear that building down . . . Oh, and I have some friends, I talk to them; but mostly just sit and look out the window.

Nothing. That's what I do. Nothing. You can't watch TV; them girls—especially the colored devils—are yelling and screaming all day and night, too.

Sit. I sit in the TV room; I sit in the recreation room; I sit outside on Broome Street; I sit in the park on Grand Street; I just sit. Oh, on Thursday's, I go to the King County Hospital—to the alcoholic ward. Otherwise I just sit. . . . unless, of course, I'm drinking. Then it's another matter.

Walk around, usually. Yesterday I walked all the way to 42nd Street and back. . . . There isn't much else for me to do.

I don't go nowhere. I sit in the dayroom. Talk to a few of the ladies, watch TV. That's about it.

Sources of Disruption

Although the operations at the Shelter follow a routine time schedule, the "normal" day also includes occasional disputes, fights among the women, and other problems that create disruption.

Policemen and matrons at the Shelter said that the women, especially those with a drinking problem, frequently become abusive, threatening, and occasionally violent:

There's a lot of fights . . . a lot of fights. . . . It gets nasty. Especially when the [welfare] checks come in on the Bowery. When there's money around the men buy the women drinks. They come back here and get nasty. . . . They fight like cats among themselves.

Theft is evidently the major cause of fighting among the women. In addressing the problem of stealing personal belongings, one caseworker said:

There's a lot of stealing around here. There's always some stealing but you can't do much about it. . . . The personal belongings of these women are important to them, probably the only thing they have. That's why they carry all their belongings, what little they've got, with them, even when they go to the restaurant. Of course we always lock the sleeping rooms every day, but that don't seem to stop the thievery.

The matrons reported that homosexuality was an occasional problem in handling Shelter women. When complaints of homosexual activity occur, the usual practice is to reassign the suspect client to separate quarters.

Regarding drug use, casewokers explained that addiction is rarely a problem among Shelter women. Known addicts are immediately referred to other agencies, and those women who are drug users seldom behave in abusive or violent ways. Regarding sexual behavior, informants indicated that only a small minority were practicing prostitution.

Shelter Staff

Professional Staff. The Shelter is operated with a staff of five professionals: the director, a case supervisor, two senior caseworkers, and one junior caseworker. All five had held previous positions in other divisions within the Welfare Department.

While the staff seemed to "know" the behavior and habits of their clients in the professional sense, each staff member voiced the opinion that the Shelter personnel were not particularly suited or qualified to handle this type of case. As one senior member of the staff remarked at the time of the exploratory investigation:

> To be frank, most of us don't have the background. I've been here two years but I have a major in economics. Caseworkers are just assigned to the Shelter—it's ridiculous. These cases should be handled by an MSW with special training in alcoholic women . . . someone with training in medical social work.

At the same time, some staff reported that their ineffectiveness in working with Shelter clients was in part due to personality conflicts. Explaining his situation, one caseworker commented:

> I'm getting out [of the Women's Shelter]. . . . [I'm] going to something else in a year or two. At first it was very interesting but it gets boring after awhile. . . . I can't get along with these women. You know, some people can't get along with them at all.
>
> I really don't have the patience sometimes to work with these women.

With the exception of special requests, caseworkers are assigned to the Women's Shelter by the EAU. According to one source, members of the EAU night staff who work especially well with the women or who do not like night work are the most likely to receive Shelter duty. In questioning staff and administrators about job assignment, it became increasingly clear that professional qualifications per se played a relatively minor role in determining assignment to the Shelter. In speaking of the issue of recruiting qualified personnel for the Shelter, the director remarked: "We have a pretty high turnover rate here. I don't know that the department really killed itself trying to recruit."

Recruiting qualified personnel for the Shelter is further complicated by the fact that, from a professional standpoint, the Shelter is not a particularly desirable assignment. Most caseworkers remarked that the Shelter woman is one of the most difficult and "trying" types of client to handle. One worker remarked: "You just can't develop a meaningful relationship with them. It's hard to handle women like that. . . . I don't know whether it's due to their alcoholism or not. I suspcct so."

The Matrons. The Women's Emergency Shelter employs twelve matrons, at least two of whom are on duty during the day. Shifts are allocated on the conventional 8-hour basis. One matron explained her duties:

> We do no social work here. We maintain the place and the people. We make sure order is kept. We cooperate with the caseworkers. We don't overstep our part. . . . We do the best we can.

The role of the matron includes duties of a peacemaker, housekeeper, and maid. If a dispute erupts among the women, she acts as arbiter; when the women lodge complaints about their treatment at the Shelter, she extends a sympathetic ear; if medical problems arise, she summons a doctor; if a client's personal problem reaches acute proportions, she calls a social worker; and if the facilities are in a state of disorder, she acts as the official cleaning lady.

Although the matrons do not serve the clients in a professional capacity, it became increasingly evident throughout the project that the women perceived the matron as a powerful figure in the organizational structure. Indeed, some women indicated in various ways that the matron wielded more power than the casework staff. This observation is not altogether surprising, however, in view of the fact that it is the matron who distributes most of the goods and services provided in the Shelter. Such commodities as cigarettes, ice cream, and candy are particularly precious, and it seems to make little difference whose command or generosity makes these items available–it is the matron who dispenses them, and she inevitably received the credit.

> Well, she's just as nice as can be. Why, she brings us some cookies and juice every night. Every now and then she gives me a cigarette, too.
>
> Oh, she's just a wonderful thing. She brought me dinner when I was sick.

While the matron enjoys a certain halo effect in her role as quartermaster, at the same time she receives the blame for the variety of decisions that limit the clients' freedom. The following exerpts from field notes illuminate the flow of "negative halo effects":

> There just ain't no good reason why we have to have the lights off by 10. None. She's just plain mean, that's why.
>
> On Wednesday, the caseworker evidently told the matron, Mrs. B, that Mrs. N should not be assigned to the lower sleeping quarters. . . . Later, Mrs. N remarked: "Oh, she's a goddamn devil, she is. Pardon me, I don't swear you know, and I don't like to say anything bad about anybody. . . . I wanted to share a room with Lillian. She and I are good friends, you know. And that bitch, pardon me, said that the caseworker had given her orders that I couldn't room with

Lillian. Well, she's a damn liar, excuse me; I hate to say it, but she *is*. . . . She doesn't like me; it's a darn shame; she doesn't like me. . . ."

Today Mrs. E. approached me for a favor. She reported that the matron had taken a strong dislike to her. It was for this reason, Mrs. E feels, that she would not honor her request to switch sleeping rooms. I checked with the caseworker and asked why Mrs. E was not permitted to change rooms, and it was explained that beds are presently assigned in the room Mrs. E requested. It was an interesting situation because Mrs. E blames the matron for denial of her request even after I later explained that all beds were presently filled in that room.

Special Service Policemen. At least one policeman is on duty at the Shelter at all times. According to their handbook, their function is "preventative protection," and they have the authority to place a client under arrest if "circumstances, in the opinion of the officer, warrant it." Generally speaking, the officer on duty assumes the role of watchdog over the Shelter, inspecting the rooms periodically for various types of contraband (especially alcohol), monitoring the flow of visitors to and from the Shelter, and occasionally subduing an aggressive client. During the period of the study, interviewers witnessed one violent scene.

As I entered the TV room, Mrs. G was hurling insults, though she seemed not to be addressing them to any particular woman. A few moments later, Mrs. S, who had been drinking most of the day, entered the room. Almost immediately, Mrs. G began directing her insults at Mrs. S. A short time later, Mrs. G, unprovoked, leaped from the couch and assaulted Mrs. S in a stranglehold. At that moment, the policeman on duty raced to the rescue. He grabbed Mrs. G by the throat and threw her across the room. (Notably Mrs. S took this opportunity to strike a blow with her purse on Mrs. G's forehead.) Again, the policeman grabbed Mrs. G and this time tossed her into the hallway. At last, he pushed her down a short flight of stairs, yelling, "Goddamnit. You get the hell out of here and don't you come back." That ended the incident and the policeman returned to reading the evening paper.

Among the women, opinions about the policemen seemed to be determined by whether they have experienced some "run-in" with an officer. Observers reported that one officer was seen by the women in a particularly unwholesome light:

He's always saying mean things about the women.

He'd hit me if he dared. . . . He hit two women who were walking down the stairs. . . . One of them was in the hospital for three weeks. . . . There's no need for a stick in here.

In contrast, one caseworker reported to observers that

Many of them [Shelter women] have quite a relationship going with the police. They think of them as public servants and will usually call them if they need help. The men [Bowery men] certainly don't see them as helpers. When some of the women go out, they'll stick close to the side of the street where the police call boxes are.

Medical Services

A physician is on duty at the Shelter each morning during the regular working week. Although medical facilities are limited to a small examination room, the medical services given to the women are perhaps the most successful part of the total program at the Shelter. A substantial number of newly admitted clients enter the Shelter with a variety of ailments, the most common being malnutrition (avitaminosis), skin disorders due to poor personal hygiene, respiratory ailments, and venereal disease. For this reason, it is standard practice to require all new admissions to undergo medical examination.

Women with acute medical problems arising from prolonged drinking are often referred to the Alcoholic Clinic at King's County Hospital in Brooklyn. At the time of the pilot study, several women were undergoing aversion treatment. But clients are not required to undergo alcoholic therapy, and for this reason a woman's attendance at the Clinic is usually sporadic.

Psychiatric Services

A psychiatrist visits the Shelter on a weekly basis, though he acts as a consultant only and provides no psychiatric treatment per se. If a client shows signs of a severe psychiatric disorder, institutional treatment is recommended. A recommendation by the psychiatrist, however, seldom results in actual hospitalization: "Hospitals are sometimes reluctant to accept Welfare clients, and, of course, most institutions are seriously overcrowded, which limits acceptance to those with the severe disturbances."

According to a Shelter psychiatrist, the prognosis for treatment of these women is poor. He characterized the women in the following way:

> I could speculate about it. . . . I would guess that they are particularly more self-defeating than other people. They have a greater feeling of failure. You know, it takes a lot of effort to wind up on the Bowery . . . at the Shelter . . . it really takes work . . . you have to want to go there . . . you have to work at it.
>
> These people are at the lowest level of existence. . . . And for long-term chronic schizophrenics . . . who can't function on their own . . . even with a tremendous effort made at a day hospital with a good rehabilitation program . . . you can have this kind of program without hoping for even a good percentage of good results. The people at the Shelter are not temporary cases with temporary problems. . . . They're long-term problems with chronic difficulties in managing in the community.

Most of the people here are on the borderline between being in the community and being out of the community. This is the last place to go before being sent to a hospital or elsewhere. Rehabilitation is a tremendous effort and useless. . . . They aren't terribly motivated.

Alcoholics Anonymous

Eash Sunday and Tuesday, members of Alcoholics Anonymous (AA) hold meetings at the Shelter which are conducted in the traditional manner of most AA organizations. Women with drinking problems are encouraged to attend AA meetings even though it is recognized that these women are unlikely to develop any long-range commitments to the program. The underlying assumption is that discussion of one's drinking problem at any level constitutes an initial step toward permanant sobriety.

Observers at the Shelter reported that most women appeared to view their involvement in AA in a serious light, and a few women identified AA as their only organizational affiliation in recent years. But while women show evidence of a serious attitude toward AA, observational reports indicate that the spirit of fellowship, which is perhaps the hallmark of AA organizations, seemed to be absent among the Shelter group. Rather, women seemed to view their fellow members as a disinterested audience. Although no statistics on post-Shelter drinking are available, it is notable that the bulk of clients who regularly return to the Shelter are those with long-standing drinking problems.

Most caseworkers estimated at least one half of Shelter clients were chronic alcoholics, and the substantial majority had experienced some type of acute drinking problem at one point in their lives. In fact, caseworkers tended to assign special significance to excessive drinking as a cause of the present predicament of these women.

Yes, I think their problems are caused by alcoholism.

It's due to her alcoholism . . .

She brought it all on herself with her drinking . . .

I think the kind of person you find around the Bowery—men and women—are mostly alcoholics. If you could take away their drinking, they would never have had the problems they have.

[Regarding a twenty-five year old client, one worker remarked] "Sure, she's a chronic alcoholic. She told me that she gets drunk once, sometimes twice, a week."

Not unexpectedly caseworkers took a rather dim view of the chances of recovery for these women:

I'm afraid they're pretty much hopeless cases.

When you have an addict, you get him away from dope and he goes through a withdrawal period. How can you get an alcoholic in an environment like this (the Bowery) to withdraw from alcohol? . . . You can't.

Note

1. The colorful history of the Bowery is described in detail by Alvin F. Harlow, *Old Bowery Days*, New York: D. Appleton, 1931. See also Elmer Bendiner, *The Bowery Man,* New York: Thomas Nelson and Sons, 1961, and George Nash, *The Habitats of Homeless Men in Manhattan*, New York: Columbia University, Bureau of Applied Social Research, 1964.

6 Social Characteristics of Shelter Women

In this chapter selected characteristics in the life histories of Shelter women will be described, including their demographic characteristics, family backgrounds, and marital histories. Attributes of Shelter women are contrasted with those of Camp LaGuardia men in an attempt to identify sex differentials in the antecedents of homelessness. Finally, for illustrative purposes a few case histories are presented.

Demographic Characteristics

Clients of the Women's Shelter and Camp LaGuardia tend to be middle-aged (see Table 6-1), but Camp men are somewhat older than Shelter women (mean ages are 54 and 47, respectively). it should be pointed out, however, that men under 30 years of age are seldom referred to Camp LaGuardia by the Men's Shelter whereas the Women's Shelter has no similar policy. Hence, the difference in age between the two samples is in part explained by different admission policies. In view of this fact, the mean age for a random sample of 203 Bowery men was also computed. (Data on Bowery and Camp LaGuardia men were available from the Homelessness Project.) The mean age for the Bowery sample (53) was only slightly lower than that of the Camp LaGuardia men.

Almost half (44 percent) of the Shelter women were blacks. According to the 1960 census, approximately one of every four New Yorkers was black. Thus it appears that blacks are overrepresented among homeless women in the city. However, in light of the overrepresentation of blacks in the lower socioeconomic strata, this finding is not altogether surprising. Somewhat more unexpected was the finding that the proportionate representation of black women at the Shelter is greater than that for black men at Camp LaGuardia. Only one in four Camp residents is a black.

Regarding marital status, at least three observations are worthy of mention. First, none of the respondents was living with a spouse. Second, most of those

---

Portions of this chapter and Chapter 7 have been expanded and altered somewhat in two journal articles: "Women on Skid Row," *Quarterly Journal of Studies on Alcohol* 34 (December 1973): 1228-1243; and "Comparison of Self-Rating and Quantity-Frequency Measures of Drinking," *Quarterly Journal of Studies on Alcohol* 35 (December 1974); 1294-1306. Reprinted by permission from Quarterly Journal of Studies on Alcohol, vol. 35 pp. 1294-1306, 1974. Copyright by Journal of Studies on Alcohol, Inc., New Brunswick, New Jersey.

Table 6-1
Selected Demographic Characteristics of Shelter Women and Camp LaGuardia Men[a]

Characteristic	*Women's Shelter*	*Camp LaGuardia*
Race, Total	100%	100%
White	56[b]	75
Negro	44[b]	25
Nativity, Total	100	100
Foreign-born	10[b]	21
Native-born	90[b]	79
Northeast	37	54
Midwest	15	4
South	37	21
West	1	0
Marital Status, Total	100	100
Never married	23[b]	53
Married		
Divorced	29[b]	10
Separated (including desertion)	40[b]	27
Widowed	8	10
Religious Preference, Total	100	100
Protestant	44	42
Catholic	35[b]	53
Other	7	3
No preference	14	2
Age, Total[c]	100	100
Below 25	4	0
25-34	10	1
35-44	42	5
45-54	20	22
55-64	14	48
65 and above	10	24
Income (per Month Average), Total	100	100
Less than $100	89	57
$100-$500	10	43
Above $500	1	0
Education (Years Completed), Total	100	100
8th grade and below	25[b]	56
Some high school	38[b]	24
High school graduate	29[b]	15
Some college or graduate	8	5

[a]Total sample size: N = 52 (Shelter Women); N = 199 (Camp LaGuardia). "No response" categories were not used in computing percentages. Therefore, the total N varies slightly.

[b]Differences between Camp men and Shelter women are statistically significant at the .05 level.

[c]Mean ages: 47.1 (women); 54.0 (men). The difference is significant at the .05 level.

who had been married at least once reported that the marriage had ended in separation or divorce. Thus marital instability is a prominent feature of these populations. Finally, although the homeless men and women were maritally unattached, they had arrived at this status by different routes. Over three-fourths of the Shelter women had been married, compared to less than half of the Camp LaGuardia men.

Compared to the Camp LaGuardia men, the Shelter women are more likely to be nativeborn and are better educated. Although both samples are heavily concentrated in the lowest income category, the homeless woman is worse off than the Camp LaGuardia man; very few of the women (11 percent) have over $100 disposable income per month, but almost half of the Camp LaGuardia men report that much income. Finally, the Camp men are somewhat more apt to be Catholic than are the women. Although there is no reason to assign special importance to this difference, it is noteworthy that the rate of drinking pathologies is generally higher in Catholic populations than among Protestant groups.

Family Background Characteristics

Table 6-2 summarizes findings on selected aspects of the family backgrounds of Shelter women and Camp LaGuardia men.

Demographic Characteristics

The parents of homeless men and homeless women differ in several respects. First, homeless women are far less likely than homeless men to have a parent who is foreignborn. Approximately three-fourths of the women have nativeborn parents, as compared to slightly over half of the men. Second, findings on religious background of the parents indicate that more Camp LaGuardia men than Shelter women come from Catholic homes.[a] Finally, while information on education of parents for Camp men was not available, the data for Shelter women show a heavy concentration of cases in the lowest categories of educational attainment. Since education is closely related to income, it is therefore not surprising that 8 out of every 10 Shelter respondents reported that the family income during their childhood was "average" or "below."

---

[a]Several women made comments during the interview indicating that their parents had forced them to attend church. Statements such as the following suggest that antichurch sentiments are especially strong among some women:

I had my belly full of church when I was a kid.

I went to Synagogue once or twice and that's because I *had* to go. But I didn't care for it. That ritual. It's phony. I finally got fed up and told them I won't go anymore; I don't want any part of that life.

It was a lot of nonsense. I finally came right out and told them I ain't never going to church again.

Table 6-2
Selected Characteristics in the Family Background of Shelter Women and Camp LaGuardia Men[a]

Characteristic	*Women's Shelter*	*Camp LaGuardia*
Father's Nativity, Total	100%	100%
Foreign-born	27[b]	45
Native-born	73[b]	55
Mother's Nativity, Total	100	100
Foreign-born	19[b]	46
Native-born	81[b]	54
Father's Religion, Total	100	100
Protestant	35	43
Catholic	33[b]	53
Other	20[b]	4
No preference	12	0
Mother's Religion, Total	100	100
Protestant	52	43
Catholic	35[b]	54
Other	12[b]	3
No preference	1	0
Parents' Religious Attendance, Total[c]	100	100
Regularly (almost every week)	65[b]	83
Sometimes (more than a few times per year)	4	–
Infrequently (once or twice a year or never)	18	17
Not certain	13	–
Father's Education, Total	100	–
8th grade and below	48	–
Some high school	8	–
High school graduate	8	–
Not certain	25	–
Never knew father	10	–
Some college or college graduate	1	–
Mother's Education, Total	100	–
8th grade and below	54	–
Some high school	15	–
High school graduate	4	–
Some college or college graduate	2	–
Not certain	25	–
Family Stability, Total[d]	100	100
Stable home	46[b]	65
Broken home	54[b]	35
Reason for Broken Home, Total	100	100
Death of one or both parents	34[b]	68
Divorce or separation	26	15
Other (including desertion)	40[b]	17

Table 6-2 continued

Characteristic	*Women's Shelter*	*Camp LaGuardia*
Age at Family Breakup, Total	100%	100%
Before birth	15	9
1-3 years old	22	28
4–10 years old	37	31
11 years and older	11	32
Not certain	15	0
Family Size (of Orientation), Total	100	100
1-2	28	20
3-4	34	28
5 or more	38	52
Perception of Family Income, Total	100	–
Far above average	6	–
Somewhat above average	16	–
Average	27	–
Somewhat below average	18	–
Far below average	33	–
Parental Participation in Voluntary Organizations, Total	100	100
Yes	25	22
No	65	67
Not certain	10	11

[a]Total sample size: N = 52 (Shelter Women); N = 199 (Camp LaGuardia). "No response" categories were not used in computing percentages. Therefore, the total N varies slightly.

[b]Differences between Camp men and Shelter women are significant at the .05 level or beyond.

[c]Categories for men and women not strictly comparable.

[d]$\chi^2 = 5.34; df = 1; P < .05$.

Family Stability

A number of studies of homeless men have assigned special significance to the broken home as an etiological factor. This point of view has been particularly prominent among those who have embraced the "undersocialization hypothesis," in which various social pathologies, including homelessness, are seen as an outcome of early-life and family deprivations. Straus describes it as a syndrome which includes a wide variety of atypical conditions and relationships with normal society, such as:

Deficiently socialized persons are usually deprived of the opportunity of sharing experiences with others, of belonging to social groups and participating in social activities. They are deprived of certain important satisfactions, such as affection . . . the feeling of security, the rewarding aspects of identifying with others and the like. The satisfaction of these personal needs usually comes only through association with other people. Such associations are normally found in the parental home, in the marital home, in schools, in employment situations, in church participation and in community life. These are the very institutional situations in which the experiences of homeless men are incomplete. . . .[1]

With reference to the role of family instability per se, Pittman and Gordon comment:

On the most crucial plane of personality development, the loss of parents leaves a void in the existence of identification models which the child uses in shaping his role conceptions. . . . The absence of one or both parents creates a condition in which the problems of socialization are multiplied, especially in the economic sphere and the realm of identification models, ego ideals and role conceptions.[2]

Despite the alleged theoretical significance of family stability during childhood in the etiology of homelessness, past empirical studies of the relationship have produced contradictory evidence. Pittman and Gordon found that nearly 4 out of every 10 chronic police case inebriates in Monroe County (Rochester), New York, came from broken homes. Straus observed a positive relationship between instability in the parental home and male homelessness, and Dunham commented that the typical background of the homeless man includes a broken home.[3] Other studies, however, do not provide strong support for the relationship between family instability and subsequent homelessness. Bogue's survey of Chicago skidrowers revealed that less than 25 percent came from broken homes, and a study of homeless migrant laborers found that less than one in every five men reported that they were reared in families in which one or both parents were missing.[4]

More recently Bahr compared skid-row men to a control group comprised of working-class men and found no difference in the proportion of men whose background included a broken home. He concluded that ". . . much of the apparent evidence for an association between broken parental homes and . . . homelessness has been based on a misperception of what constitutes 'high' rates of family stability, a misperception due mainly to the usual absence of comparative data from control samples.[5]

Although Bahr's observations suggest that the broken home is not an important factor in the creation of male homelessness, data in Table 6-2 indicate that this is not the case for homeless women. On the contrary, over half of the Shelter women reported that they were reared in a family where one or both parents was missing. Apparently family instability is more directly related to homelessness among women than among men.

In order to further test this relationship, the Shelter women were compared to respondents in the three Manhattan census tracts which served as research sites for the Urban Disaffiliation Project. Samples from all three tracts were well matched on the broken-home attribute. Proportions of women from broken homes ranged from 24 to 34 percent, compared to 54 percent among Shelter women. Thus, the broken home is significantly more characteristic of Shelter women than of either skid-row men or other low-income women.

Other differences between the male and female samples are associated with the broken-home factor. Again referring to Table 6-2, it can be observed that while homeless men from broken homes are slightly older than the Shelter women at the point of family disruption, significant differences exist between the two samples in the reasons accounting for family instability. Over two-thirds of the men reported a broken home as due to death of a parent whereas approximately the same percentage of women indicated a broken parental marriage due to divorce, separation, or desertion.

Families interrupted by the death of a parent may be seen as qualitatively different, both preceding the loss and in subsequent adjustment by family members, from families in which the "loss" of a parent is due to divorce, separation, or desertion. Thus, the "type" of broken home may be a significant variable in examining the relationship between family instability and various social pathologies, including homelessness. In fact, comparisons of the Shelter women with the respondents in the three Manhattan census tracts suggests that the shelter sample is indeed atypical with respect to the high proportion of "voluntarily" broken homes among its clients. In all three tracts less than one-fourth of the women who reported broken homes during their youth identified divorce, desertion, or separation as the reason for the broken home.

Although detailed empirical data about early-life and family experiences are not available in the present study, qualitative material from the interviews with Shelter clients sheds some light on the nature of parent-child relationships of these women. The following cases illustrate two general types of parent-child relationships that were found in the early-family experiences of Shelter women. The first case exemplified the child neglect-parental irresponsibility syndrome; the second, a parent who was domineering and a strict disciplinarian. In both cases, the parental marriage was broken during the respondent's early childhood.

Mrs. C. Mrs. C, age 45, white and currently divorced, was born and raised on Milwaukee's South Side. In reflecting on her early childhood, she reported that her life was filled with "unhappiness and misery" because of her father's irresponsibility and heavy drinking. She commented, "My dad worked with the railroad and was gone a lot. Ma said she thought he was seeing and going around with other women. He used to stay in Chicago for a whole month. Never sent money or nothin'. Then when he did come home he'd be drunk and mean. Once he beat Ma up and my brother Harry tried to stop him. He broke Harry's jaw. . . ." During the period while her father was away Mrs. C reports that her mother was neglectful of the children. "We weren't brought up. We just grew up. Period. She gave us no upbringing at all. I did what I wanted. . . ."

When the respondent was 11 years old, her father deserted the family. She has not seen him since that time. Five years later, however, her mother was contacted by prison officials informing her that her husband had been sentenced to thc Wisconsin State Prison on charges of armed robbery.

Two years after her father's desertion her mother remarried and the family moved to Gary, Indiana. A year later the marriage ended when it was learned that her stepfather was not legally divorced from his second wife. Regarding her stepfather, she said, "He was no good, either. Hardly ever worked. He used to beat us kids just like my ol' man did." At the age of 16 Mrs. C left home. Hostility toward her parents is clearly evident in her statement, "They gave me nothin', absolutely nothin'. I finally got fed up. . . . My mother, she was a weak woman."

Mrs. E. Mrs. E. age 39, white, and widowed, was born and grew up in the Bronx. Her father was an architect, employed at first with an architectural firm in Manhattan and later establishing his own "highly successful" business.

Mrs. E reported that the first 10 years of her life were filled with happiness. "Life was good, then. I had everything." When the respondent was 9 years old, however, her mother apparently decided that she would resume work at a Manhattan hospital where she had been employed before the respondent was born. Her parents quarrelled over this issue for two years: "They used to fight every day. I couldn't stand to listen to them. My daddy said that he thought her place was at home with me. . . ." Eventually her parents were divorced, and child custody was given to the mother. Mrs. E saw the breakup of her parents' marriage as a major turning point in her life: "Just wasn't the same. I started hating a lot of things." She said that her mother became a domineering, aggressive woman and described her relationship with her mother as an unhappy experience: "I just couldn't get along with her. She always nagged . . . she meddled in my affairs . . . she told me what to do . . . she told me what friends I could have. . . . I grew to hate her *intensely*. I still hate her." Since she left home at age 18, the respondent has not seen her mother.

Marital Backgrounds

The marital histories of Shelter women and Camp LaGuardia men differ in a number of ways (see Table 6-3). First, Shelter women are more apt to have been married, and second and third marriages are more frequent among them than among the skid-row men. Only one percent of the men had been married three or more times, compared to nearly 20 percent of the women. It seems that marital experiences of most homeless men are such that they inhibit their interest in subsequent marriages, but negative marital experiences among Shelter women apparently do not prevent them from trying again. Also, these differences may reflect the greater cultural emphasis on marriage for women.

Detailed information about the marital experiences of homeless men and women were not gathered in the present study, but there were some questions

Table 6-3
Selected Characteristics in the Marital Background of Shelter Women and Camp LaGuardia Men[a]

Characteristic	*Women's Shelter*	*Camp LaGuardia*
Number of Marriages, Total	100%	100%
One	60[b]	82
Two	22	17
Three	13[b]	1
Four or more	5	0
Reason for Marital Breakup (First Marriage)[c]	100	–
Death of spouse	10	–
Divorce	31	–
Separation	18	–
Desertion	28	–
Other	13	–
Number of Children, Total[d]	100	100
None	14[b]	42
One	30	18
Two	18	18
Three	15	10
Four	13	8
Five or more	10	4
Spouse's Education, Total	100	100
8th grade and below	35	42
Some high school	10	22
High school graduate	23	27
Some college or graduate	18	9
Not certain	14	0
Problems during First Marriage:		
Disagreements over wife's working	100	–
Yes	25	–
No	75	–
Disagreements over childrearing, total	100	–
Yes	28	–
No	72	–
Disagreements over sex, total	100	–
Yes	36	–
No	64	–
Disagreements over spouse's drinking, total	100	100
Yes	36[b]	14
No	64[b]	86
Disagreements over absence of either spouse, total	100	100
Yes	47[b]	30
No	53[b]	70

Table 6-3 continued

Characteristic	*Women's Shelter*	*Camp LaGuardia*
Unfaithfulness (either spouse), total	100%	–%
Yes	62	–
No	38	–
Disagreements over in-laws, total	100	100
Yes	32[b]	16
No	68[b]	84
Disagreements over financial matters, total	100	–
Yes	39	–
No	61	–
Ever Lived with Another Man/Woman as If They Were Married (Cohabitation), Total	100	100
Yes	65[b]	21
No	35[b]	79

[a]Total sample size: *N* = 52 (Shelter Women); *N* = 199 (Camp LaGuardia). "No response" categories were not used in computing percentages. Therefore, the total *N* varies slightly.

[b]Differences between men and women are significant at the .05 level or beyond.

[c]N = 40 (married women); *N* = 94 (married men).

[d]Includes children born out of wedlock.

about marital problems. It is noteworthy that the marital problems of homeless men were significantly different from those reported by the women. For example, reported marital disagreements over the drinking of either spouse were significantly higher for Shelter women (1 out of 3) than for the homeless men (1 out of 8). In addition, quarrels over the prolonged absence of either spouse and disagreements over in-laws were more characteristics of the marriages of Shelter women than of Camp men.

More than half of the Shelter women said that infidelity was a marital problem, and in asides to the interviewers, they almost invariably pointed to unfaithfulness as the major reason for the breakup of their marriages:

He cheated on me. I never did, at least while I was married to him.

I caught him playing around with other women, so I left him.

I met him and some woman strolling down Broadway arm in arm. . . . Well, that was the end of that!

It got so she was even callin' him at home. She didn't even pretend to have the wrong number. Well, one day I answered the phone and said, "Listen, Sister. If you want that good-for-nothing, you take him' . . . He never set foot in the door again.

In addition to blatant infidelity, disagreements about the absence of either spouse from home were a significant problem for almost half of the sample. Almost every respondent in this category felt compelled to explain why the absence of the spouse (invariably the husband) created marital tensions. One Shelter client, who had perhaps more "experience" with marriage than other women (five husbands), explained the problem of a "missing husband" in this way:

> . . . Gone for three and four weeks at a time, he was. . . . . You heard the bit about "lipstick on the collar," haven't you? Well, I even found a tube of lipstick in his shirt after he'd come back. . . . Told me he'd been taken to the hospital in Brooklyn. . . . I knew better. So much for husband number two, huh!

A similar theme is found in the comments of other respondents. For example,

> I used to get lonely. He'd be out to sea. Sometimes, I guess he was gone for two or three months. I'd get letters, but you can't talk to a piece of paper. . . . Then when he was home, we'd quarrel over every little thing.
>
> He just wore me out. Couldn't keep up with a man like that. He told me once that if I wouldn't go out places with him he'd go alone. He did too.

Apart from unfaithfulness and the related matter of absence of spouse, however, most of the items on marital problems were endorsed by about one-third of the Shelter women.

The Shelter women were much more likely than Camp LaGuardia men to admit that they had lived with a person of the opposite sex without being formally married. Two-thirds of the women admitted these "informal" marriages, in comparison to only one-fifth of the Camp men.

Finally, Shelter women were more likely than Camp men to have large families. Substantially more men than women reported that they were childless, and at the other extreme, the women were twice as likely as the men to have four or more children. One-fourth of the Shelter sample had that many offspring.

Social Contact

One of the distinctive characteristics of homeless people is their apparent lack of contact with friends and relatives. Most studies of the homeless man indicate that subsequent to his move to skid row, he experiences almost no contact with family, relatives, and previous acquaintances.[6] As the data in Table 6-4 indicate, a similar attenuation of former ties occurs for the homeless woman. In fact, she is perhaps even more isolated from past family and interpersonal relationships than her male counterpart.

Table 6-4
Measures of Social Contact with Family and Friends for Shelter Women and Camp LaGuardia Men[a]

Measures of Social Contact	*Women's Shelter*	*Camp LaGuardia*
Location of Closest Child, Total[b]	100%	–
New York	33	–
New York metropolitan area	10	–
Other	50	–
No information	7	–
Frequency of Contact with One or More Children, Total[b]	100	–
No contact	22	–
1–10 times per year	25	–
1–7 times per month	10	–
Once a week or more frequently	43	
Last contact with Relative, Friend, or Children, Total	100	100
Within the past year	37	39
1–3 years ago	23	22
More than 3 years ago	28	39
Not certain	12	–
Relative Seen Most Often, Total	100	–
Husband or children	26	–
Sibling	12	–
Relative or in-law	12	–
No one	50	–
Number of Close Friends in New York City, Total	100	100
None	57[c]	80
1–2	29[c]	13
3 or more	14	7
Number of Persons in Bowery Known by Name, Total	100	100
None	61[c]	21
1–5	27[c]	22
6 or more	12	58
Desires More Friends in Bowery, Total	100	100
Yes	29	26
No	71	74
Do You Have Someone You Can Confide in and Tell Your Troubles to, Total	100	–
No one	61	–
Friend	27	–
Relative	6	–
Other	6	–

Table 6-4 continued

Measures of Social Contact	Women's Shelter	Camp LaGuardia
Number of Personal Letters Received per Month, Total	100%	–
None	75	–
1-5	10	–
6 or more	15	–
Number of Conversations with Others (Day Preceding the Interview), Total	100	100
None	20[c]	8
1-5	60[c]	39
6-10	19	23
11 or more	1[c]	30

[a]Total sample size: N = 52 (Shelter women); N = 199 (Camp LaGuardia). "No response" categories were not used in computing percentages. Therefore, the total N varies slightly.

[b]N = 30.

[c]Difference between men and women is significant at the .05 level or beyond.

In terms of contact with children, for example, approximately half of the Shelter women reported no contact at all with their children, or saw them, on the average, from 1 to 10 times a year. In part, this lack of contact may be due to the fact that most of the children of these women do not reside in or near New York City. But many of the women made comments during the interview suggesting major disagreements with their children, and a surprising number of respondents expressed great hostility toward their children. Fieldwork notes written during the last week of data gathering throw some light on the underlying reasons.

> . . . Although most women who have been married and had children express genuine interest in seeing their sons or daughters on a more frequent basis, at least ten women have shown marked hostility toward their children during the interview. . . . The specific circumstances which have led these women to "excommunicate" themselves from their children are varied, though they all have in common one feature, namely that . . . all these women view their children as "having turned against them." In one instance a woman lost custody of her infant daughter because her older son complained to legal authorities that she was an unfit mother. Still another client points to the fact that her "very own daughter put her own mother in an institution for the mentally insane."

More extreme, however, is the case of Mrs. C, who has not seen her daughter in almost 10 years. This case is particularly remarkable because the respondent lived in a residential hotel situated less than two blocks from her daughter's apartment for 8 of these years.

Mrs. C., born and raised on a farm in central Iowa, married her husband in 1926. They moved to Kansas City shortly after the marriage and six months later the respondent gave birth to her only child. Soon after she learned that her husband had been having relations with another woman; she left him immediately. She remarks, "It took me many years to get over that."

Mrs. C raised her only daughter until age 15, supporting herself as a legal stenographer; her daughter continued her schooling at a girls' finishing school in Upstate New York. Mrs. C explains why she sent her daughter to a private school: "I always tried to give her the best I could. I'd always wanted to send her to a good school, too. I figured if I could do something good for her she'd be able to take care of herself later on." At the same time, however, Mrs. C implied other reasons for sending her daughter away, namely, that "I'd always been tied down, even when I was a girl," and "she was an independent child, you might say, and I guess I just didn't have what it took to discipline her right. . . ." When her daughter graduated from school, she returned home to live with her mother. It was at this time when their relationship began to take a turn for the worse, partly due to the daughter's obstinance and partly due to the client's heavy drinking. On one occasion, her daughter found Mrs. C with another man and "raised such a commotion that management asked me to move out of the building." On still another occasion her daughter stormed into Jack Dempsey's restaurant, where Mrs. C was having dinner with a friend, and called her "a slut, a damned good-for-nothing alcoholic mother . . . in front of everybody there." In summarizing her present relationship with her daughter, she remarks, "She won't have anything to do with me, and I don't care. I don't care if I ever see her again. Nobody deserves a girl like that."

The Shelter women appear to have fewer active friendships than Camp LaGuardia men. Significantly more men than women (80 percent versus 57 percent) reported having at least one close friend in New York City; women were much less likely than men to have acquaintances in the Bowery district (61 percent compared to 21 percent); and they reported fewer conversations on the day preceding the interview. Six of every ten Shelter women said that they had no one in whom they could confide, and three-fourths of them said that they never received personal letters from family or friends. Thus, present findings seemingly point to the fact that the homeless-women population is at least on an equal plane with the homeless men in terms of the frequency of contact with family members, relatives, and previous friends.

In the course of interviewing the Shelter sample, project members were struck with the fact that not only did a large number of women report no close friends or acquaintances but also that they preferred to avoid close interpersonal associations. Statements such as the following are illustrative of this sentiment:

I want to be independent. I don't want nobody; I don't need nobody.

I want . . . to be alone, to have my own place, a room. . . . I don't want to associate with others. Period.

I don't associate with people. That's my motto.

I get insulted by other people, so I go it alone–always.

I want to be left alone. Why can't people let me be?

I don't have any friends. . . . I stopped being friends with people 15 years ago, and I intend to keep it that way for another 15 years.

I want to be by myself, maybe have my own little place where I can be all alone–with nobody around.

Notes

1. For a discussion of broken homes as related to alcoholism and problem drinking among men, see Howard M. Bahr, "Family Size and Stability as Antecedents of Homelessness and Excessive Drinking," *Journal of Marriage and the Family* 31 (August 1969): 477-483.

2. David J. Pittman and C.W. Gordon, *Revolving Door, A Study of the Chronic Police Case Inebriate*, Glencoe, Ill.: The Free Press, 1958, pp. 80-81.

3. R. Straus, "Alcohol and the Homeless Man," *Quarterly Journal of Studies on Alcohol,* 7 (June 1946): 360-404; and H. Warren Dunham, *Homeless Men and Their Habitats: A Research Report*, Detroit: Wayne State University, 1963.

4. Donald J. Bogue, *Skid Row in American Cities*, Chicago: Community and Family Study Center, University of Chicago, 1963; and Gerald R. Garrett, "The Migrant Laborer: A Sociological Study," unpublished master's thesis, Washington State University, Pullman, Washington, 1966.

5. Howard M. Bahr, *Homelessness and Disaffiliation,* New York: Columbia University, Bureau of Applied Social Research, 1968, p. 178.

6. Leonard Blumberg, et al., *The Men on Skid Row*, Philadelphia: Department of Psychiatry, Temple University School of Medicine, 1960; Donald J. Bogue, *Skid Row in American Cities*; and Howard M. Bahr, *Homelessness and Disaffiliation.*

7 Drinking Patterns of Homeless Women

Homeless men on skid row are popularly stereotyped as excessive drinkers; the nature of the public stereotype of homeless women is less clear. In fact, there is some question as to whether stereotypes of homeless women exist at all. Even other Bowery residents, who daily confront these women, hold divergent views. Their descriptions of homeless women provide no clue to the salience of drinking; instead, they illustrate styles of homelessness, often yielding contradictory images:

> . . . Old ladies with shopping bags. Oh, yes . . . bandages on their legs.
>
> Prostitutes. Every one of 'em.
>
> . . . Harmless. And, helpless, too. . . .
>
> No, they ain't drunkards. They're pickpockets, thieves, and panhandlers . . . well, most of them, at least.
>
> Just lost souls. Maybe God forgot about them.

While drinking may not be perceived as the dominant characteristic of the homeless women, the fact of the matter is that the skid-row way of life places heavy emphasis on drinking. Since most of these women, at least those in the present study, spend a large part of their daily lives in or around the Bowery district, it might be expected that a disproportionate number of them would exhibit patterns of heavy drinking.

In this chapter the drinking behavior of Shelter women will be described and compared with the drinking practices of homeless men.

Extent of Drinking

Two measures of current drinking status were used in this study: (1) the respondent's perception of the extent of her drinking; and (2) a quantity-frequency (*Q-F*) index based on her reports about the amount of alcohol consumed over a standardized time period. Since drinking status is a major variable in the hypotheses to be tested in this chapter, the rationale underlying each of these measures is outlined below.

Measures of Drinking Status

Perceptions of current drinking activity were measured by two items. First, the respondent was asked: "Do you ever have occasion to use alcoholic beverages such as liquor or 'mixed drinks,' wine, or beer; *or* do you drink at all?" If the respondent gave an affirmative reply, she was asked, "Well, then, all things considered, would you say you presently drink quite a lot, moderately, or very little?" On the other hand, if the answer to the first question was no, the interviewer then asked, "Well, then, have you ever drunk in the past even though you don't drink now?" Note that the initial item, which separates current drinkers from abstainers, leaves open the possibility that alcohol may be consumed for reasons other than social drinking. Thus, on three occasions women were classified as drinkers even though they claimed that they used alcohol for "medicinal" purposes only. This then led the interviewer to inquire further as to the extent of alcohol use, which, in the above cases, ranged from a "teaspoon of whiskey for relieving headaches, sorethroats, and coughing spells" by one respondent to "a pint of wine every evening as a tranquilizer before bedtime."[a] In sum, then, it was thought that the initial item might minimize the loss of respondents who were, in fact, current drinkers, but, for one reason or another, excluded themselves from the "drinking" population. Second, special consideration was given to labeling the actual drinking categories in the perception item, the most critical being the "high" category. The general concern here stems from previous survey and epidemiological studies on drinking which suggest that women in the interview or questionnaire situation are more likely than men to underrepresent the extent of their drinking. It was decided, therefore, that the label, "quite a lot," carried fewer negative implications than the more widely used, "very heavy" or "heavy" classifications.

The second measure of drinking status, the quantity-frequency index, was designed as a more objective classification of drinking status, though it, too, was based on information supplied by the respondent. The index was constructed on the basis of two items. The first question tapped how often the respondent drank on the average; the second, the type and amount of beverage usually consumed on drinking occasions. The beverages were then translated into "ounce equivalents" of alcohol according to the following standard:

1 ounce beer = 1 ounce equivalent
1 ounce wine = 4 ounce equivalents
1 ounce spirits = 10 ounce equivalents

Thus, it can be seen that a one-ounce shot of whiskey, for example, represents the same alcohol content as a 10-ounce bottle of beer.

Typically women reported the extent of their drinking in terms of glasses,

[a]Still another respondent initially classified herself as an abstainer, restating (and misinterpreting) the question, "Do I drink? Absolutely, no." In questioning the interviewee as to her past drinking practices, however, it was found that she currently used whiskey as a mouthwash. When asked how often she used whiskey for this purpose, she said, "I like to wash my mouth every hour or so. . . ." Interestingly the respondent reported that she always swallows it "cause it ain't polite to spit it out!"

shots, bottles, or fifths of specific beverages. The following standards were employed in translating these measures into ounces of beverage for subsequent conversion into ounce equivalents:

1 cocktail or shot of whiskey (or spirits) = 1½ ounces of spirits
1 glass of whiskey (or spirits) = 2 ounces of spirits
1 glass of wine = 4 ounces of wine
1 glass of beer = 7 ounces of beer
1 can or bottle of beer = 12 ounces of beer
1 fifth of spirits = 26 ounces of spirits
1 quart of spirits = 32 ounces of spirits
1 bottle of wine = 16 ounces of wine

Using both the amount of alcohol ingested (ounce equivalents) and the frequency of imbibing (daily, three times a week, once a week, and so on), a quantity-frequency quotient was then computed for each respondent. The resulting value indicated the number of ounce equivalents of alcohol a respondent consumed on a weekly basis. Using previous investigations of skid-row drinking practices as guidelines,[1] the following classifications were devised: (1) In order to be classified as a "heavy drinker,' the respondent's *Q-F* quotient had to be at least 400 ounce equivalents per week (which equals slightly less than 1½ cases of beer); (2) for "moderate" drinkers, 140 to 399 ounce equivalents; and (3) light drinkers, under 139 ounces.[2]

Table 7-1 summarizes the current drinking patterns of Shelter women and Camp LaGuardia men. The findings reported below pertain to the hypotheses about differences in drinking between the two samples.

First, using comparative data on perceptions of drinking status, no support is found for the hypothesis that drinking is more pronounced among homeless men than homeless women. In fact, quite unexpectedly, the two samples are well matched in all drinking classifications. Approximately one-third of the women (compared to one-fourth of the men) considered themselves heavy drinkers, another third were moderate drinkers, and nearly 40 percent of both samples were light drinkers or abstainers. Thus, on the basis of self-perceptions, it might be concluded that homeless men and women do not differ significantly in the extent of their drinking.

However, data obtained by the quantity-frequency (*Q-F*) measure reveal major differences between the two samples, the most striking of which is the proportion of respondents classified as heavy drinkers. On the *Q-F* index almost half of the men are classified as heavy drinkers, compared to one-third of the women. At the other extreme, 10 percent of the men and nearly 25 percent of the women are light drinkers. Thus, use of the *Q-F* index as the indicator of extent of drinking reveals that patterns of heavy drinking are more characteristic of homeless men than of homeless women.

The differences in the distribution of respondents on the two drinking

Table 7-1
Measures of Drinking Status for Shelter Women and Camp LaGuardia Men[a]

Measure of Drinking	*Women's Shelter*	*Camp LaGuardia*
Perception of Current Drinking, Total	100%	100%
Quite a lot (heavy)	32	26
Moderate	31	35
Very light (light)	18	22
Abstainer	19	17
Previous Drinking by Abstainers, Total[b]	100	100
Quite a lot (heavy)	50	10
Moderate or light	50	80
Total abstainer	0	10
Current Drinking Status by *Q-F* Index, Total	100	100
Quite a lot (heavy)	32	47[c]
Moderate	26	26
Very light	23	10[c]
Abstainer	19	17
Lifetime Drinking Status, Total	100	–
Quite a lot (heavy)	55	–
Moderate	20	–
Very little	25	–
Total abstainer	0	[5][d]

[a]*N* = 52 (Shelter Women); *N* = 199 (Camp LaGuardia Men). "No response" categories were not used in computing percentages. Therefore, the total *N* varies slightly.

[b]N = 10 (Shelter Women); *N* = 39 (Camp LaGuardia Men). Significance test not computed due to small sample size.

[c]Differences are significant at the .05 level.

[d]Comparable information for the Camp LaGuardia is available for abstainers only.

indices prompted further analysis of the congruence of these two measures of current drinking status. An ordinal measure of association (gamma) was used to reveal congruence. The results are reported in Table 7-2.

It was expected that relationships between self-report and objective measures of drinking would be lower for women than for men due to greater public disapproval of drinking—especially heavy drinking—among women. However, among women the congruence between the self-perception of drinking status and the extent of drinking as indicated by the *Q-F* index was higher than among the skid-row men.

It appears that homeless women who see themselves as light drinkers are far less likely than homeless men to report quantities and frequencies of drinking that qualify them for "heavy" or "moderate" classification on the *Q-F* index.

Table 7-2
Perception of Drinking by Quantity-Frequency Index for Drinkers, Women's Shelter and Camp LaGuardia

	Self-perception					
	Women's Shelter[a]			Camp LaGuardia[b]		
Quantity-Frequency Index	*Heavy*	*Moderate*	*Light*	*Heavy*	*Moderate*	*Light*
Heavy	76%	18%	11%	85%	53%	31%
Moderate	12	64	11	10	44	38
Light	12	18	78	5	3	31
Total	100%	100%	100%	100%	100%	100%

[a]Gamma = .82.

[b]Gamma = .58.

Among those women who perceived themselves as light drinkers, 78 percent reported drinking patterns which resulted in the comparable category on the *Q-F* index.

Even more interesting is the finding that homeless men who misperceive their drinking activity tend to do so in the direction of public morality, that is, view their drinking as being more within the pale of "respectability" than it really is. Over half of the men who described themselves as moderate drinkers were classified as heavy drinkers on the *Q-F* index, but only 3 percent of the self-defined "moderate" category were "light" drinkers on the *Q-F* index. On the other hand, Shelter women who defined their drinking status as "moderate" but were in another category on the *Q-F* index were evenly divided between heavy and light drinking; approximately one-fifth of them misperceived in either direction. Thus homeless women who misperceive the extent of their drinking seem just as likely to underreport as to overreport.

On the basis of the above findings on current drinking practices, the following conclusions can be made: (1) there are no significant differences between homeless men and women on the extent of drinking when self-perception is used as the measure of drinking status. (2) On the other hand, when a quantity-frequency index is employed, patterns of heavy drinking are shown to be more characteristic of homeless men than homeless women. (3) The congruence between self-perception and quantity-frequency measures of drinking is considerably higher for Shelter women than for Camp LaGuardia men. Moreover, the magnitude of difference is large enough to suggest that heavy drinking is, in fact, more characteristic of homeless men than homeless women, thus supporting the hypothesized differences between the drinking behavior of these two populations. (4) Finally, not only is the homeless man much more likely than homeless women to misperceive his drinking status, but he is also more likely to underreport the extent of his drinking.

"Lifetime" Drinking Patterns

In addition to obtaining information about current drinking practices, drinking histories were compiled for Shelter women. Using the current drinking status as a starting point, the respondent was asked whether she had drunk "heavier" or "lighter" in the past, or, in the case of an abstainer, whether she had ever drunk at all. A series of probe questions followed which ultimately provided a self-report drinking status for every year of the respondent's life, from her initial drinking experience to the present.

Thus, each respondent's entire drinking career was depicted. From this, it was possible to observe whether a woman had ever exhibited heavy drinking patterns, regardless of her present drinking status. Since the antecedent variables associated with heavy drinking are thought to exist in the backgrounds of all who have ever drunk heavily, the variable "ever drunk heavily" is a more relevant measure than current drinking status for the study of etiological patterns. The findings on "lifetime" drinking (Table 7-1)[b] show that many Shelter women who are not heavy drinkers presently have been heavy drinkers at some time in their lives. Over half (55 percent) of the Shelter women are or had been heavy drinkers in the past, as compared to the one-third who were heavy drinkers at the time of the interview. Moreover, while nearly one-fifth of the respondents are indentified as current abstainers, *all* have been drinkers at some time. Since comparable information is not available from the Camp LaGuardia sample, the conclusion that homeless men and women do not differ in terms of their lifetime drinking status is unwarranted. Nevertheless, the data reported here firmly establish the fact that heavy drinking is a highly prominent feature of the homeless-women population.[c]

Characteristics of Drinking

Studies of homeless men typically have examined various characteristics of drinking patterns. These analyses usually have been justified on grounds that knowledge of what a person drinks, where he imbibes, and with whom he drinks reveals much about the role of alcohol in the life of that individual. Since little information on the current drinking practices of homeless women is available

---

[b]Comparable data for Camp LaGuardia men were not available except for abstainers. However, since the findings for women indicate that their drinking has been heavier in the past, it might be presumed that this is also true of Camp LaGuardia men. Findings on the previous drinking patterns of current abstainers among these men seemingly point to this conclusion inasmuch as almost all (90 percent) reported that they had drunk in the past.

[c]In reviewing past studies on skid-row drinking practices, it would appear that most researchers have assumed that the present pattern of drinking by homeless men represents the high point in their drinking career. Although investigators have, in a few instances, ascertained whether abstainers have imbibed in the past, longitudinal data on the extent of drinking at various points in the lives of homeless men are rarely encountered.

in existing literature, brief attention will be given to describing some of the more salient features of the drinking behavior of this population. Findings are summarized in Table 7-3.

Beverage Consumption

According to popular stereotype, the most distinctive feature of drinking among skid-rowers is heavy consumption of wine (commonly labeled the "wino syndrome"). While it is undoubtedly true that a fair number of skid-rowers consume wine at various times in their drinking careers, findings in the present study lend almost no support to this belief for either homeless men or women. Less than one-fourth of the Camp LaGuardia men and approximately one-third of the Shelter women reported wine as the most frequently consumed beverage alcohol. Instead, the group preference for men is apparently beer, while for the women it is liquor or "mixed drinks." Interestingly, beer, the most frequently consumed beverage for the men, is the least frequently consumed by the women.

Data were also collected on the money Shelter women spent on alcoholic beverages (Table 7-3). Findings indicate that spending patterns were almost equally divided between three categories: approximately one-third reported no expenditures, another one-third spent from $1 to $10, and still another third reported expenditures in excess of $10 (in no case higher than $20). Although these findings show that the amount of money spent on alcohol is not great by absolute standards, it should be remembered that most of these women reported an average monthly income below $100, which means that a woman even in the "middle-expenditure bracket" could be spending as much as 50 percent of her disposable income on alcoholic beverages.

In the course of gathering interview data, many interesting (though mostly fictitious) beliefs about the virtues or detrimental effects of alcohol were revealed. For example, one woman who was currently an abstainer remarked, "I used to drink that wine, yes the wine. . . . I quit. It was eatin' my brain away, little by little." Other women mentioned the following as reasons for avoiding alcohol:

It thickens the blood
. . . Makes me constipated.
. . . Gives you diarrhea.
. . . Damages the lower intestine.
. . . Brings out the devil in people.

On the other hand, some women commented on the more positive aspects of alcohol:

Whiskey, yessiree, Man's best friend;
. . . Relieves the aches and pains, a lot better than aspirin, too.

People should take a spoonful of whiskey just before . . . [a meal]. Makes the food digest better.

Whiskey's a good tonic. Makes a body feel good all over. . . . A real eye-opener, too!

Table 7-3
Selected Characteristics of the Drinking Histories of Shelter Women and Camp LaGuardia Men[a]

Characteristic	*Women's Shelter*	*Camp LaGuardia*
Most Frequently Consumed Beverage[b]		
Beer	17%[c]	37%
Wine	32	24
Spirits (including "mixed drinks")	39	31
Combination of above	12	8
Money Spent on Alcoholic Beverages Per Week[b]		
None	32	–
\$1–\$10	32	–
More than \$10	36	–
Usual Place of Drinking[b]		
Home	24	–
Bar or tavern	15	–
Street or park	24	–
Other (incl. combination of above)	36	–
Drinking Pattern[b]		
Alone	50[c]	36
With others	40[c]	54
Both alone and with others	10	10
Age of First Drink[d]		
10–15	8	–
16–17	17	–
18–19	25	–
20–21	31	–
22–24	13	–
25 or after	6	–
Age at Onset of Heavy Drinking[e]		
Under 20	0	16
20–24	18	25
25–29	18	11
30–34	32	13
35–39	21	8
40 or older	11	28

[a]N = 52 (women); N = 199 (men).

[b]Information pertains to current drinkers only. N = 42 (women); on cells which contain data for Camp LaGuardia men, N = 129 unless designated otherwise.

[c]Differences between men and women are significant at the .05 level.

[d]N = 51. Mean age is 19.2 years; median, 19.0.

[e]N = 28 (women); N = 104 (men). Mean age: 32.1 years (women); 28.0 years (men). Difference is significant at the .05 level. Median age: 32.0 (women); 28.5 (men).

As might be expected, women's beliefs about the evils or virtues of alcohol tended to coincide with present consumption practices.

Drinking Companions

Evidence from a number of studies of skid-row subculture suggest that much of the drinking done by homeless men takes place in the company of others. Wallace, for example, asserts that practically all drinking on skid row is done in groups.[3] Observations on bottle-gang behavior seem to support this viewpoint.[4] On the other hand, while group drinking may be characteristic of the homeless man, there are good reasons to suspect that homeless women, especially those who exhibit patterns of heavy drinking, are less inclined to drink in the company of others. First, general literature on problem drinkers and alcoholics points to the fact that solitary drinking is far more characteristic of women than of men.[5] Second, since the Shelter women tend to know fewer people on the Bowery than Camp LaGuardia men, this would seem to reduce the general probabilities of their having drinking companions.

Data in Table 7-3 provide support for this hypothesis. Exactly half of the women, compared to slightly more than one-third of the men, are solitary drinkers. Conversely, 40 percent of women and 54 percent of the men drink primarily in the company of others. Although the percentage differences in both cases reached statistical significance, the difference is not so great as to suggest that the drinking patterns of homeless women differ vastly from homeless men.

Given the fact that one of every two Shelter women is a solitary drinker, the question can be raised as to where these women do most of their drinking. Findings in this regard (Table 7-3) reveal that the women were evenly distributed as to the location of the usual place of drinking. Approximately one-fourth drink at home, another one-fourth drink in "unstructured drinking places" (streets, parks, doorways, etc.), and slightly more than a third drink in a variety of other places (social gatherings, restaurants, etc.).

Excerpts from field notes help to illuminate certain features of the drinking contexts for some of these women:

Friday I [the researcher] visited the Crazy Horse Tavern near Broome Street during the late afternoon hours. . . . Five of the Shelter women arrived (separately) over the course of the first hour. Except for Miss G, the women did not intermingle with the men. Miss S, who sat isolated in a corner booth for the entire time, promptly dismissed two men who approached her for a drink, yelling "Get Lost!" (One man was apparently so startled that he fell down!) The other three women remained completely isolated, two of them sitting at opposite ends of the bar; the other, in a booth near the window. On one occasion, Mrs. D created quite a commotion among the men when she apparently got confused as to which rest room was for the ladies, accidentally walking into the men's room. The bartender was especially perturbed, muttering to me "Women! They're more trouble than they're worth. Got no business being in here." Miss G, on the other hand, approached almost every man in the bar, asking each (in very unpolite tones), "buy the lady a drink." Only one man consented, later refusing to buy her a second. She left immediately.

. . . As far as tavern-drinking is concerned, the women I observed, for the most part, did not intermingle with the men. With few exceptions, the men made no attempts to interrupt the solitude of these women.

On other occasions field workers observed women who drank primarily in a park near the Shelter. These observations are particularly interesting because they suggest that these women are not insensitive to the pressures of social disapproval of "drinking in public."

Many of the Shelter women who drink heavily spend a good deal of time sitting in the park on Grand and on doorsteps near the Bank just off of Bowery. . . . It is especially interesting to watch their drinking behavior in these contexts. Oddly enough, these women go through a "predrinking" ritual before every drink. For example, Miss R, who usually drinks in the park, takes a drink if—and only if—there is no one in the immediate vicinity. Typically she looks around, first looking up the street, then down, and occasionally even behind her bench; if no one is near, she "sneaks" a drink from her wine bottle (disguised in the proverbial "brown bag") by holding her coat up around her face. . . . Even more interesting is the drinking behavior of Mrs. D, who hides her drinking from public view by squatting near some bushes near the playground.

Finally, observational reports on drinking activities indicate that these women, unlike many skid-row men, do not participate in "bottle gangs." In fact, women who were seen drinking in parks and on the Bowery itself almost invariably drank alone. One field worker noted:

Although I have observed many of the women drinking in the park and near the Shelter itself, I have seen nothing that could be interpreted as the counterpart of the skid-row man's "bottle gang." In a few instances I noted women drinking with another man, but never more than one at a time. . . . On one occasion Mrs. W tried to "bum a drink" from a group of men passing a bottle near the Bank; she was refused, however. . . . In sum it appears that most, if not all, of the "public drinking" of these women is a solitary experience.

Age of First Drink

Most of the Shelter women took their first drink between the ages of 19 and 20 (Table 7-3). A comparison of the mean age (19.2) to that of other female drinking populations reveals almost no differences. For example, the mean age of first drink in Lisanky's female alcoholics and problem drinkers is approximately age 20; in Cramer and Blacker's study of female drunkenness offenders, 19.3.[6]

Although data on age of first drinking experiences were not available from the camp LaGuardia sample, information from other studies provides a basis for comparison with men. Lisansky reports that the mean age of first drink for outpatient male alcoholics is 17.0 years.[7] A population more comparable to skid-row men, however, is chronic drunkenness offenders studied by Pittman and Gordon.[8] Most of these men had their initial drink in "early adolescence." Thus, the comparison or findings of Shelter women suggests that there is nothing atypical about the age of their first drink.

Onset of Heavy Drinking

A number of studies in which various alcoholic populations have been compared report that the onset of heavy or excessive drinking almost always occurs at an earlier age, on the average, in men than in women. Lisansky, for example, reports that outpatient alcoholic men in her study began drinking heavily at approximately age 27 compared to slightly later than age 31 for the comparison sample of female alcoholics.

In order to test the hypothesis that the onset of heavy drinking occurs earlier in homeless men than in homeless women, a comparison of the age of onset of heavy drinking between the Shelter and Camp LaGuardia was made (see Table 7-3). Findings show that approximately one-third of the women began drinking heavily before the age of 30, compared with over half of the Camp sample. Almost one-third of the women, however, experienced the onset of heavy drinking between the ages of 30 and 34. The overall difference between the two samples is reflected in the mean ages for onset of heavy drinking, age 32 for the Shelter women compared to 28 for the men (a difference statistically significant at the .05 level). Hence, the findings provide support for the hypothesis that the onset of heavy drinking occurs at a later age, on the average, in the lives of homeless women than homeless men.[d]

Concluding Observations

Having described and examined the drinking behavior of homeless women, and, in the previous chapter, their social characteristics, a few summary statements are in order. We have demonstrated that homeless women differ from homeless men on skid row in a number of respects. Demographically, homeless women are somewhat younger than homeless men, and they are more likely to be native-born. Financially, homeless women are worse off than skid-row men,

---

[d] Findings from the Homelessness study indicate that the median age at onset of heavy drinking for the Bowery sample is 24.5 years. A comparison to the median age for Shelter women (32.0) suggests that the difference between homeless men and women may be even greater than that reported above.

and they are much more likely to come from a broken home, especially one that has been broken due to divorce or desertion. Although both populations are maritally unattached, they have arrived at this status by different routes. Homeless women are much more likely to have been married at least once, whereas homeless men are more likely to have remained single throughout their lifetime. As for patterns of affiliation, the attenuation of former ties among homeless women closely resembles that among homeless men. Neither the women nor the men have much contact with their families, relatives, or previous acquaintances. In addition, available evidence on the early-life histories of Shelter women suggests that they have long histories of limited social involvement.

Heavy drinking is clearly a distinctive feature of both the homeless-man and homeless-woman populations. Findings on the extent of drinking by the two groups, however, apparently vary according to which measure of drinking status is used. The perceptual measure of current drinking employed in this study revealed that patterns of heavy drinking among homeless women were on an equal plane with homeless men. However, findings from the quantity-frequency index indicate that heavy drinking is somewhat more characteristic of homeless men than women. A subsequent comparison of the two measures suggested that the skid-row man is much more likely than the homeless woman to misperceive the extent of his drinking. Almost always his "misperceptions" take the form of underreporting his drinking, whereas women are just as likely to overreport as they are to underreport their drinking status. This finding can be viewed with special significance inasmuch as it throws light on the general validity of perceptual measures of drinking. Thus, the findings in this study suggest that future researchers investigating the drinking behavior of homeless men would be unwise to rely solely on perceptual measures of drinking status. For homeless women, however, it apparently makes little difference as to which measure is used; both yield approximately the same results.

Finally, the drinking histories of homeless women differ from homeless men on two important characteristics. First, homeless women are much more likely to exhibit solitary patterns of drinking than are skid-row men, which suggests that drinking by these women tends to be less convivial in nature than among the men. Second, the onset of heavy drinking occus at a significantly later age in homeless women than in homeless men. Although the age of onset of heavy drinking has been shown to be an important variable in the "skid careers" of homeless men, findings in this study suggest that the age at onset of heavy drinking apparently does not influence the "skid careers" of homeless women in any significant way. The "skid careers" of both early- and late-onset heavy drinkers, as measured by affiliation patterns (cohabitation history, membership in voluntary associations, and regularity of church attendance) showed no appreciable differences. These findings suggest that women who experience an early-onset of heavy drinking are no more likely than late-onset heavy drinkers to have an early arrival on skid row.

Notes

1. Howard M. Bahr, *Homelessness and Disaffiliation*, New York: Columbia University, Bureau of Applied Social Research, 1968; Donald J. Bogue, *Skid Row in American Cities*, Chicago: Community and Family Study Center, University of Chicago, 1963.

2. These *Q-F* index categories represent a slightly lower alcohol-equivalent level than was used in classifying the Camp LaGuardia sample. This reduction can be justified on grounds that existing literature indicates women drinkers usually drink smaller quantities than men. See J.L. Horn and K.W. Wanberg, "Symptom Patterns Related to Excessive Use of Alcohol," *Quarterly Journal of Studies on Alcohol*, 30 (March 1969): 35-58; K.W. Wanberg and J.L. Horn, "Alcoholic Symptom Patterns of Men and Women: A Comparative Study," *Quarterly Journal of Studies on Alcohol*, 31 (March 1970): 40-61; K. Wanberg and J. Knapp, "Differences in Drinking Symptoms and Behavior of Men and Women Alcoholics." *British Journal of Addiction*, 64 (1970): 347-355.

3. Samuel E. Wallace, *Skid Row as a Way of Life*, Totowa, N.J.: Bedminster Press, 1965.

4. W. Jack Peterson, "The Culture of the Skid Road Wino," unpublished master's thesis, Washington State University, Pullman, Washington, 1955; E. Rubington, "The Bottle Gang," *Quarterly Journal of Studies on Alcohol*, 29 (December 1968): 943-955; Gerald R. Garrett, "The Migrant Laborer: A Sociological Study," unpublished master's thesis, Washington State University, Pullman, Washington, 1966; W. Jack Peterson and Milton A. Maxwell, "The Skid Road 'Wino,' " *Social Problems*, 5 (Spring 1958): 308-316.

5. Horn and Wanberg, "Symptom Patterns Related to Excessive Use of Alcohol"; Wanberg and Knapp, "Differences in Drinking Symptoms"; E. Lisansky, "Alcoholism in Women: Social and Psychological Concomitants," *Quarterly Journal of Studies on Alcohol*, 18 (December 1957); 588-623; Barry A. Kinsey, *The Female Alcoholic: A Social Psychological Study*, Springfield, Ill.: Charles C. Thomas, 1966.

6. M.J. Cramer and E. Blacker, "Early and Late Problem Drinkers among Female Prisoners," *Journal of Health and Human Behavior*, 4 (Winter 1963): 282-290, and "Social Class and Drinking Experience of Female Drunkenness Offenders," *Journal of Health and Human Behavior*, 7 (Winter 1966): 276-283.

7. Lisansky, "Alcoholism in Women."

8. David J. Pittman and C.W. Gordon, *Revolving Door: A Study of the Chronic Police Case Inebriate*, Glencoe, Ill.: The Free Press, 1958.

8 Summary and Speculations

This concluding chapter is in two parts. First, we discuss disaffiliation among "independent" women in the tract samples. Then the "institutionalized" homeless women at the Pioneer Hotel are treated separately. In each part we attempt to tie our findings to possible action programs aimed at reducing involuntary disaffiliation.

Disaffiliation among "Independent" Urban Women

One of the major findings was the direct relationship between formal affiliation and extent of activity. Affiliated women do a wider variety of things, and do them more frequently, than disaffiliated women. There is no reason why this need be so. A disaffiliate may walk in the park, go shopping, go to the theater or to films, clean her home, listen to the radio, or participate in many other activities just as well as a person with many formal ties. But although there is no *necessary* correlation between affiliation and activity, in fact the presence of a roommate or the fact that one is employed or involved in formal organizations increases the probable range and frequency of social activity. Thus the people with the most "free" time—the fewest social obligations—are the *least* likely to take advantage of the range of activities which the city offers.

The disaffiliated women we studied are multiproblem women. They manifest feelings of deprivation, both with respect to their own past and to significant others in the present. They are lonely, poor, sick, and afraid. They resent the physical decay of their surroundings, and the growing number of thieves, muggers and addicts who prey on them. They ask for better police protection but have little faith that the city government will aid them.

Some of the isolation of aged women in Manhattan is voluntary, but even that is compounded by fear, poverty, and illness. The institutionalized Shelter women receive better health care than many of the poor disaffiliates in the census tract samples. Their social isolation not only means that there are no companions for activities, but also that if anything happens, there is no one to notice or care immediately. Thus, much of their isolation is protective, and their shrinking from use of the recreational, educational, or transportation services of the city is a function of fear and poverty as well as age and ill health. The constricted social networks of these women represent a failure of delivery of social and human services, of democratic representation, and of governmental responsibilities to the disadvantaged.

Many of the disaffiliates we interviewed are talented people. Their experiences are interesting, and they are capable of making positive contributions to the lives of other people. They are prevented from making those contributions by their isolation from other people, an isolation that comes to be ingrained via defensive living in a threatening context. To a certain extent, protection can be bought. Merely increasing the incomes of the disaffiliated women would increase their level of affiliation.

The importance of reading, watching television, and listening to the radio—all activities carried on in the safety of one's room—reflects the women's desire for social involvement within the constraints imposed by their threatening environment. Perhaps more attention should be given to orienting media programming for the aged, and less to reaffirming the youth-centered culture.

Many women objected that they had been forced to retire, or complained that the work they were doing was not what they would like to do. Many of the disaffiliated might be reinvolved by increasing job opportunities for aged women, either by specifically earmarking certain jobs for them or by establishing legal quotas assuring that a certain proportion of all, say, teachers or clerks had to be women over a certain age.

Most of the disaffiliates wanted better housing, and some form of part-time employment might be linked to acceptance into better-quality housing, thereby serving to integrate elderly women into social (work) groups and solve their housing problems at the same time. Another way to combine activity and affiliation might be to lower the level of risk associated with venturing away from home by the provision of escort service. Many of the women fear to trouble others, so the service should be linked to a housing establishment, just as doormen or elevator operators come with an apartment building. Thus, without the loss of face associated with admitting she was dependent or afraid, a woman might use the house's escort service to take her when she wanted to go and pick her up when she was ready to return. Such services could be provided by volunteer groups, community agencies, or church groups without any additional allocations of public funds.

The outlook for reintegration of many of the disaffiliated women is fairly positive in light of the analysis of dominant predictors of current affiliation rank. Current income, age, and health status—all elements of a woman's present status—were far more important than the so-called "background factors" in determining her disaffiliation. This is essentially a happy conclusion for therapists because while they can do nothing to alter a woman's social background, the nature of her present circumstances is subject to change. The important role of income is especially reassuring, since it is so readily manipulable.

Disaffiliation among Shelter Women

A primary purpose of the study of Shelter women was to learn if their backgrounds differed from those of homeless men. As compared to residents of

Camp LaGuardia interviewed during the Homelessness Project, the Shelter women proved to be poorer, younger, better educated, more often black, and more frequently married. Three-fourths of the homeless women had been married, compared to less than half of the Camp LaGuardia men. Moreover, second and third marriages were common among the women. The homeless men seemed to have lost interest in marriage after a negative initial experience, but Shelter women had kept trying. Informal, relatively long-term liaisons were also much more common among the homeless women than among homeless men. Two-thirds of them reported participating in "informal marriage," contrasted to one-fifth of the homeless men.

Also, the Shelter women were more apt to have children; childlessness was three times as common among the men, and those who had children had smaller families than did the Shelter women. Like homeless men, the women had long histories of limited social involvement by the time they arrived at the Shelter, and drinking was a severe problem. However, the Shelter women were much more likely to drink alone, and onset of heavy drinking occurred later for them than for homeless men.

As for background characteristics, over half of the Shelter women came from broken parental homes, compared to only about one-third of the Camp LaGuardia men. The high proportion of broken homes in the backgrounds of Shelter women suggests that the experience of a broken home is indeed a predisposing factor to homelessness. Also of interest was the contrast between homeless women and men in reason for dissolution of the parental home. Among the men, death of a parent was the dominant reason; among homeless women, divorce, desertion, or separation accounted for most of the parental breakups.

Comparisons of Shelter women and other respondents in extent of youth affiliation revealed that the disaffiliation of Shelter women may not be attributed to their lifelong patterns of avoidance of memberships. In youth they were just as involved in voluntary associations as were women in the other samples. Assessment of the affiliative histories of subsamples revealed that, within samples, the disaffiliates manifested lower employment rates than the affiliates, and were also less likely to belong to voluntary organizations, but they did not differ from the more affiliated in lifetime profiles for church attendance, occupational status, or family affiliation.

The salience of the broken home in the family of orientation, combined with the important role marital crises seem to have played in the personal histories of Shelter women, suggested that for women homelessness mainly derives from difficulties experienced in performing the major female roles of wife and mother. For males, homelessness is linked to failure in occupational roles combined with nonperformance or failure in marital roles.

For women, occupational roles seem relatively unimportant as antecedents of homelessness. Instead, it is the dissolution of marriages–divorces, desertions, separations, and widowhood–which seems to be most salient. Of course other factors such as heavy drinking, ill health, and poverty are associated with homelessness for both males and females. But it was evident that for women the dominant process leading to homelessness was the marital experience, as opposed to the occupational history for men.

Our interview schedule was not designed to provide a systematic evaluation of the Shelter program, but researchers' observations and the comments of the women interviewed led to several conclusions: (1) The physical facilities of the Shelter, and especially its location in the Bowery, were not appreciated by the women. (2) The recreation and rehabilitation programs provided at the Shelter were viewed as ineffective by both staff and clients. (3) Staff members were frequently ill-trained and unmotivated for work with homeless women; several indicated that their professional training might be put to better use in a different type of social work. (4) Clients viewed the staff as not caring about them but merely putting in their time to draw their pay. (5) The absence of a viable rehabilitation program was viewed by the women as evidence that society had given up on them. (6) Clients and staff expected clients to fail, and the atmosphere of pessimism and apathy with which the Shelter seemed charged made psychological rehabilitation almost impossible. (7) Despite a strict schedule for rising, eating, or going to bed, there were large blocks of time when the women had nothing to do.

The Women's Shelter seemed much less efficient than Camp LaGuardia. Inmates at Camp LaGuardia like the food there; and they talk about the healthful surroundings. The Shelter women report fewer acquaintances and friends, and they talk to other people less than Camp LaGuardia residents. Camp LaGuardia is very successful at providing adequate recreational facilities, medical services, and personal security. The inmates indicate that the staff takes good care of them, and chances for getting a job upon leaving the camp are fairly good. In contrast, the residents of the Women's Shelter are very negative about facilities and treatment.

One aspect of the Camp LaGuardia program which might be adopted for the Women's Shelter is the resident work program. It is explicit policy at the Camp that every capable man be assigned to a work detail, and in fact even the disabled men receive some assignment. Sometimes the job assignments are artificial, designed only to keep the men "interested and occupied," but the universal work assignment helps the men pass time and serves to legitimate the Camp to the tax-paying public. Moreover, the jobs at Camp LaGuardia are paying jobs, with income and responsibility differentials which, while small, provide symbolic distinctions and a status system. At the Women's Shelter, only one status was apparent, that of dependent client. Time hangs heavy for the Shelter women. A few maintain employment on the outside, but within the Shelter program itself there aren't even make-work jobs. For most of the women, the recreation therapy of bingo and cards is no substitute for active work. So the women sit. They have only a few activities; watching television, walking, and visiting the park are the most common "active" pastimes.

While programs aimed at helping the women structure their time would be an improvement, even within the present structure there are ways in which the women might be helped. For example, field workers were struck with the patronizing spirit that often characterized the caseworker-client relationship. Witness, for example, some statements made by caseworkers and clients at the Emergency Assistance Unit and at the Shelter:

Well, Miss S, that's just one of those things that just can't be helped. Things always work out. Just think about that for awhile.

You just go on back and watch TV. You'll feel better then.

I been waiting here since 11:30. . . . And he keeps saying, "pretty soon, ma'm. Pretty soon."

The patronizing attitude was reflected even more clearly in the "rehabilitation" programs in operation at the Shelter, most of which amounted to little more than playing bingo interspersed with a game of cards.

The philosophy underlying these programs has evidently been one of entertaining the women in hopes that some positive benefit will appear. During the exploratory investigation in 1968, many women made comments that not only summarized the extent of their interest in such programs, but simultaneously captured the essence of the "therapeutic environment" at the Shelter.

AA? Sure. I go. I'll take donuts over cookies–anyday. What program? . . . Bingo bores me.

Passing out a bar of soap and a wash cloth ain't my idea of rehabilitation.

They play games. Now, isn't that nice!

At the time of the study, the gloom and pessimism surrounding the Shelter program was such that efforts at helping the clients to reconstruct their lives seemed bound for failure. Neither the professional staff–supervisors, caseworkers, and physicians–nor the nonprofessionals–matrons, police officers, and clerks–voiced much hope for significant improvement in the life circumstances of these women. As one caseworker put it: "Anything we do here is useless. . . . I guess they just want to be lost souls, and that's it. . . . They want to be away from it all, and they're just as happy about it. They are hopeless cases, at best."

APPENDIX A

Data Collection

Construction of the Interview Schedule and Training of Interviewers

The Urban Disaffiliation Project was designed to provide knowledge about disaffiliated urban women comparable to that obtained in the previous studies of homeless men. Its immediate antecedent was Columbia University's Homelessness Project (MH-10861), and the life-history interview schedule used in that study of Bowery men was adapted for use with female respondents.

Changes in that instrument reflected our perceptions of women's more diverse means of social mobility and the wider variety of roles available to them than to males. Also, the fairly cumbersome questions used to identify drinking histories and lifetime church attendance patterns of skid-row men were modified considerably. Finally, some items were added simply because the base of knowledge about the activities of homeless women was so much smaller than for homeless men. Therefore considerable qualitative material was sought, material that had already been available for men when the initial life-history interview schedule was designed in 1965 and 1966.

Specifically, the most substantial additions to the instrument used among the homeless men were: (1) a series of questions about the occupations of several key relatives (daughter, mother, son, husband, brother) thought essential to charting the social mobility of women; (2) a page of questions about women's reasons for taking and leaving jobs; (3) questions about perceived disaffiliation or loneliness; (4) items about aspirations and feelings about the several major roles women may occupy in our society; (5) a series of questions about functions of alcohol for the respondent; and (6) a page of questions about the activities of the previous day.

The completed first draft of the interview schedule was used in training interviewers, and their reports of difficulties with the instrument led to several revisions. Thus, interviewer training and pretesting were combined, a procedure used successfully in the Homelessness Project.

Criteria for selecting among applicants for interviewer positions on the project staff included (1) extent of formal training or experience in interviewing and (2) educational background, with the social and behavioral sciences preferred. Of the 19 interviewers selected, all were at least 21 years old, and all but three were women. Fifteen held bachelor's degrees, and most of these were graduate students, usually in sociology, although the fields of education, social work, and medicine were also represented.

Although most of the staff had had previous interviewing experience, a 3-week period was devoted to in-depth training of interviewers. In addition to lectures and discussions devoted to the instrument itself, much of this time was devoted to reviewing principles of interviewing, techniques of establishing rapport with respondents, and strategies for gaining entree.

The first stage in the training process was the presentation of a general overview of the study during an initial orientation meeting. Objectives of the research, methods, and theoretical orientation were outlined, and each interviewer agreed to read the project proposal.

There followed a series of five 2-hour meetings devoted to discussion of interview techniques. Demonstration interviews were conducted by experienced interviewers illustrating the "do's" and "don'ts" in questioning respondents. Particular attention was given to techniques for gaining rapport, handling inconsistent or contradictory responses, strategies for probing, and to general approaches for questioning respondents on personal or sensitive issues. Special emphasis was also placed on ways of gaining entry into a respondent's home under a variety of conditions such as those posed by a particularly stubborn doorman, an intercom system, or the potential respondent answering through a closed door. In general we tried to anticipate irregular conditions that might be particularly problematic for interviewers.

Next interviewers received a draft of the instrument, and particular items were reviewed. Frequently the rationale for inclusion of particular items was discussed in the interest of standardizing interviewer response. Members of the staff then conducted an interview in a contrived situation using another staff member as a respondent.

Practice interviews were conducted over a 3-day period until each interviewer had achieved an acceptable level of facility with the instrument. All practice interviews were checked by supervisors, and an attempt was made to assess differences in the recording performance of interviewers, i.e., in the extent to which interviewers differed in recording the details of a respondent's answer to the open-ended questions. This was done by means of a demonstration interview; each interviewer was asked to imagine that the replies in the demonstration were those given to her in a real interview situation. Results from the experiment revealed there to be no major difference in the general *theme* of recorded material, but sizable disparities in the amount of detail recorded. Some of these differences were due to differential skills in taking dictation. Interviewers whose recording of detail was inadequate were given additional training and practice until their performance reached an acceptable level.

Interviewers then went out to interview under actual field conditions. Each of them completed at least two interviews with nonsample women (usually residents of hotels on the upper West Side) who consented to be interviewed. Thus prospective interviewers had practice in door apporaches as well as in going through the instrument. This first major pretest produced 20 interviews. Results of these interviews were used in revision of the instrument, and after more practice interviewing among the staff there was a second pretest in which 26 elderly women were interviewed. Extensive debriefing sessions highlighted several limitations in interviewer technique or instrument construction. Where possible, these were corrected, either by additional changes in the instrument or by more interviewer training.

After the interview schedule had been put into final form, there were more training sessions. At this point there were relatively few problems because there had been no substantial changes in the instrument, and most of the discussion centered around problems of gaining entrance and of maintaining rapport. As the data collection proceeded, periodic staff meetings were held in which workable strategies were shared and new problems considered. As the schedules were completed, a staff member checked them for omissions and errors. Sometimes results of this audit revealed the necessity for interviewers to contact the respondent again, and try to obtain missing or illegible information. This practice helped to reduce response error and nonresponses in the completed instruments.

Universe and Sampling

In each census tract, the initial objectives were for researchers to familiarize themselves with the tract, to learn about the kind of people who lived there, to enumerate households and, where necessary, to draw floor plans of buildings for future sampling. As an aid in the enumeration, maps of each tract were obtained from Columbia University's architecture library. These maps identified every building on each block by building number and also provided information about the number of floors in each building.

Preliminary trips to the research site provided a general overview of the area. Subsequent field trips produced written descriptions of each building. Building superintendents, residents, patrolmen, and business and hotel managers were interviewed in the effort to learn about the residents of the tract and their dwelling places.

Once the purpose of the study was explained to them, most of the managers and/or owners of the hotels and apartment buildings were willing to cooperate. However, in all the tracts we were unable to gain access to residents of one or more large hotels, and in tract 159 there were some apartment buildings to which we were never admitted. In tract 76, where almost the entire residential population were hotel dwellers, the refusal of the management of one hotel to let us have the names or room numbers of their permanent residents was particularly unsettling, and throughout the summer various project personnel including the project director and two field supervisors returned again and again to the hotel in unfruitful attempts to persuade the management to change its initial posture. Indicative of the extent of lack of cooperation accorded us there was the fact that three visits to the hotel were necessary before the "clerk" admitted that he was, in fact, the "manager."

Some other hotels had managers who, at first, were suspicious, hostile, or upset in other ways but who eventually "came around" following repeated visits by the field supervisor. Moreover, two hotels where the management were initially cooperative found it necessary during the course of interviewing to limit or prohibit our access to their residents, allegedly in response to complaints by one or more residents that they were being "bothered" by the interviewers.

Tract 76

Tract 76 was the first tract in which we interviewed, and the data gathering there was designed as an exploratory study of the most disaffiliated women available. Accordingly, the sampling universe was defined to include only those women who lived alone. In addition, potential respondents had to be at least 45 years of age, and if they lived in hotels, they had to be "permanent residents." One of the hotels in the area refused to cooperate in the study, but the mangements of nine others graciously supplied the names of their residents who met the above criteria. The total sampling universe consisted of the names of 228 women. Each name was assigned a random number, and with the aim of finally obtaining about 100 completed interviews, a sample of 134 was drawn. It later developed that only 79 of these met the criteria for inclusion in the sample and were accessible to contact. Eventually 64 of these 79 potential respondents were interviewed.

Interviewers continued to work in tract 76 throughout the summer, even though the main focus of data gathering shifted to tract 56 and later to tract 159. In the other tracts, arbitrary criteria for designating a potential respondent "inaccessible" were adopted; if a certain number of calls did not produce a contact with the person supposedly living in a household, that person was deemed inaccessible. In tract 76, however, contacts were continued throughout the data-gathering phase of the project. The intent was to see just how many of the women could finally be interviewed. Details about the attrition of the sample appear in Table A-1.

Tract 56

Tract 56 included many apartment buildings. Following enumeration of the units in the tract, approximately one-third of the enumerated units were drawn as the sample. Procedures for the nonhotel units were somewhat different than for the hotel residents. In hotels, thanks to the preliminary work with the manager, we were able to obtain the names and room numbers of occupants who

Table A-1
Statistics on Sampling Universe and Sample, Three Tracts

Research Site	*Tract 76*			*Tract 56*			*Tract 159*			
Population Characteristics	*Women aged 45 and over living alone*			*Women aged 45 and over*			*Women aged 45 and over*			
Sampling Universe										
Source	Names from management of hotels	Enumeration of apartment houses, rooming houses	Total	Names from management of hotels	Enumeration of apartment houses, rooming houses	Total	Names from management of hotels	Names from management of large apartment buildings	Enumeration of small buildings	Total
Size	211	17	228	88	588	676	574	1487	1422	3483
Sample Drawn	134	8	142	88	200	288	143	372	357	872
Inaccessible[a]	39	4	43	14	29	43	48	142	226	416
Ineligible[b]	19	1	20	4	122	126	6	77	90	173
Net Available Sample (units)	76	3	79	70	49	119	89	153	41	283
Potential respondents	76	3	79	70	50	120	90	156	42	288
Refusals	14	1	15	27	11	38	36	49	18	103
Interviews completed	63	2	64	43	39	82	54	107	24	185

[a]In tract 76, inaccessibility included being unable to speak English, being mute, moving out or going away on vacation and not returning during the summer in which we collected data, being extremely ill (usually this meant hospitalized–many of the respondents are "sick" a great deal of the time), or being a potential respondent in a hotel which was closed to the interviewers before data collection was completed. The last of these was a problem only in tract 76. In the other tracts, inaccessibility also included total lack of contact with the respondent after five attempts at different times of the day and on different days.

[b]Criteria for eligibility included being female, 45 years of age or over (except in the Shelter, where clients of all ages were eligible), residing in the tracts (or being a client at the Shelter), and in tract 76 only, living alone.

were likely to meet the criteria for inclusion in the sample. In the apartments, however, we had no idea of the age or sex of the occupant, and in many cases we did not even have a name. Workers devoted a great deal of time to contacting building superintendents or other informants in the building and to checking mail boxes and nameplates so that we might have a name to use on the letter introducing the potential respondent to the research project.

In general, we had little difficulty in learning the number of units in a building. Getting names for the preliminary letters (and to expedite telephoning for appointments) was often a different matter. In one building where there was strict security, doormen, and three sources of names (mail boxes, an alphabetic directory, and a house phone directory), the enumerator proceeded as follows:

I used the house phone listings, so I could get at least a "floor plan" of the building, so that in case I couldn't get all the names as well, I would at least be able to figure out the appropriate apartment numbers. I got about one-third of the names. Then the superintendent's sister-in-law saw me and apparently figured out what I was doing. She told the doorman to tell me (doorman himself was very cooperative) that I shouldn't be doing that. Another doorman and maintenance man also told me that what I was doing was not allowed and that I couldn't go upstairs either—no soliciting, no getting names, etc. I pretended to wait around to see the building superintendent (who wasn't in just then) and proceeded to get the floor plan from the house phone listing as surreptitiously as possible by just wandering around and glancing at it now and then. Finishing that, I left saying that I couldn't wait any longer for the superintendent, and that I'd come back another day to speak to him. After I left, I figured out the rest of the apartment numbers.

I returned later that evening and found different doormen on duty. I sat down on the pretense that I was waiting for someone. . . . I said I was early, giving me an excuse to stay there 30 or 40 minutes. The doorman near the entrance where I sat was *very* nice. We chatted and got fairly friendly. He was sympathetic because I had to sit around and wait. Every once in a while I would get up and go look at the phone directory on the wall. I'd written down the apartment numbers for which I needed the tenants' names and would memorize the names in groups of three or four, and then go jot them down. It must have looked like I was nervous; I kept jumping up and down. The entire operation took about 40 minutes. I finally left on schedule. (I said I'd wait til 8 or so and then leave.)

Letters were sent to all units. Where we didn't have a name, the letter was addressed to the "occupant" of the unit. After allowing a day or two for the potential respondent to receive the letter, an interviewer made a personal call or telephoned. The interviewer had to determine for each unit whether one or more residents of that unit met the criteria for inclusion in the sample, and, if so, to arrange an interview with them. If not, she was to extricate herself gracefully and move on to the next unit. Only about one-third of the selected units had a female resident aged 45 or more. In cases where there were two or more eligible respondents in a unit, all were to be interviewed, if possible.

There were eight hotels in tract 56, accounting for well over 2000 units. Most of these units were for transients only, and one of the hotels had an all-male clientele. The management of another hotel absolutely refused to cooperate in the study. Women 45 and over living as permanent residents in the other six remaining hotels were potential respondents. As it turned out, most of the aged women living alone were concentrated in two of these six hotels; of the 88 names obtained from these six hotels, all but 10 were concentrated in two hotels. Because the total sampling universe of women aged 45 and over living in the hotels as permanent residents was so small, no attempt was made to sample. Instead, interviewers attempted to contact all 88.

Although technically that list of 88 women included all women aged 45 and over living in the hotels, in fact women who lived alone were somewhat overrepresented. This was due to the fact that the names were obtained in two separate enumerations, one for women living alone and another later for women living with someone. When the second attempt to get names was made, the management of one of the large hotels had decided their contribution to the project was already sufficient and refused to provide the requested list of names of women aged 45 and over living with someone.

Of the 88 names provided by hotel managers, 70 proved eligible and "accessible" respondents. Interviews were completed with 43 of these 70 women, for a completion rate of 61 percent. Experience in tract 76 had demonstrated that continued work with the refusals might have produced another 9 or 10 additional interviews and raised the overall completion rate to about 76 percent. However, since a major effort was underway to convert refusals in tract 76 and much work remained in tract 159, we elected not to do the intensive and expensive followup necessary to secure those additional 9 or 10 respondents in tract 56. Instead, interviewers were transferred to tract 159. The completion rate among nonhotel respondents in tract 56 was a fairly acceptable 78 percent (39 out of 50). For further details about attrition of the sample, see Table A-1.

Tract 159

In tract 159 a 25 percent sample of all eligible respondents was drawn. Prior to sampling, an extensive, time-consuming enumeration was necessary. The enumeration in tract 159 was in two stages: One, for the "large" buildings (defined as those buildings with more than 40 residents), and another for the "small" buildings. In the former, we tried to obtain names of all potential respondents who were 45 years of age and older. This meant contact with building superintendents, hotel managers, apartment house managers, owners, and real estate agents. Obtaining the lists of possible respondents and permission to enter the large buildings to interview them took more than a week of full-time activity by the field supervisor.

The responses of managers, "supers," doormen, and realtors to the project were, at best, neutral. We obtained permission to work in most buildings despite frequently expressed skepticism about the project or negative feelings about social research in general. A strong bias toward action with concrete, tangible results was evident among the "gatekeepers" we contacted. Many times they asked, "What good will it do?" "How will it help us?" Managers, owners, and doormen constantly assured us that the elderly women in their buildings would not want to talk with us; their withdrawal from relatives and friends was described at great length, and the usual conclusion was: "They won't let you in." Varying degrees of isolation were described, ranging from women who "never leave the hotel" to women who worked and led active lives, "even though they are of retirement age."

In the smaller buildings the procedure was to make a careful enumeration of all housing units. These were then sampled, and direct contact was attempted with the residents in the units selected in the sample. Our enumeration of small buildings produced a total of 1422 units. Security was so "tight" in the area that often getting in the front door of one of the smaller buildings was a major obstacle. To minimize entry problems, the 1422 units in small buildings were divided into 356 clusters of four units each, the idea being that any door we had to get through would have at least four potential respondents on the other side. The 356 clusters of four units each were numbered, and the table of random numbers was used in selecting one out of every four of them. The 89 clusters selected represented 356 households.

On account of the very large sample, the "inaccessibility rule" was applied very strictly in tract 159. In other words, after an interviewer had made five unsuccessful attempts to contact an occupant either by telephone or in person (including at least two evening or weekend approaches), that unit was defined as inaccessible. In the small buildings where the sampling universe had consisted of dwelling units rather than names, there were many units occupied by young people or by males only. Often it was possible to determine whether a particular unit contained an eligible respondent by asking building superintendents or other tenants. Once the samples were drawn, field workers were sent to attempt to get names of the occupants of the units included in the sample. Mailboxes, nameplates, and informants of various kinds were used. Names were also obtained by the use of an address directory rented from the telephone company. As in the previous tracts, letters explaining the project were sent to all potential respondents (or occupants of all units drawn). Where no name was available, the letters were sent to the "occupant" at the particular address.

The manager of the largest hotel in the tract refused to give us access to his list of residents but agreed to place our letters of introduction in every fourth mailbox of all women 45 and over who lived in the hotel. There was a total of 111 names, indicating that there were approximately 450 eligible women living in the building. After much negotiation the manager finally provided us with the names of the women who had received the letters, and we were able to telephone them for appointments.

After deletion of ineligible and inaccessible persons, the total available sample in tract 159 consisted of 288 women. Interviews were completed with 185 of these, for a completion rate of 64 percent. Details of sample attrition in each of the kinds of units in the tracts (hotels, large apartment buildings, small buildings) appear in Table A-1.

Gaining Entree

Each potential respondent was sent a letter on the official stationery of the Bureau of Applied Social Research informing her of the study and requesting her cooperation. The letter stated:

> The Bureau of Applied Social Research of Columbia University is conducting a research study of the life-styles, problems, and experiences of women living in Manhattan. The study is being sponsored by the United States Department of Health, Education, and Welfare. We are talking with a representative sample of the women in your neighborhood. You were among those selected as part of the sample. Successful completion of the research depends on successful interviews with the people selected, so it is very important that we have the opportunity to talk with you.
>
> Within the next few days you will be visited by one of our interviewers. Your cooperation with her will help extend scientific knowledge of the lives and problems of women in today's changing world. All of your replies, of course, will be held in strictest confidence and no one will be identified with her responses.
>
> Most people we have interviewed have found the experience rewarding, and we hope you will, too. Thank you very much.

The letter was signed by a female "staff administrator," so that any fears about possible interaction with males as a result of the project might be minimized. Initially a telephone number was included in the letter, but enough women called to refuse that in subsequent letters we tried to make refusing a little more difficult for them by omitting the telephone number.

Interviewers had been trained by approaching nonsample residents "cold" and attempting to gain entree and to complete an interview. They found that the preliminary letter was quite helpful in facilitating entrance. One-fourth of the respondents were interviewed the first time they were approached, half required from two to five approaches, and approximately one in every five women interviewed required at least five approaches. The typical refusal in tract 76 was confronted four or five times during the summer by at least two different interviewers.

The door approach was a major hurdle. Residents of Manhattan frequently are reluctant to open their door to strangers, and aged women living alone are (with some justification) among the most suspicious and fearful of populations. To obtain an interview, it was necessary to allay a potential respondent's fears as quickly as possible. The preliminary letter helped. Frequently we telephoned for appointments, and this eased door-approach problems considerably. The image presented by interviewers of personable, neatly dressed, "straight" young women was in our favor, and the talents of interviewers themselves in answering questions about the project and showing a genuine interest in the potential respondent were most helpful.

A high refusal rate was anticipated. Aged women living alone tend to be seriously undersampled even in studies of the aged. Data gathering was begun with the sample of isolates so that a maximum time period was available for repeated approaches, if necessary. In addition, we felt there was a psychological advantage in beginning with the "hardest" population, reasoning that interviewers would quickly gain experience with the most difficult problems they were likely to face in the remaining weeks of interviewing.

Interviewers were instructed to keep the door approach brief and to say as little as possible until they had reached face-to-face contact with the respondent. They were furnished with identification papers which they frequently presented to respondents to legitimate their presence. Moreover, since the majority of the completed interviews involved more than one personal contact in addition to the letter, potential respondents had a chance to get used to the idea of the interview as well as to become familiar with the interviewer.

Women gave a wide variety of reasons for refusing to admit the interviewers. Some claimed they were "just too busy" with their own affairs and felt they had nothing to gain in participating in the interview. Others were simply afraid—muggings and robberies were common in the neighborhoods where we worked—and sometimes the potential interview was a casualty of the protective mechanisms used by the women to survive in such a neighborhood. Also, some women insisted they knew little of importance and recommended someone else more informed, and no amount of persuasion could change their minds. Another factor was the habitual isolation and privacy of some of the women. After many years of being ignored, a sudden confrontation with a stranger who wants to ask questions can be an alarming incident. Perhaps the least threatening alternative in such a situation would be to avoid entanglement entirely, and unless the potential respondent had other strong reasons for cooperating (such as loneliness which might be relieved by a talk with a sympathetic young person), a refusal was likely, simply as a continuation of a long-established application of the principle of privacy.

Despite valiant explanations and justifications by the interviewers, many of the women saw little purpose in the study. There were comments such as: "Give these women money, forget studying them. We know what's wrong with them. They're poor."

Finally, there was the very real threat that a woman's carefully supported rationalizations about herself might be exposed if she participated in an interview. At times, even after an interviewer had gained entrance and begun to ask questions, the interview would be broken off because the respondent found that the questions were more "personal" than she was prepared to answer. Sometimes women offered transparent excuses to prevent discussion of any kind; others were willing to talk in the doorway on an informal basis, or perhaps in the lobby, but were not willing to submit to a formal inteview. The obvious recording of responses was often threatening, at least initially.

As a last resort, interviewers would offer to pay for an interview, but even that worked fairly infrequently. Much more successful were offers of lunch–and several interviews took place during or after a lunch paid for by the interviewer. Interviewers who had to return several times sometimes took small gifts or flowers, but these were the unusual cases; most of the time the interviewers were able after two or more attempts to establish sufficient rapport to be admitted into the respondent's room and there complete an interview lasting from 1 to 3 hours.

The Interview

In discussing the conducting of the interview itself, we will drop the framework of discussing the tracts separately. With the exception of interviews in which a roommate or husband was present, which could not have occurred in tract 76, the situations described below might have happened in any of the three tracts. None of the cases below pertain to Shelter women. The setting for interviewing at the Women's Shelter was unique, and it has been discussed in detail elsewhere in the book.

There were a wide variety of reactions to the interview itself. Many women complained about its length. There were also criticisms of certain portions of the interview schedule. Among these "problematic" sections were the systematic and detailed migration and occupational histories, which respondents found tiring; the attitude questions, which some of them found frustrating; and, most especially, the fact that we ungallantly inquired about a woman's age. Several respondents refused to tell their age, and sometimes elaborate inventions were built into migration or marriage histories to prevent interviewers from estimating a woman's age accurately.

In most cases, rapport increased during the interview. Frequently after the interview (or during it) respondents showed interviewers their photographs, provided light refreshment in their homes, or accompanied interviewers to a nearby coffee shop. Sometimes interviewers received apartment tours and were shown cherished collections.

Reactions to the interview can be grouped into a number of categories by (1) respondents' reactions at the beginning of the interview, (2) the general tone of the interview itself, and (3) the nature of the termination of the interview. Initial reactions can be divided into those situations in which the interviewer was admitted immediately, and those in which she was obliged to overcome hostility or suspicion or other types of resistance before getting started. Once into the interview, there were some situations where rapport increased and others where it deteriorated. Finally, the termination of the interview sometimes was abrupt and cold, and at other times there was a conscious effort by the respondent to lengthen the interview, to keep the interviewer longer, or to establish a longer-term relationship with her. These variables, taken together, produce the typology shown in Table A-2. The types may be briefly described. Type 1 is the individual who, against her better judgment, submitted to an interview. It turned out to be just the kind of negative experience she expected, and frequently the type 1 respondent terminated the interview before the schedule was completed. Women of type 2 also found the experience essentially a negative one, but having involved themselves in it, played the role to the end. The type 3 respondent, the woman who tries to prevent the departure of the interviewer despite initial resistance and deteriorating rapport, is almost a nonexistent type, although the woman who refused to complete the interview and then subjected the interviewer to a half-hour harangue about the infringement of her privacy and the insensitivity of the research directors might be included here.

Table A-2
Typology of Respondent Reactions to the Interview

Initial Reactions:	*Resistance*		*No Resistance*	
Rapport during Interview:	*Deteriorating*	*Not Deteriorating*	*Deteriorating*	*Not Deteriorating*
Termination of Interview				
Encouraged	Type 1	Type 4	Type 7	Type 10
Accepted	Type 2	Type 5	Type 8	Type 11
Resisted	Type 3	Type 6	Type 9	Type 12

Type 4 may be represented by women who, although initially suspicious, allowed the interview to begin and enjoyed it, or at least related well to the interviewer, but for some other reason, such as fatigue, wished to have it over quickly, and sometimes broke it off. Type 5, the respondent who enjoyed the interview enough to let it take its natural course despite her initial doubts, was probably most common among those who were initially resistant. Type 6 includes those women who not only let the session run its course, but once involved with the interviewer, did all they could to prolong the encounter.

Type 7 represents those women whose expectations were violated. They began the interview willingly, but were dismayed when it turned out to be more personal than they had anticipated, and they reacted by terminating the situation. Others whose expectations were violated did complete the situation, although they still were disturbed. Type 9, like type 3, is probably an empirically null case.

Most frequently the respondents fell into types 5, 11, and 12; that is, women who initially seemed friendly and who happily completed the schedule or actively tried to continue contact after the formal interviewing was completed, appeared more frequently among the respondents than did representatives of the other types. Nevertheless, the length of the instrument created some who actively sought termination (type 10) even among those who enjoyed the interviewing experience.

We do not have frequency distributions of the way respondents from various tracts were distributed among the 12 cells of the typology in Table A-2, because the typology was developed after the data collection was completed. Thus, information on the three dimensions of the typology was not recorded systematically for all respondents. However, sometimes it is possible to classify a respondent on the basis of an interviewer's summary comments. The examples which follow illustrate most of the types of respondent reaction identified in the typology.

Regretfully Involved (Type 1)

The first five pages of the interview was conducted with me on one side of the chained door and Mrs. Wilson on the other. After her "errand man" called that he was coming up, she let me in. She explained that she never lets anyone cross her threshold. Near the end of the interview she became tired and asked exactly what it was we were trying to get at and looked at my letter of introduction. Then the "errand man" returned and in the process of their conversation she said that she never should have let me in. Although she wouldn't answer the last page of questions, she was quite congenial and pleasant as I left. She took my name and the Bureau's name and number. Two days later the respondent called the office to find out if I were really an interviewer and what we were really trying to get at with our questions. She said she was sorry that she had let me in, was feeling ill, and that she should have called the security guard. She said that I had asked many questions which were none of my business.

My Civic Responsibility (Type 5)

When the researchers telephoned to make the appointment, she was quite resistant, and she kept putting off the interviewer. When the final appointment was made, she said she could spend only an hour, but in the end she granted more than twice that much time. Part of her initial negative attitude resulted from a bad experience she had had with a reporter for the *Daily News.* She was stopped on the street and asked for her opinion on some issue; the next day her statements appeared in the newspaper along with her picture. She was shocked and outraged that they had taken her picture without her permission.

At the outset Mrs. Queen told the interviewer that she would not reveal anything about her age, and "tantalized" the interviewer with the statement that she had been in the theater. She said that when people learned that she had been in the theater, they were anxious to know all about it, but that she was even more anxious not to reveal the details. She also refused to answer any of the questions in the marriage section of the interview schedule that had to do with either sex or drinking.

The most touchy part of this interview was the section containing the attitude statements. Several of these she absolutely refused to answer, calling them "silly" or "ridiculous," and she objected to the wording of several others. The interviewer described the situation at the end of the interview in these words.

> She said the only reason that she let someone come to interview her was that she was a bit curious about the kinds of questions they'd ask. I think she more or less prepared herself for a Kinsey-type questionnaire. She said she thought the next time she would probably refuse. She said she'd done her service by going through this particular interview. She equated it with voting, as sort of an obligation one has to get rid of.

Helping the Elderly (Type 5)

When Miss Cheshire, a hotel resident about 57 years old, was contacted by telephone, she declined to have interviewers visit her. She said that she didn't let anyone into her room, being afraid of muggers and the like. However, she had no objections to being interviewed over the telephone. At the time of the initial call, the researcher at the telephone did not have an interview schedule, and so she made arrangements for Miss Cheshire to be telephoned again the following day.

The next evening a different interviewer telephoned from the hotel lobby. Miss Cheshire seemed quite upset when it was suggested that, given the length of the instrument, she might want to come down to the lobby and be interviewed. She asked for an explanation of the purpose of the project, what the questions might be, and said that she was in her pajamas and didn't want to leave her room. Then, quite suddenly, she changed her mind and said she would come down. As the interviewer described the event:

> We sat in the lobby for the duration of the interview, and were quite fortunate that there was no one else around. During the beginning of the interview, the respondent was quite hesitant in answering some of the questions, especially the one about how often she goes someplace away from this neighborhood; she does go to business every day, and she doesn't want anyone to know how often she's out of her apartment. She says that that's very dangerous information to

give anybody, and preferred that I write "no comment." Also, she wasn't particularly eager to tell me the different types of things she did with her day . . . at this point of the interview she asked for my identification, saying that these were quite dangerous questions I was asking. And didn't I know that? However, after I assured her that the answers would go no further than her, me, and the computer, and also when I assured her of what a great help she would be, she continued through the remainder of the interview, very cheerful. . . . The respondent was quite eager to do anything she could to help the elderly; as she said, she was now reaching the age where she would start thinking about how she was going to spend her later years. She complained, many times, about the high rents, and about how she would have to find a more reasonably priced apartment, if she was going to be able to live comfortably in her later years.

Protecting Privacy (Type 7)

Mrs. Turner inspected the interviewer's credentials and admitted her. She responded well to questions about the neighborhood but cooled noticeably when the questioning moved to matters such as family background, religion, and her own age. Questions on occupation and education of her parents and brothers made her very resentful, and she asked what all that had to do with the neighborhood. The explanation that the backgrounds of its residents are legitimate elements of neighborhood composition was not adequate. Mrs. Turner was convinced that her privacy had already been violated, and that the rest of the instrument contained items that were even more personal. "These things," she remarked, "I don't even discuss with my own family." The interviewer was convinced that the respondent accepted the fact that her answers would be anonymous, but her "strong sense of privacy" and "narrow definition of what are matters for public discussion" made it impossible for her to continue. There were things she simply would not discuss with strangers, and much of the information we were seeking fell into that category. Besides, she stated that the introductory letter had grossly misrepresented what we intended to ask. She had intended to inform on the neighbohood, not on herself. The interviewer commented:

She was lovely. I respected her. . . . She had a forthright opinion about the whole thing, and she was expressing it. . . . Are her areas of inviolability really larger than usual? They may be larger than other respondent's, but are our other respondents typical? . . . She said that she came from a good Jewish family, and there are simply matters that are not for throwing around for just anybody to see. And details about her family that she would not tell her neighbors, she certainly wouldn't tell me.

An "Annoying" Respondent (Type 8)

Miss Stiles came to the door and immediately closed it to put on some clothes. She seemed very cooperative until I began to ask the questions. Almost immediately she became belligerent, and nervous, laughing and continuously commenting on the stupidity of the questions. She wouldn't tell me her age, her parents' religion or her own, her father's specific occupation or any *specific* job she's held. . . . I tried repeatedly to emphasize her anonymity and the general importance of the survey, but the respondent was strictly critical, finding excuses for any question she did not wish to answer. She shouted, shrieked, laughed and fumbled. She was a very ill-kept, ill-tempered respondent, and also a bit overparadeful and uppity about the extent of her education and her "respect" for religion (meaning she would not answer those questions). At the end of the interview, however, she relaxed, smiled strangely and said she hoped my next interview was not as annoying as she had been.

The Painful Past (Type 10)

Mrs. Reeves answered my questions quite readily . . . until we got to the migration history, which was pretty spotty, and then she became a little tired. . . . When I got to her job history, she refused to say any more other than that she has been in show business. Although her voice had been quite shaky throughout the interview, it seemed to get a more emotional quality at this point. She talked to me at some length about how she didn't feel that it was good to dig into a person's past, and make them bring up and think about things that they would rather not think about. She said, "For example, when you pray, you pray for your parents, but it's kind of a habit, and you don't have to stop and think where they were born, how often they went to church, what they did." She said these kind of things bring back memories, and that when you become old, you've just got to face the truth that you're no longer important, but that you're put into the background. She said that when you become old, that you don't count, except for what you can do for the few years you have left, in helping younger people fulfill dreams that they have. She currently gives several [music] lessons a day. She'd given one this morning, and had three more to give this evening. She talked, for a time, about her [deceased] husband's memorial [anniversary] which . . . will be Friday. She says on this day she cancels all appointments, and such things, and spends the day in church and at the cemetery. She says she'd just rather not think about this, and all the other things in her past, because she needs all the strength that she can muster up just to keep going from day to day.

She wanted me to be sure and tell the people who write these questions that she didn't feel that the best way to get answers was to ask people these types of questions about the past, which would get them all excited, to such an extent as to actually unnerve them. Mrs. Reeves became very emotional. . . .She said that she would appreciate it if I didn't ask her any more questions about the past, but she offered to answer any question about social conditions, and that type of thing, and very graciously did answer some questions about conditions in the neighborhood, and also I was able to fill in the page about her financial situation. . . . She refused my offer to come back at another time, saying that she didn't want to answer any more questions. . . . She said that she was sorry that she couldn't go on. I probably could have pressed her, but I don't think it's my job to hassle little old ladies. She said goodbye, and said that she hoped that I didn't get any more assignments like herself, that I just got nice little old ladies from now on. I apologized for having upset her, and she said that she would get her cup of coffee, and try and settle down before her lessons this evening.

The Appreciative Respondent (Type 12)

Mrs. Thomas kept the interviewer waiting in the hotel lobby for half an hour. When she came down, she was elegantly dressed in a long flowing flowered dress, a pink floral hat, pink earrings, and high pink spiked shoes. According to the interviewer, "She gave the impression of being about 60 years old, as her face had no wrinkles at all and she had a size 10 figure. However, as it turned out, this woman is about 80 years old." At first Mrs. Thomas invited the interviewer to have cocktails before dinner; she presumed that dinner would precede the interview. After it was explained that the interview required a quiet place and concentration, they went up to her hotel room.

Her small room was cluttered with hundreds of books and papers. Most of the latter were newspaper clippings about herself. She has written and produced plays, lectured on a variety of topics, and published several articles. Her window was open, and on the window sill were fruits, fruit juices, and two eggs. She said she used her window as a refrigerator, and that she had no extra electrical outlets in the room; she was afraid that with all her papers lying about it would be dangerous. Occasionally she uses her flatiron for cooking eggs, which she considers a real treat. Many of her books and papers were stored in a room in another hotel. She hated to leave them there, but felt that she could no longer live in the hotel because of lice and cockroaches there. She said that the lice were all over her books and although she made repeated attempts to make the Board of Health do something about it, nothing was ever done. In desperation, she moved out of that hotel into her present room. She has been back to look at her works only a couple of times.

She told the interviewer that she was very optimistic about science, and that was why she was willing to be interviewed. She even attributed the failure of her marriage to the fact that her husband could not understand her interest in the social sciences and in helping people.

The interview with Mrs. Thomas lasted 3½ hours. When it was over, she accompanied the interviewer to the hotel lobby and bought her blueberries and ice cream. In parting, she expressed her gratitude and offered to pay the interviewer 10 dollars.

The Jewish Mother (Type 12)

Mrs. Stein welcomed the interviewer and was extremely cordial and cooperative throughout a 4-hour interview. The session lasted so long because Mrs. Stein, a

71-year old widow, was so hospitable. The interviewer described her as "about the most typical Jewish mother I've run across," and commented:

Mrs. Stein insisted that I stay longer than I should have, and showed me pictures and her plants and things, which I did not mind, except that the interview was taking too long. She started to talk about a neighbor, whom she called a "kvetch," and told me that a kvetch was somebody who was complaining when there wasn't anything to complain about. She said, "Well, I must be made of iron, because if I don't sleep a full night, or if I don't feel well, I say, 'I'll take it as it comes,' and I go on. I don't like to burden other people with my bad feelings, or the way I'm thinking today."

Refusals

Refusals were considerably more common among the women in the hotels than among those living elsewhere in the neighborhood. We continued our practice of checking back on refusals, hoping to catch them in a different mood or that a different interviewer would have better results with them. In part, the number of such callbacks was a function of the mildness of the initial refusal: the nicer the previous contacts had been, the more apt we were to try to change the woman's mind. The following examples of women who were finally placed in the refusal category illustrate the researchers' conduct and provide an idea of the kinds of women we confronted.

Mrs. C. 7/29: She wouldn't answer her door; I called up on the house phone—she won't talk in person, only on the telephone (even the *maid* doesn't see her in person).

8/26: Mrs. C refuses to let anyone come up to her room, wouldn't complete phone interview—she seems quite deaf.

Miss L 7/7: Refused, saying "invasion of privacy, don't you think?" She knew this was voluntary, said she dreaded next year's census.

Miss M 7/17; 7/17, 7/18: "Do Not Disturb" sign on door. 7/23: Slammed door on interviewer. 7/25: Maid thought Miss M was in, but she didn't answer phone. "Do Not Disturb" sign was up. 7/29: Saw interviewer's folder and promptly slammed door, yelling, "I haven't . . . !"

Miss A 7/18: She came up behind the closed door when I knocked, asked "who is it?"; when I answered, she said "can't hear you" and walked away from the still-closed door. We repeated the ritual twice, beginning with the knock.

7/23: She said she was expecting a phone call, couldn't be interviewed at the moment, and couldn't give us another time.

7/25: Voice contact through door–she wouldn't respond after asking "who is it?"; later on the phone she said over and over that she doesn't want to be bothered–ultimate exasperation and refusal.

Miss Y 8/19: Lived 26 years in hotel–is from San Antonio; loves living in New York, thinks anyone who gets lonely in New York is nuts–it's their own fault; she goes out all the time–especially to Belmont and Acqaduct; she loves New York, every dirty inch of it (a paraphrase of her comments). She said she would like to participate but has absolutely no time available; she wrote us a letter of regret–wouldn't budge over the phone (Her letter: "Thank you but my time at present does not allow me to have an interview.")

Miss Z 8/18: Not interested; she resents our contact with her (by letter) because she doesn't let anyone know where she lives and we had her room number on the letter. She thinks it's too personal–she's enraged.

Mrs. G 7/16 (A.M.): Contracted Mrs. G. She was just on her way out and said to come back when I'm in the neighborhood. I couldn't get an appointment because she is always "going out on calls." She had received our letter but I believe this was a put-off."

7/16 (P.M.): She was on her way out again. She expressed enthusiasm about the study, but I felt that she was not going to grant an interview; her "business" is a front.

7/23: Home, but dog was sick and she refused to be interviewed. Refused to give appointment but suggested we try again Friday, 7/25.

7/25 (A.M.): I thought I saw her in building, but she didn't answer prolonged ringing.

7/29: Talked to her on intercom–no time, no appointment–and she turned the intercom off.

8/7: Telephone approach. Absolutely refused. She could not understand why we were so adamant. Would not give reason for refusal. When pressed, she just said that someone was ringing her bell and hung up.

Mrs. D. 8/7: I telephoned, and learned that Mrs. D is in South America for the rest of month. Her sister is staying in the apartment. She seemed the right age (would not reveal it over phone) but will not consent to an interview on the grounds that she is a "creative person" and does not want to be put into a statistic. She would not consent to a telephone interview and requested that we do *not* call again. She has just come home from the hospital and may be returning there again soon.

Mrs. E 7/23: Wouldn't answer initially, was on way to work, rather hostile (8:30 A.M.).

8/7: I telephoned at 3:15 P.M. After I identified myself, she screamed, "I have no time, forget it, good-bye." Hung up. She sounded young, so I thought I'd call back to ask her age—did not get a word in. She just screamed "Please stop calling! I said stop calling!" and hung up.

Miss T 7/18: Would not be interviewed today or next week, but I will return Monday, 7/28.

7/22: I had to reassure her that it was confidential and apolitical; she may need further persuasion; the next interviewer to contact her should apologize that I was unable to return.

8/7: Miss T absolutely refused. I tried several tactics. She objected to the fact that we had her name, that we were interviewing "old women" in her building (something she did not consider herself), that she might be put into a category. After several explanations, she said that I would make a good salesman, but that she just did not want it, we should find someone else.

Mrs. C 7/17: After loud and prolonged knocking, I heard the chain being slipped on; after this tip off, I called "Mrs. C!", but she wouldn't answer.

7/22: (P.M.) Knocked on her door. No answer. I then called up from lobby, and via phone got "am not feeling well, maybe in a few days." I don't want to have to try her again, but someone else might. Call first, she doesn't answer the door.

Nature of the Interview: Interviewer Evaluations

About half of the respondents in all the samples were described by interviewers as "very frank and cooperative." As might be expected, respondents in tract 76, where one of the criteria for inclusion in the sample was that the woman live alone, were somewhat more "resistant" than respondents in other tracts. Part of the difference in proportions of "resistant" respondents interviewed may also stem from the fact that we were more persistent in tract 76, less likely to take no for an answer, and hence some women finally yielded an interview despite a "resistant" attitude which in one of the other samples might have caused her to be considered a refusal.

In terms of economic status, the tracts may be ranked as follows: highest status: tracts 159 and 56; moderate status: tract 76; and lowest status: Pioneer Hotel. The distribution of interviewer evaluations of respondent cooperativeness and accuracy clearly reflect these status differentials. For example, over 70 per cent of the respondents in the higher-status tracts were described in general as giving "accurate" answers, as compared to 64 percent of the women in tract 76 and only half of the Shelter women. The differentials in accuracy were especially noticeable with respect to migration histories and job histories (See Table A-3).

Table A-3
Selected Characteristics of Interviews as Reported by Interviewers

Variable	*Tract 76*	*Tract 56*	*Tract 159*	*Pioneer Hotel*
Evaluation of Respondent's Attitude				
Very frank and cooperative	53%	59%	46%	54%
Average	19	24	31	23
Compliant but uncommunicative	9	11	9	14
Resistant	17	6	11	2
Not evaluated	2	–	3	8
Accuracy of Answers in General				
Accurate	64	79	72	50
Fair	30	20	21	38
Very rough or meaningless	6	1	4	8
Not evaluated	–	–	3	4
Accuracy of Answers on Social Contacts				
Accurate	63	68	68	42
Fair	28	31	26	42
Very rough or meaningless	9	1	3	12
Not evaluated	–	–	3	4
Accuracy of Migration History				
Accurate	47	65	61	48
Fair	38	22	29	31
Very rough or meaningless	16	13	8	17
Not evaluated	–	–	3	4
Accuracy of Job History				
Accurate	44	63	63	40
Fair	44	28	23	37
Very rough or meaningless	11	9	11	19
Not evaluated	–	–	3	4
Existence of Unusual Situations Which Might Affect Accuracy of Interview				
Yes	22	22	23	8
No	73	78	72	85
Not evaluated	5	–	4	8
Respondent's Clarity of Thought				
Made sense	77	87	87	58
Occasional lapses	16	11	9	27
Generally confused	8	1	2	8
Not evaluated	–	1	3	8

Table A-3 continued

Variable	*Tract 76*	*Tract 56*	*Tract 159*	*Pioneer Hotel*
Respondent's Contact with Reality				
Normal	83%	90%	89%	54%
A few bizarre ideas	9	9	7	31
Somewhat delusional	8	1	1	6
Not evaluated	–	–	4	10
Respondent's Physical Appearance (Dress, Grooming)				
Uncared for, unkempt, dirty	5	1	2	33
Poor but well-kept	19	10	6	25
Average	59	55	54	33
Exceedingly proper	16	32	30	2
Bizarre or incongruous	2	2	1	–
Not evaluated	–	–	8	8
Respondent's Physical Condition (Health, Physique)				
Incapacitated	6	5	3	1
Poor, sickly	14	10	2	23
Fair	19	17	19	29
Good	36	39	42	33
Excellent	25	29	28	4
Not evaluated	–	–	8	10
Condition of Respondent's Apartment				
Dirty and disorderly	11	5	2	–
Disorderly	17	10	8	–
Clean and neat	59	74	75	–
Not evaluated	13	11	15	–
Adequacy of Apartment Furnishings				
Poorly furnished and equipped	34	11	4	–
Average	38	32	27	–
Well furnished and equipped	19	45	54	–
Not evaluated	9	12	16	–
Length of Interview				
60 minutes or less	5	12	22	6
65–100 minutes	38	18	29	23
105–140 minutes	30	27	30	35
145–180 minutes	14	22	11	17
Over 3 hours	14	18	7	15
Not recorded	–	2	1	4

Respondent's "clarity of thought" and "contact with reality" also follow class lines, with almost 90 percent of the higher-status respondents "making sense," while only three-fourths of the tract 76 women and 58 percent of the Shelter women were described in those terms. "Contact with reality" shows a similar pattern.

The physical appearance of Shelter women was much worse than for the respondents in the other tracts—fully one-third of them were described as "uncared for, unkempt, or dirty." However, respondents in tract 76 were almost as likely as Shelter women to be described as manifesting poor health. There were fewer "incapacitated" women at the Shelter than in tract 76, but that reflects the fact that Shelter women have been "screened" by the EAU, and the "incapacitated" among them have been sent elsewhere.

A remarkably high proportion of women in tract 76 lived in unsatisfactory conditions (one in nine lived in a "dirty and disorderly" apartment, compared to less than half that many in the other tracts), and their furnishings were inferior, with one-third (compared to one-ninth or less in the other tracts) of the units described as "poorly furnished and equipped."

Interviews were shortest in tract 159, where over half of the interviews were completed in 100 minutes or less, and only 7 percent lasting over 3 hours. In the other research sites, at least twice that proportion of lengthy interviews took place.

Data Collection at the Women's Shelter

The data analyzed in the chapters about Shelter women derive from four distinct sources: (1) interviews with Shelter women, (2) content analysis of case files, (3) observation during field work, and (4) interviews with a sample of homeless men (conducted during a previous project). Procedures of data collection for each type are discussed separately below.

Preparation of the Interview Schedule and Interviews with Shelter Women

The preparation of the life-history interview schedule took place in the spring and summer of 1969. The instrument was patterned closely after the interview schedule used in the earlier Homelessness Project. Maintenance of a high degree of similarity between the two schedules was critical if direct comparisons of the life histories of homeless men and women were to be made; thus changes in the original instrument tended to be limited to additions or modifications necessary to adapt it to female respondents.

The interview schedule used at the Women's Shelter was almost identical to that used in interviewing women in the Manhattan census tract samples. Most changes in the Shelter instrument were on items related to household activities and living arrangements that were inappropriate for Shelter respondents. A few modifications were also made on items pertaining to the drinking history.

Pretesting Phase

The final interview schedule evolved from two preliminary drafts, each of which was given a rigorous pretesting. The pretests were conducted as follows: After each draft had been criticized by senior members of the staff, the interviewers conducted trial interviews using another staff member. Staff meetings were later held in which "problematic" items were discussed. Following revisions, interviewers were dispatched to a nonsample census tract where they interviewed two or more "willing" respondents, usually elderly hotel dwellers. The final version of the instrument was produced after results of the second pretest of this type were evaluated. A random sample of over 50 women living in hotels in midtown Manhattan (tract 76) were interviewed before data collection began at the Women's Shelter. Although an additional pretest was conducted at the Shelter, no changes were made in the instrument apart from deleting items that did not apply to homeless women.

Selection and Training of the Interviewers

Three male interviewers were used in collecting data at the Women's Shelter. (Approximately two-thirds of the interviews were conducted by Garrett, who directed field work at the Shelter.) Originally it had been planned that female interviewers would handle all the interviewing at the Shelter, the strategy being that the woman-to-woman relationship would present fewer obstacles in gaining rapport and in soliciting frank responses in pretesting the interview schedule at the Shelter; however, female interviewers reported that they encountered serious difficulties in getting the women to cooperate. A report from the interviewers describes the initial problem:

> . . . We asked the women if they would like to talk to us as interviewers and went around the room [Shelter, day room] until we found one who was willing to be interviewed. This took about four tries each. The women were not unfriendly, but were reluctant to be interviewed. Though [the respondents] . . . were pleasant to talk to, they were not able to cope fully with a formal interview schedule. . . . A more profitable approach, perhaps, would be to drop the formal interview altogether, and if these women are to be included at all, strive to gain rapport on a personal level . . .

Later a second attempt was made by a male interviewer. His evaluation of the Shelter women was strikingly different from that of female interviewers.

I arrived at the Shelter shortly after lunch. . . . Later one of the caseworkers provided me with a group introduction. The caseworker singled out a client and explained that I wished to speak with her. She immediately asked, "What for?" The worker replied that I would explain that to her in private (most of the women in the dayroom seemed very curious, several of them asking me "What you want to see Jane for?") . . . All things considered, the interview went very well. The respondent was cooperative, fairly articulate, and frank in expressing her opinions. . . . At the end of the interview, she remarked, "I certainly have enjoyed talking with you. Maybe we can do this again sometime. . . . Why, I feel as if I've known you for years." . . . As we entered the dayroom, the women seemed even more curious than before. One lady asked the respondent, "Who's your gentleman friend, honey?" The respondent, at first pretending to ignore the question, finally replied, "He's *my* boyfriend–nosey!" As soon as I helped Mrs. U to her chair, two ladies inquired if I would be interested in talking with them now. I explained that it was nearly dinner, but that I would do so on Monday. (They insisted that I write their names down so as not to forget.) I spent the next half-hour chatting with the women in the dayroom. They were very open and willing to discuss almost any aspect of Shelter life, especially staff.

Although the reasons why male interviewers were more successful than the experienced female interviewers in questioning these women are not readily apparent, one caseworker suggested that this was due to the fact that women were more accustomed to dealing with a masculine figure both on the Bowery and in the Shelter itself. Still another caseworker commented, "these ladies are more responsive to men because they come from a masculine society; in fact, many of these women even behave like men."

Thus, on the basis of field work reports during the pretesting of the interview schedule and discussions with the casework staff, it was decided that male interviewers would be used in collecting data from the Shelter women.

Since all three interviewers had had previous experience in interviewing, the need for a formal training program was not critical. Each interviewer, however, was required to interview two females on the project staff before he began work at the Shelter, and his performance and interview schedule was commented upon by a senior member of the staff. During actual field work, it became standard practice that each completed schedule be audited by a supervisor as soon after the interview as possible so that errors or omissions could be caught early.

Selecting the Respondents

A sampling procedure was not used at the Shelter. Instead an attempt was made to interview every woman who was officially admitted to the Shelter over a period of 2 months. A current list of clients was obtained from the Shelter records clerk before interviewing began; new clients were added to the list at the beginning of each day. In the course of two months, 61 different clients were admitted to the Shelter; 52 of these (85 percent of the total) were interviewed.

Failure to interview nine clients came as a result of unusual circumstances. Seven of the nine entered the Shelter during the late evening hours, but checked out shortly before breakfast. Another woman, admitted during the afternoon, withdrew her claim five minutes after check-in when another client refused to let her use the bathroom facilities. The ninth client omitted from the study was taken to the hospital on the first day of interviewing. After the third day of hospitalization, she committed suicide.

Although interviews were conducted with all available Shelter women over the 2-month period, some may question whether this group of women is representative of the annual Shelter population. That is, it is possible that there are seasonal variations in "type" of client at the Shelter. According to members of the Shelter staff, however, this possibility appeared highly remote. Many of the clients in service during the summer of 1969 visited the Shelter regularly throughout the year. In fact, approximately half of the women interviewed were "semipermanent" residents of the Shelter.

The Interview

All interviews were conducted in the Women's Shelter. Few difficulties were encountered in locating prospective respondents, inasmuch as most of the women remained in the Shelter dayroom during the working day. On a few occasions it was necessary to conduct an interview during the early morning or evening hours; several women were employed, and a few others spent most of the day panhandling in lower Manhattan.

Since many of the questions in the schedule were highly personal, it was necessary to rent a room from the hotel so that privacy could be assured. Several women were reluctant to enter rooms in the hotel that were not officially part of the Shelter facilities. Excerpts from fieldwork notes recount some of the more interesting situations.

Our room is located at the end of the main hallway on the first floor, about eight rooms down from the casework office. Nevertheless, this area of the building is "off-limits" for clients, and several women (mostly newly admitted ones who have not seen us before) are reluctant to be interviewed in other than an "official" casework room. We make it standard practice to always leave the door open during the interview, which serves, in some small way, as a visual reminder that things are on the "up-and-up." (It is comforting for the interviewer, too.) Approximately once every hour, however, the special-service policeman will walk by the door, ostensibly en route to the toilet; but his ominous glance into the room suggests otherwise. Last week I interviewed one of the Shelter's more "seasoned" and outspoken clients. As the officer casually strolled by the room, the client look up, stopped in the middle of a sentence, and yelled at the officer, "Get your ugly puss out of here, dogfacc. Ain't nothin' going on in here you need to know about!"

This afternoon I interviewed a client who, during the early part of the interview, was unusually restless. For the first twenty minutes, she sat "perched" on the edge of the chair. Her eye movements went to the bed, then to me, and then to the door. I contrived an excuse to stop the interview by mentioning that I was unusually thirsty, asking if she, too, would like a soft drink. We sat and chatted (she drank four cokes). She seemed more at ease then, so I proceeded with the interview. (In the course of the interview she revealed that she had been raped twice in the previous evening. . . .)

Interview time ranged from a low of 55 minutes to as long as 3½ hours (mean length was 2¼ hours). Some respondents were more talkative than others, and some were far more efficient in recalling specific details of their life history. Table A-4 represents a summary of interviewer ratings of various aspects of the interviews and the respondents.

It was the interviewers' judgment that respondents as a whole were cooperative and more than willing to give answers to the questions on the schedule. Only in one instance was a respondent unusually resistant, though she became considerably more responsive and frank later in the interview. However, in many cases it was necessary to deviate from customary interviewing procedures. The following account illustrates one such case.

The respondent, now age 69, is remarkably alert and active for her age. . . . She has an extensive work history, mostly as a stenographer for various Wall Street and Madison Avenue law firms. . . . Although the client had been reasonably cooperative and frank for the first twenty minutes, she became unusually abrupt when I began asking her about her marital life. Finally, when I asked her, "well, then, what about your husband?" she turned to me, showing great hostility, and said, "Now listen here. I just don't want to talk about him. That's been a *long* time ago, you understand! And I just wanna forget about that. So don't ask me anymore questions about marriage. I was married in 1923 and it's over and I just don't want to talk about it." Thinking that I might return to these items at a point when rapport was better, I proceeded with the interview. A half-hour later I again returned to the marriage items, and again the respondent became hostile, even more so than before. I continued with the remainder of the items since I did not want to risk losing the respondent altogether. Finally, at the end of the interview, I again returned to marital history. Predictably, she became upset; I asked why she got so emotional about her husband. "Because he was a miserable, good-for-nothing bastard, that's why." I pretended to be very upset that she would not talk about her husband (though not so emotional so as to be intimidating): "Now, get this straight, once and for all. I don't care about your husband, and I can understand why you don't want to talk about him. But, at the same time, this information is important to the study. I may as well not even bothered interviewing you. I'll leave out no less than 7 pages of interview. You know, sometimes it helps to think out painful experiences, get them off your mind, air your feelings." The change in the respondent was remarkable: [after a long pause] "Maybe you're right. Maybe I should have done that 40 years ago. . . ." Over the course of the next hour the respondent unfolded the incredible story of her marriage. . . .

Table A-4
Postinterview Evaluation by Interviewers

Item	*Percent (N = 52)*
Overall Attitude of Respondent	
Very frank and cooperative	54
Average	23
Compliant but uncommunicative	14
Resistant	2
No rating supplied	8
Estimated Accuracy of Responses (General)	
Accurate	50
Fair	38
Very rough or meaningless	8
No rating supplied	4
Estimated Accuracy on Specific Portions of the Schedule	
Migration history	
Accurate	48
Fair	31
Very rough or meaningless	17
No rating supplied	4
Social contacts	
Accurate	42
Fair	42
Very rough or meaningless	12
No rating supplied	4
Job history	
Accurate	40
Fair	37
Very rough or meaningless	19
No rating supplied	4
Interview Interruptions	
Yes	8
No	85
No information supplied	8
Respondent's Clarity of Thought	
Made sense	58
Occasional lapses	27
Generally confused	8
No rating supplied	8
Respondent's "Contact with Reality"	
Normal	54
A few bizarre ideas	31
Somewhat delusional	6

In two cases it was necessary to interview respondents over the course of a week due to health problems, and three respondents made verbal sexual overtures toward an interviewer during the interview. Most of the respondents, however, presented no unusual problems in the interview situation.

Although most statements by respondents had to be accepted at face validity, it was possible to assess the reliability and validity of some responses in two ways. First, missing, incomplete, or inconsistent information could sometimes be verified by examining the client's casework folder. Often these folders were read before the interview and were helpful in providing a preinterview orientation to the client's life history. Occasionally this advance information proved useful in gaining rapport with the respondent. Second, interviewers were instructed to be alert for inconsistencies in migration, job, and marital-history items. For example, if the location of the job, considered in light of the respondent's age, was inconsistent with the migration history obtained earlier in the interview, the interviewer was instructed to probe until both charts were compatible with one another. Table A-4 presents interviewer ratings of various sections of the interview schedule. Although a few respondents were judged as substandard (in all cases these were older respondents), most seemed to give accurate, consistent life-history information. Selected items from the welfare histories of the women are given in Table A-5.

Although many Shelter clients had histories of psychiatric disturbances, only a few respondents showed any signs of bizarre or unconventional thought patterns in the interview situation. In no case was a respondent's mental state suspect to a point that warranted excluding her interview schedule from analysis. Reports from interviewers shed light on some of the unusual thoughts expressed by a few respondents during the interview:

Mrs. D, who is dressed the part of the skid-row woman . . . paused at one point in the interview: "I've looked all over for it. I can't find it. I've looked in every gutter in town. It ain't here. As soon as I find it, though, everything will be OK. My Dad told me that when I was a young girl. 'Find the cross,' he said, 'and you'll be okay.' " I asked about the cross, though the respondent's only reply was (in rather ominous tones), "The cross . . . the cross." I acknowledged that I understood and then continued questioning her on family background. . . . There were remarkably few inconsistencies in her responses. She was a bit vague on dates, though these were later substantiated in her case record.

Miss S has spent about 14 years in mental hospitals. She now appears to be fairly normal, although she is extremely limited by a very low intelligence. I do not believe that she can read, and her speech is an almost incoherent mumble. I was forced to ask her to repeat many replies. Her memory was fair, using Pioneer Hotel subjects for my reference group, although she did not seem to be able to tell me much about her stay in the mental hospitals.

Content Analysis of Case Files

Results of a pilot project conducted at Emergency Assistance Unit indicated that case files of women referred to the Pioneer Hotel contained useful qualitative

Table A-5
Selected Items from the Welfare Histories of Shelter Women[a]

Item	*Percent*
Have You Ever Received Assistance from Shelters Such as This in Other Cities?	
Yes	21
No	75
No information	4
Total	100
How Long Have You Lived Here at the Shelter (Present Residence)?	
1 day	27
2–7 days	23
2–4 weeks	19
2–12 months	6
2–3 years	14
No information	11
Total	100
Where Did You Live before This?	
Manhattan	25
Brooklyn	6
New York City (borough not specified)	39
Somewhere outside New York City	15
No information	15
Total	100
Living Arrangement Prior to Admission to the Shelter:	
Hotel	21
Apartment	21
Rooming house	23
Street, park, bus station (undomiciled)	12
Hospital	8
Friend or relative	10
Other	2
No information	3
Total	100

[a]$N = 52$

data about disaffiliation among women. While the incomplete and unsystematic nature of many case files precluded their use as the main source of empirical data on homeless women, analysis of a sample of case files provided important illustrative and comparative material to be used in conjunction with data obtained by interview.

Observation during Field Work

Although the major sources of data were life-history interviews, observational reports and field notes were especially useful for adding qualitative depth to the life histories. Moreover, the observational data provide insight into the present life situations of Shelter women, illustrating how they live, dress, and talk, their outward demeanor, and their problems.

Interviewers were given general instructions as to the type of observations that would be particularly useful; i.e., they were instructed to pay particular attention to clients' interaction with other clients, and with caseworkers, matrons, and so forth. To supplement observations at the Shelter, field workers were dispatched to various places in the Bowery area that the women often visited. Occasionally field workers questioned Bowery residents about the types of women who lived in the Bowery district. For example, here are the comments of one informant:

> . . . sitting in the park located on Grand Avenue, of the Bowery . . . "I'll tell you what I think: They're old ladies, most of them, anyway, and they carry shopping bags filled with cigar boxes. And they always have bandages on their legs! . . . Funny thing is they think they're better off than the men. They ain't. They ain't one bit better off. Worse, if anything."

The Comparative Sample of Homeless Men

Interview data from a group of homeless men were used in conjunction with the data from Shelter women in an assessment of sex differentials in the character and patterning of homelessness. The men were clients at Camp LaGuardia, an institution for rehabilitating homeless men operated by the City of New York under the administrative jurisdiction of the Department of Social Services. Data from the Camp LaGuardia residents were gathered in 1967 as part of the Homelessness Project. The Camp and the methods used in collecting data there have been described elsewhere,[a] and only a brief review is needed here.

Camp LaGuardia is located in a rural area near Chester, New York, approximately 60 miles from Manhattan. Established in 1934 when the Welfare Department acquired the site from the City's Department of Corrections, Camp LaGuardia has an upper capacity to lodge 1,050 men. All clients are referred to the Camp through the Men's Shelter in the Bowery and must meet the admissions criteria of the Shelter: age (over 50), low income, and "satisfactory" physical condition. A major ideology supporting the operation of the Camp is the alleged therapeutic value of rural life. Men in various states of debilitation are sent to the camp on the assumption that a few months of healthful living give them a "new lease on life." As in the Women's Shelter, no individual

---

[a]See Stanley K. Henshaw, *Camp LaGuardia: A Voluntary Total Institution for Homeless Men*, New York: Columbia University, Bureau of Applied Social Research, 1967, and Howard M. Bahr and Theodore Caplow, *Old Men Drunk and Sober*, New York: New York University Press, 1974, pp. 22–24 and 334–339.

therapy services are provided. Thus, the primary emphasis is on custodial functions of the institution. The Camp has a staff of approximately 50 members, including a physician, dentist, and three chaplains.

A sample of 199 men were interviewed at Camp LaGuardia. The sampling frame included all clients in the Camp during the period of data collection. Since the population fluctuates from day to day, the actual sampling units were beds, each of which was assigned a number from 001 to 1059; a simple random sample was then drawn. The length of interviews ranged from 30 minutes to almost 4 hours; the median time was 70 minutes.[b]

[b]The basic interview schedule used in gathering data at Camp LaGuardia can be found in Howard M. Bahr and Theodore Caplow, *Old Men Drunk and Sober,* New York: New York University Press, 1974, Appendix III.

Appendix B

Identification of Attitudes and Computation of Scale Scores

The instrument contained four attitude scales developed by other researchers and previously used in the Homelessness Project. These four scales, containing a total of 28 items, were the Srole anomie scale (six items), two scales created by Rosenberg–misanthropy or faith in people (five items) and self-esteem (ten items)—and a self-estrangement scale developed by Bonjean (seven items). All these scales reflect aspects of alienation, and to determine if they did in fact represent distinct dimensions, a principle-axis factor analysis was performed on the matrix of intercorrelations among the 28 items, and eight factors with eigenvalues greater than 1.0 were identified. These eight factors accounted for 54 percent of the total explained variance.

The structure of the first unrotated factor is presented in Table B-1. This unrotated factor accounted for 20 percent of the total variance and 38 percent

Table B–1
Unrotated Loadings on Factor 1 of 28 Items Related to Alienation (N = 354)

Scale Items	*Factor 1*
Anomie	
1. Most public officials are not really interested in the problems of the average person.	.36
2. These days a person doesn't know whom she can count on.	.59
3. Nowadays a person has to live pretty much for today and let tomorrow take care of itself.	.39
4. In spite of what some people say, the lot of the average person is getting worse.	.51
5. Most people don't really care what happens to the next person.	.57
6. It's hardly fair to bring children into the world with the way things look for the future.	.47
Self-Estrangement	
7. Sometimes I get restless because I can't express my real feelings when talking and doing things with others.	.54
8. I have found that just being your natural self won't get you very far in this world.	.61
9. I have found that more often than not the rules in our world go against human nature.	.48
10. When I am around other people, I try to keep in mind that saying what you really feel often gets you in trouble	.51
11. I frequently have to do things to please others that I would rather not do.	.45

Table B-1 continued

Scale Items	Factor 1
Self-Estrangement	
12. What others think I should do is usually not what I would really like to do.	.53
13. I have found that in order to get along in this world, usually you have to put on an act instead of being able to be your real self.	.53
Misanthropy	
14. If you don't watch yourself, people will take advantage of you.	.36
15. No one is going to care much what happens to you, when you get right down to it.	.57
16. Most people cannot be trusted; you can't be too careful in your dealings with people.	.66
17. Human nature is fundamentally cooperative.	-.23
18. Most people are more inclined to help others than to look out for themselves.	.14
Self-Esteem	
19. On the whole, I am satisfied with myself.	-.07
20. At times I think I am no good at all.	.39
21. I feel that I have a number of good qualities.	-.06
22. I am able to do things as well as most other people.	-.15
23. I feel I do not have much to be proud of.	.48
24. I certainly feel useless at times.	.51
25. I feel that I am a person of worth, at least on an equal plane with others.	-.09
26. I wish I could have more respect for myself.	.47
27. All in all, I am inclined to feel that I am a failure.	.54
28. I take a positive attitude toward myself.	-.18

of the variance explained by the first eight factors. While these findings suggest that, as expected, several distinct dimensions are operating, the fact that only 7 of the 28 items did not reach a loading of at least .35 does indicate that there is a great deal of common variance among the items. In short, while there appear to be several dimensions of alienation represented, each of these dimensions seems to overlap considerably with the others.

To further delimit the dimensions of each distinctive component, an orthogonal (varimax) rotation was performed, and the resulting factor matrix appears in Table B-2.

Of the eight original factors, five contained items with loadings exceeding .35. The first of these contained four of the six anomie items plus one item from the self-estrangement scale ("rules in our world go against human nature") and one item from the misanthropy scale ("no one is going to care much"). This factor was labeled "anomie."

Items with high loadings on factor 2 were five statements from the self-estrangement scale plus one item from the self-esteem scale ("I certainly feel useless"). However, the latter item loaded more heavily on factor 8. Factor 2 was labeled "self-estrangement."

Table B-2
Varimax Solution, Factors 1 through 8, for 28 Items Related to Alienation (Combined Samples, N = 354)

	Factor							
Item	*1*	*2*	*3*	*4*	*5*	*6*	*7*	*8*
Most public officials are not really interested in the problems of the average person.	*.68*	.08	.00	.02	-.02	.21	.10	.08
These days a person doesn't know whom she can count on.	.24	-.14	-.05	-.01	-.62	.23	-.02	-.08
Nowadays a person has to live pretty much for today and let tomorrow take care of itself.	.06	.09	.09	-.01	-.32	.12	.00	-.73
In spite of what some people say, the lot of the average person is getting worse.	*.56*	-.14	-.16	-.04	-.21	.01	.01	-.25
Most people don't really care what happens to the next person.	*.54*	-.18	.10	-.25	-.19	.20	.19	-.18
It's hardly fair to bring children into the world with the way things look for the future.	*.64*	-.20	.02	.10	-.09	-.04	-.21	.04
Sometimes I get restless because I can't express my real feelings when talking and doing things with others.	.19	*-.51*	-.04	.00	-.04	.15	*-.40*	-.26
I have found that just being your natural self won't get you very far in this world.	.23	-.21	.03	-.09	-.25	.26	-.23	-.18
I have found that more often than not the rules in our world go against human nature.	*.56*	-.15	-.03	.05	-.19	-.17	-.05	-.12
When I am around other people, I try to keep in mind that saying what you really feel often gets you into trouble.	.15	*-.54*	-.12	-.03	-.48	-.09	.05	.02

Table B-2 continued

Item	*Factor*							
	1	*2*	*3*	*4*	*5*	*6*	*7*	*8*
I frequently have to do things to please others that I would rather not do.	.06	-*.69*	.09	-.04	-.11	.16	.14	-.05
What others think I should do is usually not what I would really like to do.	.07	-*.60*	.06	.13	-.30	.12	-.00	-.08
I have found that in order to get along in this world, usually you have to put on an act instead of being able to be your real self.	.13	-*.47*	.16	.23	-.14	*.35*	-.28	.10
If you don't watch yourself, people will take advantage of you.	.11	-.18	.03	.01	-*.74*	.07	-.08	.00
No one is going to care much what happens to you, when you get right down to it.	*.57*	-.07	.05	-.09	-.27	.18	-.04	-.09
Most people cannot be trusted; you can't be too careful in your dealings with people.	.29	-.06	.01	.03	-*.75*	.11	-.08	-.13
Human nature is fundamentally cooperative.	-.19	-.14	-.15	*.52*	.22	.01	.27	.02
Most people are more inclined to help others than to look out for themselves.	.02	.03	.11	*.81*	-.14	.15	-.15	-.04
On the whole, I am satisfied with myself.	.09	.18	.04	.22	-.06	-.12	.21	-.07
At times I think I am no good at all.	.04	-.24	-.17	.05	.13	.19	-.07	-*.66*
I feel that I have a number of good qualities.	.08	-.07	*.79*	.22	.05	-.11	.11	.02
I am able to do things as well as most other people.	.06	-.05	.17	-.04	.98	-.10	*.78*	.04

Table B-2 continued

Item	*Factor* 1	2	3	4	5	6	7	8
I feel I do not have much to be proud of.	.10	.02	-.07	.07	-.21	*-.74*	.08	-.13
I certainly feel useless at times.	.26	*-.40*	-.07	.10	.10	.19	-.16	*-.51*
I feel that I am a person of worth, at least on an equal plane with others.	-.09	-.03	*.69*	-.21	-.00	-.09	.07	.04
I wish I could have more respect for myself.	.07	-.32	-.04	.13	-.00	*.58*	-.15	-.03
All in all, I am inclined to feel that I am a failure.	.12	-.19	-.11	-.03	-.13	*.69*	-.12	-.16
I take a positive attitude toward myself.	-.00	.02	.09	.08	.05	-.09	-.10	.01

Factors 3 and 4 each had only two items with high loadings. Factor 3 included two items reflecting positive recognition of personal worth and possession of good qualities. Factor 4 included two "people are cooperative" items from the misanthropy scale.

Factor 5 appeared to represent low faith in people and included one anomie scale item, two items from the misanthropy scale, and one self-estrangement item. However, the latter had also loaded (more heavily) on the self-estrangement scale and was designated a part of the latter scale. Factor 5 was labeled "misanthropy."

Factor 6 represented feelings of failure and low self-respect. Three items from the self-esteem scale had heavy loadings on this factor, and so the factor was defined as "self-esteem." One item from the self-estrangement scale also loaded on this factor but had loaded more heavily on factor 2.

Factor 7 had to do with feelings of competence in expressing feelings or doing things with others, but only two items loaded on this factor.

Finally, the three items with high loadings on factor 8 reflected feelings of impotence, such as inability to control the future, or inability to do constructive ("useful," "good") things. The "uselessness" item had also loaded on factor 2, but its loading was greater on factor 8.

In summary, the factor analysis yielded five factors on which three or more items had loadings of .35 or more. In cases where items loaded on two of the five factors, they were assigned to the factor on which they loaded most heavily. For the purposes of the present study, attitudes were defined by the items loading on these five factors, i.e., anomie (1), self-estrangement (2), misanthropy (5), self-esteem (6), and powerlessness (8).

The items comprising each of these scales were submitted to principle-axis factor analysis, and factor weights on the first factor were used to calculate standardized factor indices (scale scores) for each respondent. Results of the principal-axis factor analysis performed on each of the scales independently appear in Table B-3.

Table B-3
Unrotated Loadings on Factor 1 for Five Scales (Loadings Computed Independently for Each Scale)

Scale	*Items*	*Factor 1 (Unrotated)*
Anomie	1. Most public officials . . .	.58
	9. In spite of what some people say . . .	.65
	11. I have found that more often than not . . .	.64
	16. Most poeple don't really care . . .	.70
	18. No one is going to care much . . .	.68
	28. It's hardly fair to bring children . . .	.62
Self-estrangement	2. Sometimes I get restless . . .	.64
	13. When I am around other people . . .	.64
	19. I frequently have to do things . . .	.66
	23. What others think I should do . . .	.69
	25. I have found that in order to get along . . .	.67
Misanthropy	4. These days a person doesn't know . . .	.77
	14. If you don't watch yourself . . .	.82
	20. Most people cannot be trusted . . .	.84
Self-esteem	12. I feel I do not have much . . .	.78
	21. I wish I could have more respect . . .	.72
	24. All in all, I am inclined to feel . . .	.80
Powerlessness	5. At times I think I am no good . . .	.79
	6. Nowadays a person has to live . . .	.60
	15. I certainly feel useless . . .	.78

Examples of the meaning of the computed scale scores may be given, using sample items from the five scales. A single item from each of the scales appears in Table B-4, along with percentages showing the proportion of respondents in each sample that agreed with the item as stated. Thus, the positive mean anomie score of .755 reported in Table B-5 for tract 56 indicates that women in tract 56 tended to *disagree* with statements reflecting anomie, whereas respondents in the Shelter sample tended to agree with statements such as "most people don't really care what happens to the next person." In other words, a negative scale score reflects high anomie. The same type of scoring was applied to all the items; accordingly, women who tended to agree with items such as "most people

Table B–4
Proportion of Respondents Agreeing with Sample Items from Five Attitude Scales

Item	*Percent of Respondents Agreeing with Item*			
	Tract 159	*Tract 56*	*Tract 76*	*Women's Shelter*
Most people don't really care what happens to the next person (anomie)	53% (171)	34% (77)	50% (62)	61% (51)
Most people cannot be trusted; you can't be too careful in your dealings with people (misanthropy)	39% (162)	39% (79)	75% (60)	84% (49)
At times I think I am no good at all (powerlessness)	25% (169)	29% (82)	28% (60)	51% (51)
All in all, I am inclined to feel that I am a failure (self-esteem)	7% (167)	22% (80)	32% (59)	50% (50)
What others think I should do is usually not what I would really like to do (self-estrangement)	41% (155)	45% (71)	61% (57)	72% (50)

Table B–5
Mean Scores on Attitude Scales and Affiliation Rank, by Sample

Variable	*Tract 159*	*Tract 56*	*Tract 76*	*Women's Shelter*
Anomie	.0487	.7554	-.4675	-.8119
Misanthropy	.4342	.5538	-.8261	-1.3531
Powerlessness	.2412	-.0662	.0542	-.7937
Self-esteem	.3041	.4691	-.2756	-1.4154
Self-estrangement	.4123	.4198	-.5650	-1.4158
Affiliation Rank	3.3297	2.9146	2.1719	1.6538

cannot be trusted" ended up with a negative score on the misanthropy scale; those who tended to agree with statements reflecting their perceived impotence ("at times I think I am no good at all"), inferiority ("all in all, I am inclined to feel that I am a failure"), or lack of control over their own decisions ("what others think I should do is usually not what I would really like to do") received negative scores on the powerlessness, self-esteem, and self-estrangement scales, respectively.

The attitude scales discussed above were not treated extensively in the present report, in part because they represent attitudinal components of the respondent's present situation, and they seemed inapprorpriate predictors of our major dependent variable, affiliation rank. However, it may be of interest to present the intercorrelations between the attitude scale scores and affiliation rank. The appropriate correlation coefficients appear in Table B-6.

Table B-6
Intercorrelations among Five Attitude Scales and Affiliation Rank, Four Samples[a]

Variable	*Anomie*	*Misanthropy*	*Power-lessness*	*Self-esteem*	*Self-estrange-ment*	*Affiliation Rank*
Anomie		.46	.24	.42	.38	.26
Misanthropy	.59		.17	.87	.47	.22
Powerlessness	.32	.18		.24	.30	.08
Self-esteem	.55	.90	.17		.47	.19
Self-estrangement	.44	.41	.46	.49		.13
Affiliation Rank	.34	.46	.16	.39	.27	
Anomie		.47	.32	.37	.42	.04
Misanthropy	.47		.20	.88	.09	.09
Powerlessness	.57	.49		.15	.37	.28
Self-esteem	.37	.84	.52		.15	.08
Self-estrangement	.43	.52	.31	.57		.14
Affiliation Rank	.14	-.01	-.01	.01	.05	

[a]Top matrix, above diagonal = tract 159.
Top matrix, below diagonal = tract 56.
Bottom matrix, above diagonal = tract 76.
Bottom matrix, below diagonal = Women's Shelter.

The procedure of creating interval data via factor analysis and computation of scale scores weighted for the individual factor weights of each item was used with several other scales. Details of the results obtained are given in Tables B-7 through B-14.

Table B–7
Intercorrelations among Seven Items Reflecting Discrepancies between Aspirations and Achievement (Combined Tract Samples, N = 331)

Item	*1*	*2*	*3*	*4*	*5*	*6*	*7*
1. Satisfaction with housing	1.00	.04	-.08	.02	.22	-.07	.12
2. Did not intend to spend working years as she did	.04	1.00	-.15	.04	-.01	-.08	.08
3. Looking back, would rather have had another type of job	-.08	-.15	1.00	.08	-.03	.15	-.08
4. Lonely	.02	.04	.08	1.00	.18	.07	-.00
5. Participates in activities less than other women her age	.22	-.01	-.03	.18	1.00	-.11	.11
6. Thinks she should be more active	-.07	-.08	.15	.07	-.11	1.00	-.07
7. Life did not turn out as hoped	.12	.08	-.08	-.00	.11	-.07	1.00

Table B–8
Unrotated Loadings on Factor 1 for Seven Items Reflecting Discrepancies between Aspirations and Achievement, and Varimax Solution and Communalities (Combined Tract Samples, N = 331)

		Rotated Factors			
Item	*Factor 1 (Unrotated)*	*1*	*2*	*3*	h^2
1. Housing	.58	.02	-.05	.06	.82
2. Worked at intended	.36	.09	-.87	.04	.78
3. Looking back	-.45	.30	.57	.27	.58
4. Lonely	.13	.86	-.15	.15	.80
5. Participates less	.57	.57	.11	-.30	.66
6. Should be active	-.48	-.01	.08	.94	.89
7. Was life as hoped	.49	-.00	-.06	-.03	.98

Table B-9
Intercorrelations among Five Items Reflecting Discrepancies between Aspirations and Achievement (Women's Shelter, *N* = 52)

Item	*1*	*2*	*3*	*4*	*5*
1. Did not intend to spend working years as she did	1.00	-.28	-.14	-.10	.02
2. Looking back, would rather have had another type of job	-.28	1.00	.25	.27	.07
3. Lonely	-.14	.25	1.00	-.25	.16
4. Participates in activities less than other women her age	-.10	.27	-.25	1.00	-.19
5. Thinks she should be more active	.02	.07	.16	-.19	1.00

Table B-10
Unrotated Loadings on Factor 1 for Five Items Reflecting Discrepancies between Aspirations and Achievement, and Varimax Solution and Communalities (Women's Shelter, *N* = 52)

Item	*Factor 1 (Unrotated)*	*Rotated Factors*		h^2
		1	*2*	
1. Worked as intended	-.66	-.12	.05	1.00
2. Looking back	.82	.97	-.16	1.00
3. Lonely	.54	.13	.13	1.00
4. Participates less	.25	.14	-.98	1.00
5. Should be active	.18	.02	.09	1.00

Table B-11
Intercorrelations among Five Items about Frequency of Social Interaction (Combined Samples, *N* = 346)

Item	*1*	*2*	*3*	*4*	*5*
1. Number of personal letters received per year	1.00	-.13	-.06	-.06	-.03
2. Number of persons conversed with on day preceding interview	-.13	1.00	.28	.21	-.01
3. Number of persons in neighborhood known by name	-.16	.28	1.00	.29	.01
4. Number of close friends in New York City	-.06	.21	.29	1.00	-.07
5. Number of times left room or apartment on day preceding interview	-.03	-.01	.01	-.07	1.00

Table B–12
Unrotated Loadings on Factor 1 for Five Items about Frequency of Social Interaction, and Varimax Solution and Communalities (Combined Samples, N = 346)

Item	*Factor 1 (Unrotated)*	*Rotated Factors* 1	2	h^2
1. Personal letters	-.41	-.35	-.50	.37
2. Persons conversed with	.67	.66	.12	.45
3. Persons known by name	.74	.73	.14	.56
4. Close friends in city	.65	.68	-.22	.52
5. Times left room	-.04	-.16	.85	.75

Table B–13
Intercorrelations among Four Items about Frequency of Media Use (Combined Samples, N = 366)

Item	*1*	*2*	*3*	*4*
1. Number of books read in the past year	1.00	.00	.01	.16
2. Number of hours per day spent watching TV	.00	1.00	-.02	-.02
3. Number of hours per day listening to radio	.10	-.02	1.00	- .01
4. Number of movies seen in the past month	.16	-.02	-.01	1.00

Table B–14
Unrotated Loadings on Factor 1 for Four Items about Frequency of Media Use, and Varimax Solution and Communalities (Combined Samples, N = 366)

Item	*Factor 1 Unrotated*	*Factor 1 Rotated*	h^2
1. Books	.75	.77	.59
2. Television	-.09	.02	.99
3. Radio	.01	.00	.00
4. Movies	.76	.75	.58

Appendix C

Historical Sketch of the Women's Emergency Shelter

It is believed that the New York City Community assumed responsibility for providing shelter care for homeless women prior to the early 1900s. The early provisions were for temporary shelter care only, and no social service staff was utilized.

However, from available records and conversations with surviving personnel, we have ascertained that the Women's Shelter was functioning prior to 1913.

A building on East 25th Street near First Avenue, where Bellevue's current Nurses' Residence is located, was the site of one of our early shelters. The shelter was temporary and provided food and housing on a limited basis. Men and women were housed in the same building with two separate entrances on East 25th Street, one of which was reserved solely for women. Meals were served on the premises, and while this arrangement was not primarily intended for family cases, in extreme situations, provisions were made for the temporary care of families.

Shelter was considered very temporary, to meet an immediate emergency. Therefore, no provisions were made for a stay which exceeded five nights per month. During the Depression years, the shelter often housed as many as 100 women per night.

During March 1935, women were no longer housed at the Municipal Lodging House on East 25th Street. A double brownstone house at 309 West 14th Street was pressed into service for the unattached women. When the number of applicants went above the shelter's capacity, additional women were housed at the Adelphi Hotel on 23rd Street. However, the increased number of applicants, because of the Depression, soon made these two sites inadequate; therefore, the Women's Shelter moved to 630 East 6th Street. Within a short period of time, exigencies required that the Shelter return to its original location on East 25th Street where it occupied one floor.

In 1946, because of public reaction to the increasing cost of referrals of families dispossessed from their apartments to hotels, one floor at the present Men's Shelter at 8 East 3rd Street (a former YMCA) was turned over to undomiciled women and children. When public clamor was reduced in 1947, no more referrals were made to 8 East 3rd, and all unattached women were provided for on East 25th Street.

The following sketch of the Women's Energency Shelter was written by the Director of the Bureau of Shelter Services for Adults of the New York City Department of Social Services, Mr. Morris Chase, and was distributed in a mimeographed memorandum in 1970.

At the end of 1948, the Family Shelter was established at 330 East 5th Street, formerly Public School 325. In order to keep the unattached women—most of whom were alcoholics, emotionally disturbed, or transient—separate from families with children, space at Pioneer Hotel at 341 Broome Street was obtained as a temporary measure.

At the time the change to the Pioneer Hotel was instituted, the Women's Shelter program became a 24-hour program known as the Homeless Women, Emergency Assistance Unit. It serviced any emergency resulting from fires, disasters, family incompatibility, stranded people, etc., which occurred after the regular welfare center closed, as well as sheltering of homeless women at the Pioneer Hotel.

The Pioneer Hotel was considered an interim site. Continuous and intensive efforts have been made to obtain another and more adequate site with a realization of the difficulties present in trying to meet the day-to-day needs of a group of alcoholics and emotionally disturbed women. Sectors of the city where possibilities were considered rejected the idea of a domicile for unattached alcoholics and emotionally disturbed women within their boundaries. The task was made more difficult because of the need for being located within a short distance from a variety of traveling facilities as well as in an area which would be utilized by the homeless type of women. Changing municipal administrations, together with depleted municipal allotments, also made the plan a difficult one to implement. However, after intensive efforts, a building was finally located on Lafayette Street. Renovations focusing on the provisions of adequate housing with full cognizance of the essential need for privacy, on-the-spot medical and psychiatric services, meals served on the premises, and the availability of a social service staff were essentials considered in setting up the initial planning of the building. The new shelter is scheduled to open shortly.

Despite budgetary limitations resulting in a minimal operating staff and despite the limited facilities of the previous Women's Shelter, available WPA projects, Alcoholics Anonymous, and interested religious groups tried to supplement services in essential areas. These groups continued their efforts and were constantly encouraged in their work and assisted whenever possible by the small dedicated staff which serviced the old Women's Shelter.

An expanded budget, plus a markedly increased staff on all levels, will enable the new location to provide group work, recreation, medical and psychiatric services, as well as the understanding, encouragement and skilled help of caseworkers assigned directly to the location.

Appendix D

Reactions to Disaffiliation among Aged Women: The Novelists' View

This appendix is a discussion of selected aspects of the process of disaffiliation among aged women as noted by novelists. It draws upon selected works of fiction published between 1950 and 1970 which deal with the isolation and loneliness of disaffiliated or partially disaffiliated women. The objective of this research was to identify hypotheses, hunches, or alleged patterns which might serve as sensitizing devices or more fully illuminate and illustrate findings from interviews with samples of aged and isolated women living in New York City.

The universe from which our novels were drawn in some ways is not sharply defined. It certainly would not be adequate for a statistical content analysis of the incidence of the types of characters and life patterns we shall highlight. However, given our objectives, it was adequate. In part, this research grew out of a suspicion that the sociological empiricists who had studied patterns of aging might be missing something that the novelists had seen and described. Our own ultimate objectives were to gather empirical data, but we wanted to profit as much as possible from the keen eye and interpretive insight of the novelist, both in the framing of the subsequent survey and the analysis of the data generated by it.

The sources we used to find books dealing with lonely or disaffiliated women included the *Book Review Digest* for the years 1950 through 1968. The following subject headings under fiction were examined: alcoholism, aunts, death, diaries (in story form), family life, housing, homosexuality, insanity, locality (New York City), loneliness, mentally ill, middle age, mothers, narcotic habit, old age, physically handicapped, poverty, prostitution, psychological stories, short stories, sisters, social problems, spinsters, suicide, teachers, widows, women. When a book described in the reviews seemed to fit our concern with aging and disaffiliation among women, we attempted to locate and examine it. Book reviews in the *Saturday Review* between 1962 and 1968 were also scanned in an attempt to identify relevant works, and unsystematic scanning of fiction catalogs combined with simple perusal of fly leaves of books on library shelves produced additional relevant titles. The works identified were then read. Appropriate passages or insightful characterizations were noted, copied, collected, and arranged into several categories representing stages of the process of disaffiliation (disaffiliation among young women, the role of family background, spinsterhood,

---

This appendix is a project memorandum by Howard Bahr, Marcia Cebulski, Laura Kemp, Dorothy Frost, and Susan Rutherford Muller.

retirement, loss of health and normal faculties, and bereavement) and reactions to disaffiliation (living in the past, resistance to change, search for substitutes, fantasy, return to religion, superficial social involvement, stress of status, pressing need for communication, preoccupation with the affairs of others, self-pity, and unrealistic fears and misanthropy).

Reactions to Disaffiliation

Like an actress facing the stage without a part, the disaffiliated woman faces the world without a role. Through retirement, death, illness, or old age, she has lost her accustomed position, and lost with it is much of the meaning she had ascribed to life and the fulfillment she derived from it. She is forced to personally and socially redefine herself. Her success may depend on her ability to question the importance of roles or to choose new, appropriate, and workable roles which will provide meaning and lead to reaffiliation. Most of the characters included in this literature review are examples of women who chose unsuitable roles in their quest for meaning and self-esteem. They are women who sought to avoid adjustment through attempts at escape or who turned inward to the exclusion of society, thus leading for further isolation and disaffiliation. Many of the reactions to and consequences of disaffiliation discussed below are interrelated. For example, self-pity and a pressing need for communication combined with the loss of normal faculties may lead a woman to turn to animals for her friendship and communication.

Living in the Past

One common response to an isolating environment is to live in the past, so that in imagination, at least, fulfillment of the accustomed roles continues and the new alien world does not have to be faced. In the following paragraphs taken from Dickens' *Room Upstairs,* Sybil tries to disregard the handicaps which increasing age and grown children have imposed upon her continuing her role as a mother.

> She was plump at forty—where had all that flesh gone to?—puttering endlessly in the kitchen, pickling, preserving, the children knowing where to find her, knowing there was always something in the oven. She saw herself like that still. Even though you knew you were eighty, addressed yourself as Old Fool, and told people "I'm only a useless old woman," you did not completely believe it. If you did, you would not wait for death to catch you. You would go to meet it (Dickens, 1966:33).

Some women refuse to acknowledge that changes have occurred and that they must readjust. They continue to assume the roles they had shaped for themselves and in some instances accentuate these now nonfunctional roles and become preoccupied with their importance. Alma, a character in Purdy's *The Nephew,* manifested this behavior when she received word that her one interest in life, her nephew Cliff, was missing in action. The importance of her nephew's part in her life became magnified out of proportion until it became the focal point in her life.

. . . she was uneasily aware now that many of her hours were spent in a dim dream-like reshaping of Cliff's life, and her reveries themselves were often a silent commemoration of his brief career.

. . . There was hardly an hour in Alma's waking life when she did not think of Cliff. In this way, he had taken the place of her mother (Purdy, 1960:38).

Living in the past, at least in the remembered happiness of the past, may also be enacted by denying the existence of current international or political problems. Mrs. Ramsey from Stafford's "The Captain's Gift" lived in the delusion of a prewar world while evidence to the contrary surrounded her.

In spite of this substitution of the blanks for her own monogrammed letter paper, in spite of the military titles and the serial numbers which she copies down in the little box at the top of the page, in spite of the uniforms which she cannot help seeing in the square, and the newspapers and the War Bond drives, the blackout curtains at her windows and the buckets of sand in her fourth floor corridor and the ration books, Mrs. Ramsey is the one person, her friends say, to whom the cliché may accurately be applied: "She does not know there is a war on" (Stafford, 1964:165–166).

Resistance to Change

Closely allied to living in the past is the attempt to extend the present indefinitely into the future. The security of the known ends the quest for meaning, and a high value is placed on the routine and the familiar. In an example from Stafford's "The Captain's Gift," resistance to change is a refusal to be mobile, using the problem of age as an excuse: "I have never like change, and now I am too old for it" (Stafford, 1964:163). Another example:

Mrs. Cooper, 92 and in poor health, resisted the welfare workers' urging her to move into a rest home. I left Mrs. Cooper sitting on her bed. She didn't want a doctor and it was too much of an effort for her to talk. She had nothing to say. Only the enormity of her age gave her grace. She had been abandoned by her parents in 1869 and since 1869 she had lived in sombody else's home. Now she had her own home. And she wouldn't give it up for a thousand nursing homes and their Friday night chow mein suppers (Horowitz, 1960:55).

Moving to a new environment may offer many opportunities to become less isolated, but it does not affect the almost religious devotion to the continuity of daily routine.

Once having settled in Sans Souci, Nona Henry began to establish a life of routine . . . the marketing, three meals a day, the cleaning of her clothes. . . . By careful rationing and spacing, she eked out moments of companionship to make the lonely hours go by. (Armstrong, 1959: 111, 113)

Search for Substitutes

One reaction to age and loneliness is to seek a substitute, i.e., someone to whom the familiar roles can be related, someone to whom one can have a motherly, wifely, or nurselike relationship. Examples of this type of search for meaning and fight against loneliness are found in the same literary sources.

Alma was pleased, too, with having to wait on Boyd hand and foot, for at last she had a task commensurate with her energy and time, and her usual irritability and fussiness disappeared in her role as nurse. (Purdy, 1960:159)

A character in *Nightmovers* readily accepted the chance when it offered itself in the form of a young orphan claiming to be her cousin from Ireland. That he was in fact a Brooklyn boy is something the woman suspected and of which her relatives and neighbors were convinced. However, she did not care if he were lying to her as long as he would stay with her and fill up the loneliness of her life (Dunphy, 1967:41). Another example from fiction, Mrs. da Tauka, went to the extreme of actually employing a man to be her companion (Trevor, 1967:114).

Animals also are used as substitutes for human companionship. Sybil Prince's first housekeeper had a dog which occupied an important position in her life. When it was run over and killed, she wrapped it in a towel and took it to her room. "She did not cry," but locked herself up in her room all day and all night and proceeded to get drunk for the first time in her life. To her it was comparable to losing a child (Dickens, 1966:30).

Sybil Prince's second housekeeper, Dorothy Grue, also lavished her affection on a pet. Hers was Roger, a talking parakeet. Dorothy would spend hours talking to it as it sat on her shoulder. Its voice and comments copied Dorothy's, and after Dorothy died, Sybil herself came to believe that Dorothy's spirit was embodied in the parakeet (Dickens, 1966: 55, 179).

Even toy animals may serve in this way. Miss Warrender, in *The Pattern of Perfection,* replaced her dead father with a panda bear (Hale, 1960:216).

Fantasy

The disaffiliated woman is one stripped of significant roles. If she fails to achieve reaffiliation and thus attain a sense of self-worth through a means culturally defined as normal, she may turn to the past, to unrealistic but pleasing roles, or to bizarre fantasy. Almost all the fictional characters discussed here indulged in fantasy which helped maintain their self-esteem. Thus, the difference in contact with reality between Alma's preoccupation with her nephew (Purdy, 1960: 159) and another's delusion of herself as nobility is one of degree.

The woman in *Nightmovers* pranced freely in and out of fantasy. Her "cousin" Leroy shared with her an imaginary store and a guessing game of who came in each day. Her other fantasies were playful and childlike and often were joined by Leroy.

The craziest things could suddenly assume stature enough in her eyes for her to regard them in a prayerful way, almost pleading, or in a praising way. Half-blind old dogs, cats under cars, old fighters on their uppers, hags studying lacy getups for June brides, a bum on a swell street. The common, dismissed, forgotten or half-forgotten, would cause her to cross herself sometimes out of sorrow, sometimes out of horror that there but for the grace of God go I, sometimes with a smile at the resiliency of the spirit of life, and sometimes for fun, for funny make-believe, for fantasy. As when a tree she passed preened itself in the wind with a shake, she herself would feel quite grand in a flirty sort of way: "Tell the Duke I'll be right down." Music, long, open doors, fireflies. . . . (Dunphy, 1967:202)

Mrs. Ramsey, cited earlier in the section Living in the Past, is a character whose denial of the reality of the present was evidenced in every aspect of her life and which provided a refuge for those wishing temporarily to be relieved of that reality.

. . . in her house one can quite delude oneself into believing that this tranquility extends far beyond her doorstep, beyond the city, throughout the world itself, and that the catastrophes of our times are only hypothetical horrors. . . . They say they frightfully pity people who cannot have a holiday from the war in her house. . . . She speaks of Germany and Japan as if they were still nothing more than two foreign countries of which she had affectionate memories. (Stafford, 1964: 165, 166)

Mrs. Ross, of Nicolson's *A Flight of Steps,* read stories from magazines and newspapers, especially the society pages, from which she took her fantasies. She believed that she was someone wealthy and prominent, signing her name to letters with the title of Dame of the British Empire, Margaret Ross, née Cattanech, Hereditary Countess of Aird and All the Islands to the West, Lady of the Manor of Great D'Arcy (Nicolson, 1967:11). And we have already mentioned Mrs. Prince, who believed that the spirit of her dead housekeeper, Dorothy, was contained in her surviving parakeet, and thus spent hours talking to it as if it were Dorothy (Dickens, 1966:158).

Return to Religion

In the quest for meaning, some women display a renewed or newly inspired interest in religion or prayer. Clara, a neighbor of Alma Boyd in *The Nephew,* was strongly devoted to her religion, thus meeting with Alma's disapproval. But Clara saw it as a much better way of handling loneliness than Alma's own method, asserting that it was better to cling to religion than to continue to grasp at the memory of a loved one (Dickens, 1966:30).

The woman in *Nightmovers* exemplifies the same tendency in a more bizarre fashion. While remaining a practicing Catholic, she frequently experienced a desire to idolize the picture of a fish that had been on the door of her store. She occasionally considered cutting the glass and taking the fish home with her to pray over. "Pray to it as if it were her grandfather and she was a little girl again. Pray to it to send her someone like him" (Dunphy, 1967:13).

Superficial Social Involvement

The aged disaffiliated woman deeply feels the weight of time. She desperately wants to avoid boredom. One response to this particular aspect of disaffiliation is to devote energy to time-consuming activities. The woman assumes that as long as she is busy, she will be happy. Frequently this is not the case, because the activities that she chooses are meaningless and do not fill the gap in her life.

Mrs. Stewart, Hale's divorced and childless character, spent a great deal of time traveling, though it did little to relieve her emptiness and desire for companionship.

> "I don't have such a marvelous time actually," she said. "I don't know why not—God knows I try hard enough. Venice is supposed to be so heavenly in late summer, and yet I give you my word there was nobody in Venice. I've just been there. I'm going Monday to pay a rather long visit to California. San Francisco. I hope to God there's somebody there." (Hale, 1955:145)

Cornell's Mrs. Bridge "often went to Auxiliary meetings, shopping downtown, to the Plaza for luncheon, and to a number of parties, but she could no longer lose herself in these activities; the past was too much with her and also she was frequently content to stay home . . ." (Cornell, 1959:247).

Myra Russell, a widow of 59 from Blechman's *Maybe,* hoped to absorb the hours by playing cards, by attending lectures, and taking part in such protest and prevention organizations as Sanity (nuclear disarmament), Chemban (prevention of chemical pollution), Committee for the Protection of Koolie Birds, and Conserve (preservation of trees). She was extremely conscious of every minute and the need to fill it with something.

One hundred and five more minutes to go. Oh, how she'd like to stab them, strangle them, till the hours are dead and she's eaten the lonely *mole* and time, like the red-hot dinner, has vanished into her digestive system. Thank goodness for the cream puff and the catalogue and her interesting schedule or the hours would be years. . . . Though wishing to "better" herself, she often succumbs to taking sleeping pills, watching horror movies on television. (Blechman, 1967: 38)

Mrs. Prince, a character from Dickens' novel, was never able to accept the fact that a highway had been built through the middle of her estate. Although it could produce no effect, she would sit by a window making faces and shaking her fist at passing cars. Through this nonproductive activity she vented her anger and found a substitute for actively combating the loss of her property (Dickens, 1966:3).

In *Nightmovers* an aged woman exhibited a similar tendency to fill her time with unusual, unnecessary, and for the most part unfulfilling activity.

She'd taken to doing lots of fairly ordinary and easy things in the most difficult and round-about way possible. Erratic. Going to Mass in the middle of the night all by herself through today's street was doing it the hard way. (Dunphy, 1967:9)

Involvement in eccentric activities is a further manifestation of this same tendency. In one literary case a wealthy old woman began begging. Her style made her successful. Her movements were dances accompanied by the "music" of daydreams out of her past to raise her begging to a satisfying, restful, interesting, and romantic activity (Dunphy, 1967: 170, 171).

The seemingly meaningless activities mentioned above, living in the past or in fantasy, may be viewed as escapes from a life of loneliness, dissatisfaction, or boredom. Some of the fictional characters chose more self-destructive means of escape such as sleep (Gooding, 1967:49), drugs (Stone, 1967:328), sleeping pills (Blechman, 1967:19), or alcohol (Stone, 1967:224). Still others engaged in sexually promiscuous or perverted behavior (Wilson, 1959).

Stress on Status

Having lost the usual hallmarks of status with age (spouse, occupation, etc.), the elderly woman of fiction stresses whatever power and possessions she holds. A frequent preoccupation is with lawyers and wills. One of the favorite topics of conversation in the ward for the elderly in *Momento Mori* was the question of who gets what. Even among those with no possessions, a pretense was made. They constantly asked for new will forms and threatened doctors and nurses with being out of their wills (Spark, 1958:123).

A similar concern with status is evident in the *Seventeen Widows of Sans Souci.*

> The widows had their connections. They were fond of saying "my" doctor, my lawyer, my chiropodist, my butcher, my hairdresser. For they were interconnected with the economy. They consumed. (Armstrong, 1959:98)

Pressing Need for Communication

Out of touch with the world around her, the disaffiliated woman may become obsessed with the need for communication. One area in which this is particularly true is in the concern over reception of mail or phone calls. One literary example is the exaggerated importance attributed to mail delivery at Sans Souci (Armstrong, 1959).

A comment on this trait of elderly women was expressed by the young woman in *Fires of Autumn.* She remarked on her observations while living with her aunt in a small resort town where several widows stayed for the autumn:

> I had noticed before the pathetic interest all the ladies took in the arrival of the mail in the Cranford post office. I, waiting every day for a letter that never came, was particularly sensitive to a sense of mortification, bordering on panic, in others. I had heard these mothers, hanging loverlike on the caprice of their children, when faced with the empty letter box, toss out airy nothings that fooled nobody. "Oh good! Here's my copy of the Sunday *Times!* Just what I was hoping to find!" they would exclaim while unostentatiously mailing their own bulletin of news that, one feared, could be of little interest to the recipient, used to receiving its mate with inexorable regularity. (Howe, 1957:136)

Another example of this phenomenon is found in Lacy's novel *The Hotel Dwellers.* One of the employees of the Hotel Times Terrace discussed the ritual of Miss Henderson's telling the switchboard operator that if she gets any calls, she'll be in the coffee shop.

> In every hotel you see them, the lonely ones waiting for a call. I'll bet she doesn't get one phone call a month. Almost a religion with them, as if they were expecting God to phone. (Lacy, 1966:46)

Coupled to this type of behavior are hours of hopeless waiting, ways of disguising the desperate need to feel important to others; yet these mannerisms inevitably call attention to the loneliness of the aged.

Frequently these lonely women attempt to fulfill their own needs for communication at the expense of and without regard for the reactions of others. Such is the woman who, deprived of anyone to listen to her, will talk to anyone anywhere without discretion. When she finds an audience, she rambles endlessly, causing people to deliberately avoid her in the future.

Sybil Henderson, a "lonely old maid on social security" and occupant of a fourth-rate hotel in midtown New York, illustrates this need to have a listener.

> Like all lonely people Sybil was a compulsive talker—at one time she had been barred from the coffee shop for bending anybody's ear with chatter.
>
> "But you need a person to at least talk to. It's better to have someone who tells you to shut up than to have silence. My mother, may God rest her soul, thought no man was good enough for [me]. . . . Stay in one room for a couple of days and you feel you're in jail. Do you know I can't bear to return to my room right now?" (Lacy, 1966: 51, 52)

Mrs. Harriet Gregory, one of the seventeen widows housed in an apartment house in Pasadena, prattled constantly. She was rejected from most of the social gatherings at Sans Souci and felt that she had no truly understanding friend who would take the time to listen to her (Armstrong, 1959:34).

Preoccupation with the Affairs of Others

Closely related to the conspicuous need for communication discussed above is an unusual attentiveness to the lives of others. The following quotation from *The Nephew* illustrates once again the importance of mail as a sign of communion with the rest of the world and the undue concern paid to the affairs of other people.

> Watching [the postman] like this each day brought her slowly, as in a lesson to a retarded pupil, to a kind of inventory of who was left and who was dead in her immediate neighborhood, for despite her long absence from Rainbow Center, the neighbors here had been hers for life.
>
> To her mortification, she saw that the postman almost always had a letter for each house on the block but hers. (Purdy, 1960:22)

It may be noted that the information received by this type of observation may be obtained without direct contact and interaction with others. In other words, information is received without the usual verbal communication. A quote from Faunce's novel, *Those Later Years,* demonstrates how petty jealousy and self-pity can derive from this same preoccupation: "I don't know how that Sue

Reinhardt manages to get so much mail. Everybody talks about it. As for me, I just don't look for letters anymore" (Faunce), 1959:23).

In some of these novels, there was extreme jealousy of others who were loved and accepted (Swinnerton, 1967:106; Dickens, 1966:46), and sometimes there was bitterness and desire for revenge. An imposition on the woman's life, especially by the young and happy, can lead to fantasies of revenge and power. Such is the case with Miss Leckton of *The Sudden Guest,* who dreams of preventing a younger woman from meeting a lover (LaFarge, 1946:247, 248).

More commonly such preoccupation with the affairs of others is revealed in spying and gossip, i.e., in being a "nosy old lady." Mrs. Wallace of *A Flight of Steps* illustrates how this practice can become part of the ritual of daily life. Old Mrs. Wallace,

> whose mobility was much restricted by rheumatism, always had breakfast in bed, rose late, bathed, dressed, and read the morning paper thoroughly; after that it was her practice to sit in a comfortable chair by her bedroom window, a parcel of boiled sweets within easy reach, and through a very good pair of binoculars spy on her neighbors during most of the day. In the evening she watched television. (Nicolson, 1967:79)

A concern for the trivial may be a manifestation of the same phenomenon:

> To the seventeen widows living in Sans Souci, any event, no matter how big or small, was the subject of interest. Discussion ranged from such matters as on which presidents' birthdays in February would the banks close and the mail not come, to an incident of a drunken man in one widow's apartment. . . . Nona often looked out her window at the others, wondering how many of them looked out of their's as well. (Armstrong, 1959:85, 95)

Self-pity

The lonely disaffiliated woman frequently succumbs to moods of self-pity and fits of depression. Black expression of the discontent of the aged appears in the following excerpt from a letter written by a crippled old woman to her niece:

> I think we live too long nowadays, women particuarly. Pray that you won't outlive your children . . . pray that you won't find yourself someday a useless, worn-out husk condemned to the hell of individuality within your personal self with no way to get out, no way to participate in the future, a dusty piece of bric-a-brac on a shelf waiting to be swept off and broken. An old woman talking to myself—and if I talk nonsense or if I talk truth, does it matter? Who listens? Who cares? We live too long and there are too many of us. We are poisoning each other, and this wild green earth as well. (Janeway, 1959: 326, 327)

Self-pity is often linked to a woman's recollection of memories of her married life. A character in *Fires of Autumn* related how her married life compared to the lives of some of her widowed friends and then distinguished herself from those who reminisced endlessly about happy experiences with their loved ones. These reminiscences annoyed her because she could not forget the bad luck and unhappiness of her life. She was unable to break out of the destitute feelings into easier conversation. By complaining about the other's chatter, she found a means of expression, but it brought her the reputation as constant crier of "Nobody has suffered the way I suffer" (Howe, 1957:159).

Hagar Shipley said that one of her only joys left in life was complaining. But after she had, and repented, her pride kept her from apologizing. Her complaining was related to her feeling of being abused, a common correlative. In Mrs. Shipley's case, it was the result of ill feelings harbored against those who tried to put her in a nursing home (Lawrence, 1964:30).

Unrealistic Fears

Often aged isolated women are portrayed as exhibiting unrealistic fears of such things as death or social ostracism.

> The seventeen widows of Sans Souci were somewhat haunted by worry and care. The spectre of death haunted them, and the spectre of pain. The spectre of fear in many guises and the spectre of pride lest they trouble anyone, and the spectre of loneliness, lest they trouble no one and be forgotten. (Armstrong, 1959:36)

In the case of Mrs. Ross, feelings of fear and suspicion of others became extremely terrifying. Living alone amid a clutter of magazines, she thought she heard whisperings of conspirators. She was frightened by these voices but also feared leaving her room because of the taunts of the neighborhood children. She was so frightened that once when her drunken son came to visit, she failed to recognize him (Nicolson, 1967: 8, 32, 42).

Combining their suspicions of being abused and their fears of death, some of these fictional women finally came to believe that someone was planning their death. The women in the hospital geriatric ward in *Momento Mori* seriously believed that the head nurse was against them and that they'd all be dead by winter (Spark, 1958:39).

Charmian, in the same work, was convinced that the housekeeper, Mrs. Pettigrew, was going to poison her. Having no one to turn to for help, she decided to go to a nursing home (Spark, 1958: 177, 178). Another example from *Momento Mori* is Dame Lettie:

> Dame Lettie had, in the past few weeks, got into the habit of searching the house every night before going to bed. One could not be too careful. She searched the house from top to bottom, behind sofas, in cupboards, under beds. Even then there were creaks and unaccountable noises springing up all over the place. This nightly search of the house and garden took three-quarters of an hour, by the end of which Dame Lettie was in no condition to deal with her maid's hysterics. After a week of this routine Gwen had declared the house to be haunted and Dame Lettie to be a maniac, and had left. (Spark, 1958:193)

When asked if she had contacted the police concerning her suspicions,

> "The police," Dame Lettie explained with long, tired emphasis, "are shielding Mortimer and his accomplices. The police always stick toegether. Eric is in with them. They are all in it together." (Spark, 1958:193)

Sybil Prince also was afraid of her housekeeper:

> Sybil was afraid for her life. She was absolutely convinced now that Dorothy was out to kill her.
>
> It was just a question of time. And Dorothy would take her time, playing with Sybil as a cat would play with a mouse still alive in a trap.
>
> Trapped within the walls of her own house. If she wandered outside, Dorothy would hasten after her, taking her arm uncomfortably, putting a hand under her elbow at the rough spots, as if Sybil did not know every stick and stone and tuffet of this land better than Dorothy knew the runnels and open pores of her own face.
>
> She had got to be very careful. (Dickens, 1966:142, 143)

Living in fear, caution becomes the keyword. Hale makes note of this in *The Empress's Ring:*

> Since Eleanor had left, an infinite number of little precautions had come into being. There was a ritual of locking the front door (which in Eleanor's childhood had never been locked, even at night), another of dousing the fire on the hearth; everything was suspected, tested, for its safety. (Hale, 1955:128)

Summary

The present review was intended to raise questions, not to answer them. Each pattern noted by a novelist may be viewed as an hypothesis for further study. For example, to what extent do the aged "retreat" into the past when there are realistic and meaningful roles for them to fill in the present? Are fantasy, resistance to change, the search for substitutes for missing loved ones, a return to religion, or preoccupation with others functional adaptations for an aging, isolated woman? For that matter, are these patterns visible when large numbers of women are studied systematically, or are they cultural stereotypes being perpetuated by the novelists? The step from interesting invention to demonstrated social fact is a long one. It may be noted that many of the patterns observed by the novelists have also been observed in social scientific studies of residents of nursing homes, retired workers, and homeless persons. Other insights of the writers of fiction remain to be validated.

In closing the present exploratory review, let us summarize briefly the "findings" gleaned from the novels. The aged woman has three alternatives in her "choice" of residence: she can live alone, she can live with remaining living family or relatives, or she can live in a nursing home. The latter alternative usually requires an adjustment from a previous life-style which may cause a sense of marginality among the aged. As for the "living alone" alternative, it usually occurs because one's peers either have died or moved. In either case, living alone tends to create a vicious circle of increasing social isolation. Living with relatives is not always pleasant; often forced into an unfamiliar subordinate position or made to feel more of a burden than a blessing, the aged woman suffers tension and distress. When life with the elderly women becomes unbearable for the younger relatives, the third alternative is contemplated, but the aged have intense fears and anxieties about nursing homes and rarely choose to go there voluntarily.

Numerous reasons for the social isolation of aged women were described in the literature. Disaffiliation in old age may simply reflect the continuation of a lifetime pattern, as in the case of loners and spinsters. More frequently, the death of a loved one or forced retirement disrupts a previous life-style and precipitates disaffiliation. Loss of physical health also contributes to the disaffiliation of the aged.

Women's reactions to disaffiliation vary, but in general they present a bleak and gloomy picture. Finding herself devoid of her accustomed social role, an aged woman may continue to relive her old roles through past memories or by refusing to admit that changes occurred. Another method of avoiding readjustment to a new but inferior position is to resist any change—a subtle but futile attempt at trying to extend the present indefinitely into the future.

Substitutes, either human or animal, are often sought by the aged woman to fill vacuums in their accustomed role relationships. Other women use fantasy or daydreams to maintain their self-esteem. Some women find themselves restored with renewed or discovered interest in religion or prayer. Others attempt to fill their time with activity—eccentric or not, productive or not, self-destructive or not, useful or not. Elderly women often cling obsessively to any status still available to them. They find an overwhelming need for communication—waiting for mail that seldom comes, talking to others or to oneself if there is no captive audience. Another response pattern of disaffiliated women is an overconcern with the affairs of others manifested through spying, gossip, petty jealousy, and a concern for trivia. Unrealistic fears about death, injury, or persecution are not uncommon. Finally, there is the self-pity and depression that seems to weigh most heavily upon the most defenseless—the women alone who have no one willing to share the fears and frustration of their last years.

References

Armstrong, Charlotte. 1959. *Seventeen Widows of Sans Souci.* New York: Coward-McCann, Inc.

Bailey, Paul. 1967. *At the Jerusalem.* New York: Anthenum.

Banks, Lynne Ried. 1961. *L-Shaped Room.* London: Reprint Society.

Blechman, Bert. 1967. *Maybe.* Englewood Cliffs, N.J.: Prentice-Hall, Inc.

Calisher, Hortense. 1948. *In the Absence of Angels.* Boston: Little, Brown & Co; 1966. *Railway Police and the Lost Trolley Ride.* Boston: Little, Brown & Co.

Cornell, Evens S., Jr. 1959. *Mrs. Bridge.* New York: Viking Press.

Deegan, Dorothy Yost. 1951. *Sterotype of the Single Woman in American Novels.* New York: King's Crown Press.

Dickens, Monica. 1966. *Room Upstairs.* Garden City, New York: Doubleday & Co.

Dunphy, Jack. 1967. *Nightmovers.* New York: William Morrow & Co., Inc.

Faunce, Frances. 1959. *Those Later Years.* New York: Thomas Y. Crowell.

Frame, Janet. 1966. *A State of Siege.* New York: George Braziller.

Gooding, John. 1967. *People of Providence Street.* New York: Viking Press.

Hale, Nancy. 1955. *The Empress's Ring.* New York: Charles Scribner's Sons; 1960. *The Pattern of Perfection.* Boston: Little, Brown & Co.

Horowitz, Julius. 1960. *The Inhabitants.* New York: World Publishing Company.

Howe, Helen. 1957. *Fires of Autumn.* New York: Harper Bros.

Jackson, Charles. 1967. *Second Hand Life.* New York: Macmillan Company.

Janeway, Elizabeth. 1959. *Third Choice.* Garden City, New York: Doubleday & Co., Inc.

Lacy, Ed. 1966. *The Hotel Dwellers.* New York: Harper & Row Publishers.

LaFarge, Christopher. 1946. *The Sudden Guest.* New York: Coward-McCann, Inc.

Lawrence, Margaret. 1964. *Stone Angel.* New York: Alfred A. Knopf.

Nicolson, Robert. 1967. *A Flight of Steps.* New York: Alfred A. Knopf; 1967. *The Whisperers.* New York: Alfred A. Knopf.

Purdy, James. 1960. *The Nephew.* New York: Farrar, Straus, and Cudahy.

Spark, Muriel. 1958. *Momento Mori.* New York: Time, Inc.

Stafford, Jean. 1964. "The Captain's Gift," *Bad Characters.* New York: Farrar, Straus, & Giroux.

Stone, Robert. 1967. *Hall of Mirrors.* Boston: Houghton Mifflin.

Swados, Harvey. 1958. *Nights in the Garden of Brooklyn.* Boston: Little, Brown & Co.

Swinnerton, Frank. 1967. *The Sanctuary.* Garden City; Doubleday.

Thompson, Bertha. 1937. *Sister of the Road.* New York: Sheridan House.

Trevor, William. 1967. *The Day We Got Drunk on Cake.* New York: Viking Press.

White, Nelia Gardner. 1955. *The Thorn Tree.* New York: Viking Press.

Wilson, Angus. 1959. *The Middle Age of Mrs. Eliot.* New York: Viking Press.

Indexes

Index of Names

Index of Subjects

About the Authors

Howard M. Bahr is Professor of Sociology at Brigham Young University. Previously he taught at Washington State University, where he was Chairman of the Department of Rural Sociology, and at Brooklyn College of the City University of New York and New York University. As a Research Associate at Columbia University's Bureau of Applied Social Research he directed a six-year program of research on homelessness and disaffiliation in Manhattan. He has also collaborated in a series of studies of white-Indian relations in the urban Northwest, and more recently, in several studies of role relationships in modern families. He is a co-editor of *Native Americans Today: Sociological Perspectives* and *Population, Resources, and the Future: Non-Malthusian Perspectives.* His other works on disaffiliation include *Skid Row: An Introduction to Disaffiliation, Old Men Drunk and Sober* (with Theodore Caplow), and *Disaffiliated Man: Essays and Bibliography on Skid Row, Vagrancy, and Outsiders.*

Gerald R. Garrett is Associate Professor of Sociology at University of Massachusetts, Boston. In addition to his extensive work on problems of homelessness and alcoholism, he has directed or collaborated in several large-scale studies of criminology, penology, and penal reform. His other professional work includes research in deviant behavior, and in the sociology of the family.